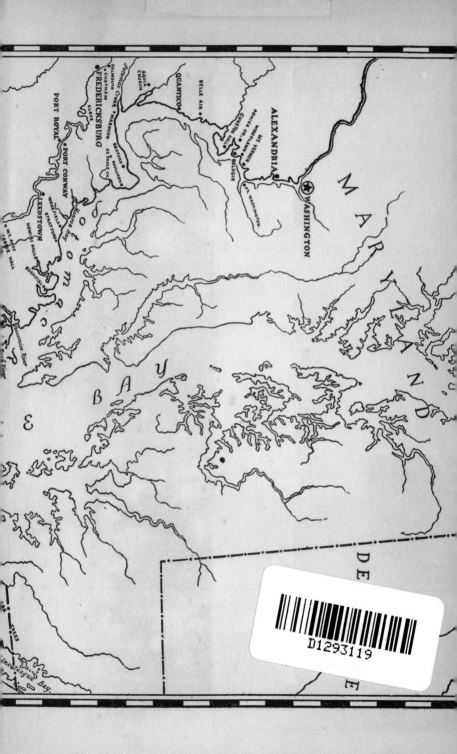

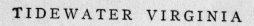
TIDEWATER VIRGINIA

TIDEWATER VIRGINIA

by

PAUL WILSTACH

Illustrated

BLUE RIBBON BOOKS, INC.

NEW YORK CITY

F
227
W7.4

PRINTED AND BOUND BY THE CORNWALL PRESS, INC., FOR
BLUE RIBBON BOOKS, INC., 386 FOURTH AVE., NEW YORK CITY
Printed in the United States of America

To
DAVID LAURANCE CHAMBERS

CONTENTS

CONTENTS—*Continued*

CONTENTS—*Continued*

CONTENTS—*Continued*

TIDEWATER VIRGINIA

TIDEWATER VIRGINIA

CHAPTER I

TIDEWATER VIRGINIA

A Great Triangle of Tides and Brine, History and Old Houses—Physical Features—How Civilization Came—Heroic Figures—Cradle of the Republic—Bridging over Three Hundred Years—A Western Mediterranean—Plantations and Towns—A Land of Acadian Simplicity—Retrogression and Renaissance.

ET us consider Tidewater Virginia.

If one asks the reasons why, is not its very name enough? Tidewater Virginia is more than a phrase; it is an entity. It is one of those magic names—like the Châteaux of France, the Castles on the Rhine, the Bay of Naples, the Canals of Venice, the Lakes of Killarney or the Spanish Main—which is both panoramic and legendary, an expectation and a promise.

Looking for the reason of the glamour of this name, one is not long in finding that Tidewater Virginia is a blend of romance and fact. But its romance is so actual, and all the facts of it are so romantic—one is so completely merged in the other; one is so identically the other—that any effort to divide them is quite as difficult as the problem of unscrambling the egg.

However unlike ancient Gaul Virginia may be in other respects—and the two are not generally, nor is there any other

17

reason why they should be, compared—nevertheless it, too, is divided in three parts. Any one native to the Old Dominion knows precisely the localities you refer to in its three great divisions when you mention Tidewater, the Mountains and South Side.

The outline of the state is roughly an irregular triangle. The right or eastern side of this triangle is Tidewater. The left or western side is the vast section known as the Mountains, where the Blue Ridge and the Appalachians, with their great valley between and with their supporting foot-hills, roll diagonally, from northern summits which look across Maryland at its narrowest into Pennsylvania, southwestward to a far corner where they taper to a vanishing wedge between Kentucky and Tennessee. Subdivisions of this major section are familiarly known as the Piedmont and the Valley. The base or southern stretch of Virginia is known as South Side, and this includes all those rolling lands across which the fresh-water rivers tumble in their journeys from the mountains down to the calm flat tidal plain.

Tidewater Virginia is an honest name. It is just what the term implies. It is all that territory of Virginia contiguous to the Chesapeake Bay. There is a detached section of it on the eastern side of the broad water, a peninsula between the Atlantic Ocean and the bay. This is called the Eastern Shore. The great bulk of Tidewater Virginia, however, is on the western side of the Chesapeake. If, on this side, the lands of Tidewater seem to leave the bay and to stretch inland, it is because the waters of the bay, too, stretch inland across the broad flat plain. Tidewater, however, reverses one's conception of a river. A fresh-water river flows to the sea; but these tidal rivers actually run over and into the land. These inland reaches are called rivers, but it may as well be admitted at once that such pretense is a pleasant fraud. These so-called "rivers" are such only by an arbitrary adoption of the term. They are really estuaries of the bay. They are brackish, when they are not downright salty. And they are tidal. Except at their heads, where the fresh waters pour into them, they have no current beyond the in and out flow of the tide. By anchoring a ship during the ebb periods it is perfectly possible to navigate it the length of any one of these rivers without any other power than the flow of the tide. If the fresh sources of any one of them, or of all of them, were to dry up, these "rivers" would remain; for they are fed less by the mountain sheds than by tidal pressure from the ocean. They are an integral part of the Chesapeake, actually they are a part of the Atlantic Ocean.

The lands of Tidewater Virginia lie along the shores of four such major rivers: the James, the York, the Rappahannock and the Potomac. The termination of the tidal reach is abruptly definite in three of them. The tides are stemmed by so-called "falls" in the James, the Rappahannock and the Potomac at or just above the cities of Richmond, Fredericksburg and Washington, respectively. And so it happens that a line drawn between Richmond and Washington, through Fredericksburg, marks the general western boundary of this section called Tidewater. Its southern side is the irregular belt of land south of the James, from the Atlantic Ocean to the continuation of the western boundary; irregular because it varies according as the length of the tidal inlets and the tidal "rivers" varies.

Tidewater Virginia at its longest is about one hundred sixty miles north and south. At its broadest it is about one hundred twenty miles east and west, but this is measuring from a point farthest east on Eastern Shore and includes the waters of the bay where it is thirty miles wide. On the western side of the bay the Tidewater country lies in a triangle whose base is the lowlands on the south side of the James and which tapers into a vanishing angle near the city of Washington.

This triangle is beyond compare more interesting to an American than any other equal area between the two oceans. In it the English made their first permanent settlement on the American continent. Here from the crudest pioneer condition flowered a civilization, and here grew a race of philosophical and practical and patriotic statesmen through whom it contributed incomparably more than any equal area to the development of the idea of independence and to the passion for it; it was a leader in the activities of the Revolution; and it was the nursery of the great contributors to the constructive organization and practical operation of the new nation.

In Tidewater assembled the first truly representative legislative body on the continent. Here was erected the first church in that area which later comprised the thirteen original states. It was here that, on this continent, the white man first exercised the right of suffrage, negro slavery was first introduced, the first free school was operated and trial by jury was first given the people. Among the names in Tidewater Virginia, sometimes representing an individual, sometimes several personages of the same name, sometimes families whose sons were distinguished in generation after generation, we find the Blands, the Pendletons, the Lees, the Carters, Patrick Henry, the Randolphs, the Harrisons, Chancellor Wythe, the Nelsons, the Pages, George Mason, the Mercers and George

CAPE HENRY LIGHT, AT THE ENTRANCE TO TIDEWATER VIRGINIA
This is the first lighthouse erected by the Federal Government in the
United States

In the Heart of Tidewater

Washington. Of the first ten presidents of the United States Washington, Jefferson, Madison, Monroe, Harrison and Tyler were born in Virginia, and, with the exception of Jefferson, all of these were born in Tidewater.

This is why Virginia has been called the Mother of Presidents; but in this, as in so many other respects, Tidewater is the Mother of Virginia. And it makes it easy to understand why this little triangle of tidal low country has been called the Cradle of the Republic.

But the glamour of history and the pomp of great names need not obscure to us the lesser glory and the greater charm of this region when setting out to explore it. Leisure and relaxation are the likeliest team to draw us along these shores. Life is less trumpet and blare than quiet routine. Blessed is this routine when not so much illuminated with heroics as glowing with the humanities. There has been vastly more years of peace than of war in Tidewater, and any one who seeks diversion here and seeks it only in the pageantry of military history is going to find much, but he is going to miss much, perhaps the more diverting part. There is the domestic pageant, too.

One of the most absorbing adventures of modern discovery must have been the experience of the first white explorers to enter these waters. They found the unfamiliar red man living his unmolested life, a curiosity of race, of character, of manner of life, of domestic and civic organization, of religion and of superstition wholly foreign to them. Forthwith the battle between white man and red man began for the possession of the waters and of the land adjacent to them. The conquest by the white was so complete that to-day, after only a little more than three hundred years, the red man is as much a curiosity to us as he was to the first of our race to sail into Tidewater.

And who were the first whites to come into this landlocked western sea? Who knows? There are conjectures. Certainty, however, attaches to no earlier enterprise than that of a party of Spaniards from Florida, who, in the course of an exploration of the north Atlantic coast, entered the capes and sailed into the bay and even up one or another of the rivers. They departed and of their experience left only the briefest mention in the chronicle of their voyage.

The next white men known to have entered these capes followed a quarter of a century later. They were the English emigrants of the London Company. They came in three little vessels—the *Sarah Constant,* the *Discovery* and the *Goodspeed.* Arriving at a peninsula about fifty miles above the mouth of the river later called the James, they there made the first permanent English settlement on this continent in 1607, and called it Jamestown after their king.

The first years on "the dear strand of Virginia, earth's only paradise," furnished few experiences, however, either to endear Virginia to them or to recommend it as a paradise. The form of government prescribed for them kept the colonists in turmoil and disorder. The Indians were aggressively unfriendly. Famine attacked them. But most devastating of all their hardships was their incapacity to cope with the climate and with the illness entailed.

There was, however, a happy ending to that tragic chapter and the colony increased in numbers, in health, in prosperity and in happiness. By the beginning of the eighteenth century Tidewater entered upon a golden age, which, too, has long since passed, but which, while it lasted, gave Tidewater an interest and a glamour and a romance that it has never lost.

The Indians were conquered and retired into the "forest" as the uncleared country was called. The pioneer's job of making the clearings had all been done, the fertile virgin soil yielded prolific crops, the cheapest labor in the world handled them, and the cheapest transportation power delivered them oversea at their market. That power blew fresh from the heavens and, bellying the sails of the tobacco-laden vessels, sped them on their voyages. Wind and water were the two free and unlimited resources which enriched the planters.

There was among the dwellers in Tidewater an intimacy with the waters, and a love for them and a dependence on them, which suggest an analogy between the dwellers about the Chesapeake and those about another and much larger inland sea, the Mediterranean. It was hardly mere fancy that gave currency to the saying that Cape Charles and Cape Henry at the mouth of the Chesapeake are the Pillars of Hercules of the West. There is in fact more than a passing similarity between these two inland seas, the lesser sea of the West and the larger sea of the East. They share the same latitude and have a similar climate. Historically each is the cradle of a great civilization, one of the ancient world, the other of the new world. On both of them to-day are seaports which are outlets for a broad contiguous territory in its oversea commerce.

And with this analogy in mind there is a temptation to particularize, for there was, indeed, in the early life in Tidewater Virginia something of the intimacy between man and water which distinguishes Venice. Just as in Venice every palace has its steps leading down into the canal and the Venetians do all their social and commercial traffic over the surface of their canals, so in Tidewater Virginia at first the plantations all had their water boundary, and the great houses stood within convenient reach of their own landings, and all the social and commercial traffic here was over the surface of the waters of their bay and its rivers.

There were several reasons for this. Every one lived and conducted his business contiguous to the water. England was the only market toward which the early planters looked, and English ships came direct to each private landing without the occasion for any road cartage whatever. There was no hinterland at first. There was land a-plenty in the preferred position on the waterside. There were no roads inland, the primeval forests screened and so protected the threatening Indians, and there was not yet occasion to drive them farther inland, clear the back lands and make more room for a population which was slow to bulge; so there was for some time no objective for roads at a distance from the water.

In the triangle which is Tidewater Virginia, there are about two thousand miles of water-front on ocean, on bay and along the shores of its tidal rivers. What was it the Indians called their bay? Mother of Rivers.

Nowhere in the tidal reaches is there between the James and the York, the York and the Pianketank, the Pianketank and the Rappahannock, or the Rappahannock and the Potomac, a land reach greater than twenty miles. Frequently it is only five miles, or less, between rivers. From which it seems a bit obvious, considering, moreover, the great acreages and sometimes mileages of so many of the colonial plantations, that it would have been difficult to keep them off the water-front had there been any occasion for it before the rising tide of population made inland holdings valuable.

And before this eventually and inevitably happened, marvelous changes came over the life on the watersides, and that golden age had dawned in Tidewater.

Log cabins gave way to brick mansions. These houses sometimes reproduced remembered features of ancestral homes in England, and even more frequently they bore the names of English homes. About them grew green lawns and brilliantly flowered gardens edged with box. A good native strain had come out of England, and under better conditions culture flowered and spread. There was a new university, the second in all the colonies; frequently the planters sent their sons to English and Scot schools and universities, but oftener a tutor was introduced on the plantation and there taught the girls and boys of the big families. The ships that went out laden with tobacco came back loaded with fineries and luxuries from the London shops: silk and satins and laces; bonnets and gloves; jewelry and silver plate; mahogany furniture; books; wines; spinets and other musical instruments; huntsmen's saddles and other gear; coaches with arms emblazoned on the door panels; all the paraphernalia of a dignified and cultured luxury. Dancing masters with their fiddles went from plantation to plantation and held regular dancing classes. The painters came and "drew" the planter and his family, and soon, in the paneled halls and above the great fireplaces, hung their portraits done by the fashionable "limners." Among them were specimens from the brushes of many American artists. But the contact with England showed in at least one English artist's visit to Virginia and in the portraits of Tidewater gentry who on visits to England sat for the great contemporary English painters.

Slave labor gave a wide margin to the planter's leisure. He devoted it to hospitality and to a repetition of the diversions traditional in England. There were fine horses, races in the field tracks, and fox hunting with horns and hounds. The players came to Alexandria and Williamsburg and repeated the comedies and tragedies of Shakespeare, Beaumont and Fletcher, Sheridan, Goldsmith and Coleman, and many other pieces currently popular on the London stage. The culmination was a life of ease and pleasure, somewhat ripe with dissipation but on the other hand little touched with puritanism, and an aristocracy of blood, wealth and culture which have left their marks in its descendants.

Then the pendulum swung. Within a century after Tidewater had reached its highest expression of civilization, its densest population and its greatest prosperity, it had degenerated into a sparsely populated, neglected, meagerly productive region, its great estates broken up or overgrown, many of its great houses gone, and had become significant largely as a memory. But what a memory!

Though hemmed about by several great units of population and a sound and hearty prosperity, at heart Tidewater retains its charm and its appeal. The charm is of its waters, its old estates, its old houses in various stages of survival or restoration, and its traditions. The appeal is of its great group of political philosophers and daring patriots, in whom every American has a legitimate pride, for the constitutional foundations and the ordered course of the Republic are his heritage from them.

Physically Tidewater is little changed. Nature is constant. Progress has remained aloof. At heart it has continued consistently pastoral. It has been the home and the delight of the country gentleman. Except at its edges it has known almost nothing at all of town or city life. At these edges, not early, though eventually, rose Norfolk and its extensive urban neighborhood, Richmond, Fredericksburg, Alexandria and Washington. Away from this rim, however, Tidewater has had merely its "crossroads," its "stores," its "court-houses," but no city and no considerable town except Williamsburg.

Norfolk is the blessed stepchild of the favorable and protected deep waters of Hampton Roads. When you visit Tidewater you will note that the physical conditions on the rivers give the reason for the position of the other cities. The York merges abruptly in union with the Pamunkey and Mattapony, and these two rivers meander northwest over gradually rolling territory. Casually it is quite impossible to say where precisely the salt tidewaters and the fresh running waters meet and blend, or where one begins or the other ends. But the tidal lengths of the James, the Rappahannock and the Potomac are limited by "falls."

Just there where the fresh waters plunge abruptly over rocky barriers into the lazy tidal calms rose Richmond on the James, Fredericksburg on the Rappahannock, and on the Potomac, Georgetown which has been absorbed by the expansions of the newer city of Washington. These cities mark the points beyond which the sailing ships could not go; the points where cargoes, discharged by the water-carriers, were loaded on wagons to be carried to the pioneers in the newly cleared hill country over roads which at first were mere trails.

These communities began merely with a wharf. To this was added a warehouse, then a custom-house, then the store and a few dwellings, and these were eventually surrounded by the demands of an increasing population.

Around the rim to-day the railways run. Along them string the few cities. And did the communities develop the railways, or the railways the communities? Did the egg produce the chicken or the chicken produce the egg? Another riddle of priority. The railways have brought a few bridges to Tidewater, but in counting and locating these bridges one is only the more impressed with the unchangingness of it. Across the Potomac there is not a single bridge below Washington. There is a threat, to be sure, for Congress has granted permission to span the river half-way along its tidal reach. However, the tides still flow back and forth undisturbed. Below Fredericksburg there was not a single bridge across the Rappahannock until this decade, when piers rose out of its waters at Tappahannock to sustain a path for the lordly motor. The only path across the York, now as when Powhatan's capital stood on its bank, is its waters. Below Richmond the James has offered no obstruction to water-craft until just now, when its mouth has yielded to the muzzle for the purposes of progress, and it is possible to wheel one's way between Newport News and Norfolk. Along four hundred miles of tidal rivers they are crossed by only two bridges.

Steam has reached Tidewater and the funnels of steamboats pour out their smoky clouds, but it is none too intimate with steam cars. Locomotives hiss about the water-fronts of Norfolk. Railway lines parallel both sides of the James but at a decent distance from its shores. Only five times in all its length do they venture to the waterside. The single line down the eastern shore reaches the water only once. A little branch line trails over from Richmond and touches the head of the York once and then runs back again. The eighty-four miles of Rappahannock below Fredericksburg are as innocent of acquaintance with the railway as in the days when it knew nothing of the noble white man. Even the Potomac sweeps up fifty mile... before the locomotive looks upon it at Pope's Creek, and then for another sixty miles it knows it no more. There is still Acadian simplicity in this land of water.

Once more, however, the pendulum has swung. There are signs of renaissance in Tidewater. Though enjoying it, the cities exist and thrive independently of it. Only Norfolk needs the sea. But there are other signs of interest, of movement, of new life. The very cities are debouching their congestion along the serene and silent shores where the tides lap, and it is a playground. The twentieth-century toy, the motor, annihilates old ideas of distance and compels new roads through waste places, and over them brings pilgrim pioneers on new voyages of discovery. The survivals among the old homes are still held by the old family line in some cases, but where holding on was too hard, new owners have come in and taken up the care. Something sentimental may have snapped, but the old houses have benefited by restoration and smilingly take on new life.

Basically this renaissance is the budding of an idea. The idea is the salvage of something precious, the salvage of something verging on disappearance. And that something is precious, moreover, because it is not only local but national, and belongs to every American.

So the physicians of the country honor their profession by reclaiming a cabin on the banks of the York where Walter Reed was born and dedicate it to the memory of that scientific practitioner and pioneer. A single munificence has made possible the restoration of an entire city, ancient Williamsburg, with the bloom that was on it in the eighteenth century, in the days when it was one of the most important civic centers of the colonies. Stratford Hall on the Potomac has at last received recognition, and a public organization has undertaken the preservation of the birthplace of the Lees—from Thomas, the acting Royal Governor, to Richard Henry Lee, with his five celebrated brothers and their grandnephew Robert E. Lee—to their memory. Wakefield, the birthplace of Washington, is emerging from its one hundred fifty years of neglect, another monument to the Father of his Country. Mount Vernon has for over half a century been the object of reverent care and patriotic interest, and now a national boulevard in the making will unite this home of Washington with the capital city which perpetuates his name.

But this renaissance of interest in Tidewater, while embellishing and preserving a few spots, is not altering it. It is still aloof from modern pressure; a retreat, when repetition irks and becomes insupportable, from crowds, hurry and the standardization of contemporary life; a haven from the throb of the twentieth century, where the past emerges from its centuries and puts on the mantle of reality.

CHAPTER II

THE EMPIRE OF THE INDIAN

What the First English Found in Tidewater—Red Men Who Were Brown though Born White—Personal Appearance—Dress and Ornament—Habits of Life—Crops and Food and Cooking—"The Earing of the Corne and the Falling of the Leafe"—Hunting—Early Camouflaging—Games—Religion—The God of Fear—War—Powhatan's Empire—Indians To-day in Tidewater.

HO has cruised about in the bays and rivers of Tidewater who has not at times felt the present slip away and the ease with which the reality of its past creeps over one? Nature rarely dates itself except in the greater cycles of cosmic transformations. A few hundred years are as the twinkling of an eye to the hills and fields, the islands and inlets, the families of trees and flowers and of beasts and birds. It is man who dates the landscape with his own contrivances, giving changing aspects to it with his architecture and engines and engineering.

But the snooper with half an eye finds that even these disappear from his outlook. He may have driven his car to the edge of a remote bluff or out on a lonely cape terminal he may have sailed or canoed into quiet waters under screening bluffs, to find himself alone with his rod and line and unaltered nature. No buildings, no wharves, no fences. There are endless such places in Tidewater. Or he may be gunning from a blind at dawn and the cool mists draw a curtain over man's handicraft and leave him alone with the dim lines where trees and land and water meet and merge, with nothing definite but the glorious glow on the eastern horizon trumpeting the coming of the sun. At such moments nature seems alone with itself, timeless, a background against which might march a procession out of any period of its past. At such a time all intervals drop away. How natural were the stag to come to the waterside, or the whoop of the savage to break the silence, or even for the Indian himself to paddle his canoe through the curtain of mist or round the point!

It's not so long ago since he was here and the white man was not. What are three hundred years in the age of these waters? The red man peopled all these shores, he had his clearings, his towns, his government, his kings and his emperor. And he is gone; he and his houses and towns are gone almost as completely as if he had never been here.

But the first English in Tidewater—Captain John Smith, William Strachey, Gent., and that honorable gentleman, Master George Percy—in their astonishment at so strange a people, left accounts of the red men, and for the sake of any who are curious, the yellow dog-eared leaves of their old chronicles make the first dwellers here live again. What the first white man to come here saw we may know.

The Indian had but little effect on the landscape. He built neither wharves nor fences. His houses were small and their components always unpainted, weathered to a tint which blended with the rustic landscape. There were so few inhabitants for so extensive an area that their clearings for fields were so few and so small that they could scarcely have disturbed the effect of universal forest. Nature, for all his influence, was virginal.

Perhaps the chief natural difference in the landscape between what it is and what it was when only the Indian roamed here, is in the trees. The forests of Tidewater to-day are almost entirely of second or subsequent growth. Natural decay, the violence of storms, or the clearing ax of the white man has swept away "the forest primeval." But we have some idea of the gigantic stature of those trees from the enormous size of the aborigine's canoes made out of the trunks of the forest trees. Master Percy remarked one "five and fortie feet long by the rule," and John Smith remarked that such a canoe bore forty men. But such a canoe did not wholly represent the longest trees, for Smith notes that the oak yielded "two foote and a halfe square of good timber for 20 yards long." Wheresoever they landed the earliest voyagers saw "the goodliest Woods as Beech, Oke, Cedar, Cypresse, Walnuts, Sassafras, and Vines in great abundance, which hang in great clusters on many trees, and other trees unknowne, and all the ground bespred with many sweet and delicate flowres of divers colours and kindes."

The number of Indians estimated as living in Tidewater at the coming of the white man was twenty thousand. They belonged to the linguistic stock of Algonquins. The population of the same area to-day is about one million. If then to-day there are uninfluenced neighborhoods where Nature still "her custom holds," how little effect must those few scattered savages have made. But because the first settlers were few the scattered twenty thousand seemed many to them when red men and white men were pitted against each other for the control of the region.

Although the Indian is habitually called a "red man" the first whites in Tidewater found him to be brown. Even observant John Smith distinguished. He noted them "of a colour browne when they are of any age but they are borne white!"

Their tall straight figures were of "a comely proportion."
Their noses were broad, flat, and full at the ends, and they
had "great bigg lippes, and wyde mouthes yet nothing so un-
sightly as the Moores." Their hair was "generally blacke,"
though no one says what color it was when not of that hue.
Perhaps the observers were too much taken up with the other
end of their heads, for though beards were few, such men as
had them, according to Smith, "weare halfe their beards shav-
en, the other halfe long." The explanation of this curiosity, or absurdity, or penalty, or whatever it was, may be in
the disastrous effect of women barbers on men, from the days
of Delilah down, since Smith adds that the Indians "for
Barbers use their Women." However, the fact that these
tonsorialists "with two shels will grate away the hayre, of any
fashion they please" may to some extent explain why their
otherwise stoical patrons were willing to compromise on half a
shave or a shave of half their face. The women cut their own
hair in many fashions; but this did not include the modern bob
or shingle since "ever some part remaineth long."

For dress they wore the skins of the wild beasts, in winter
dressed with the hair but in summer without. These skins they
ornamented with copper, some with white beads, some with
painted designs. The better sort wore handsome warm mantles
made of turkey feathers, so ingeniously wrought that nothing
was seen but the feathers. But "the common sort have scarce
to cover their nakednesse, but with grass, the leaves of trees,
or such like." When naked, or nearly so, they smeared themselves all over with a preparation made from "oyntments of
the earth and the juyce of certaine scrused roots," either from
custom or to defend themselves from the stinging of mos-
quitoes, gnats and other insects. But vanity seems to have

had its duly human part in the braves' as well as the squaws' besmirchment of themselves into this "tawny cowler, esteeming yt," according to Strachey who gave Captain John Smith a complaint for brazen plagiarism if ever one writer to another gave such:

"The best beauty to be neerest such a kynd of murrey as a sodden quince is of (to liken yt to the neerest coulor I can), for which they daily anoint both face and bodyes all over with such a kind of fucus or unguent as can cast them into that stayne, as is said of the Greek women how they coloured their faces with certain rootes called Brenthina, and as the Britaynes died themselves red with woad; howbeit, he or she that hath obteyned the perfectest art in the tempering of this collour with any better kind of earth, yearb, or root, preserves yt not yet so secrett and pretious unto her self as doe our great ladyes their oyle of talchum, or other painting white and redd, but they frindly communicate the secret, and teach yt one another; after their anoynting (which is daylie) they dry in the sun, and thereby make their skynns (besides the coulor) more black and spotted, which the sun kissing oft and hard, adds to their painting the more rough and rugged.

"Their heads and shoulders they paint oftennest, and those red, with the roote pochone, brayed to powder, mixed with oyle of the walnutt, or bear's grease; this they hold in sommer doth check the heat, and in winter armes them in some measure against the cold. Manie other formes of payntings they use; but he is the most gallant who is the most monstrous and uglie to behold."

The women were modest in their way, never appearing wholly naked, but their vanity expressed itself in pictures and decorative design tattooed on the skin. Their method, as described by Percy, was to "pounce and race their bodies, legges, thighes, armes and faces with a sharp Iron, which makes a stampe in curous knots, and drawes the proportion of Fowles, Fish, or Beasts, then with paintings of sundry lively colours, they rub it into the stampe which will never be taken away, because it is dried into the flesh where is is sered."

To harden their babies the mothers took them on the coldest mornings to the waters and plunged them in for a bath, and, moreover, they so painted and anointed them that their skins became tanned and toughened in such a manner that after a year or two no weather would hurt them.

The women wore rings and chains suspended from holes in their ears. The men had the holes but wore suspended from them, at least in cases reported by Smith, "a small greene and yellow coloured snake, nearly half a yard in length, which crawling and lapping herselfe about his necke often times familiarly would kiss his lips. Others wore a Dead Rat tyed by the taile," and so it seemed "he is the most gallant that is most monstrous to behold."

The Indians for the most part lived in loose groups called villages, and always near water. Their houses were built of flexible boughs set up in a circle and drawn together and tied at the top. This arbor they covered with bark and woven mats so thickly that it withstood all kinds of weather. But it was wretched and smoky withal, for the fire was built in the center of it on the earth, and the unchimneyed smoke dispersed in it before finding its way out through a rude hole somewhere near the top. The interior was innocent of any division, but there in the single room, some stark naked on the ground and some on frames of branches dressed with skins, slept a family numbering from six to twenty. And "he who knoweth one such house knoweth them all."

Their staple food was wild game, fish and oysters, berries, corn, potatoes, pumpkins, onions, a fruit like a muskmelon called macocks, a wild fruit like a lemon called maracocks;

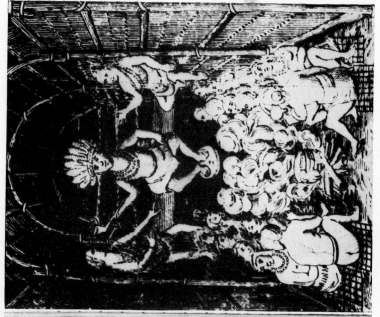

King Powhatan

Captain John Smith

JAMESTOWN CHURCH
The tower dates to the middle seventeenth century,
the church is modern

JAMESTOWN CHURCHYARD
In the clasp of the roots of the old tree are the
restored remnants of the tomb of Sarah, daughter
of an early Benjamin Harrison

in addition, in some way they had, before the coming of the whites, both peas and beans, understanding the planting and cooking of them. They seem not to have known the artful device of the scarecrow, for in the fields they set up platforms on which they themselves stood guard against birds and beasts. Or perhaps they did not know merely the inanimate scarecrow.

They were so conscious of their crops that they named two seasons for them. They had five seasons: three similar to our winter, spring and summer; and autumn which they divided into "the earing of the Corne" and "the harvest and fall of leafe."

Their cooking was simple, and none who wrote of it set down anything else so interesting to us as this, by Smith: "Tempering this flower with water, they make it in cakes, covering them with ashes till they be baked, and then washing them in faire water, they drie presently with their own heat," which is the first recipe that ever was set down for corn pone, or, if it is not, where is an earlier?

The butter of cow's or goat's milk they had not, but "butter" their rice and corn bread they did, "with deare suet."

Matches they had not, but "their fire they kindle presently by chafing a dry pointed sticke in a hole of a little square piece of wood, that firing itselfe, will so fire the mosse, leaues, or any such like dry thing, that will quickly burne." But so precious was fire that they were at great pains to preserve embers in each house at all times.

To give light in the darkness they had themselves "candells of the fattest splinters of the pine or firre tree, which will give a good cliere light and burn strongly," said Strachey, "though the matter will soon consume, for which they have many slivers ready cut out a foote long, some shorter, to be ready to light a second as soon as the first goes out." By which candles and slivers we recognize the pine-knot.

In place of a towel, such as dried themselves artificially used a bunch of feathers. Though a brave shaved with a shell for a razor, to cut his feathers he used a knife made from "the splinter of a Reed." With such a knife, too, he would cut up a deer, shape his moccasins, and fashion other skins for garments. The Indians were inveterate smokers, and I don't know whether it is more surprising to find no mention made of corn-cob pipes in the chronicles than to discover that the savage understood the molding of pipe bowls out of clay, which he baked and fortified or ornamented with a band of fine copper.

The men hunted, fished and made war; the women did all other work about the house and in the fields. The lilies (shall we say tiger-lilies?) of these fields not only labored but they in some way had the principle and practise of spinning; for "betwixt their hand and thighes, their women use to spin, the barkes of trees, Deeres Sinewes, or a Kind of grass, of these they make a thread very evenly and readily. This thread serveth for many uses. As about their housing, apparell, as also they make nets for fishing. They make also with it lines for angles."

Though their bows and arrows were uncommonly powerful, the first whites had a device for humbling their pride in them, as Master Percy paused to set down for us: "One of our Gentlemen having a Target which he trusted in, thinking it would beare out a slight shot, hee set it up against a tree, willing one of the Savages to shoot, who tooke from his backe an Arrow of an elle long, drew it strongly in his Bowe, shoots the Target a foote Thorow, or better; which was strange, being that a Pistoll could not pierce it. Wee seeing the force of his

Bowe, afterwards set him up a steele Target; he shot again, and burst his arrow all to pieces, he presently pulled out another Arrow, and bit it in his teeth, and seemed to bee in a great rage, so hee went away in great anger."

In the hunting season they abandoned the villages, many of which would band together to the number of two or three hundred braves and squaws, and set inland to the heads of the rivers to capture big game. On such expeditions they stalked the deer with fires built on the rim of a great circle. The hunters posted themselves between the fires. Then with weird noises they advanced simultaneously, driving the game to the center, where in a single morning they had no great difficulty in taking as many as fifteen.

Hunting alone the Indian used another method to entrap the ingenuous deer. He dressed himself up in the counterfeit of a deer, with stuffed head showing horns, ears, eyes and mouth. "Thus shrouding his body in the Skinne by stalking, he approacheth the Deere, creeping on the ground from one tree to another. If the Deere chance to find fault, or stand at gaze, he turneth the head with his hand to his best advantage to seeme like a Deere, also gazing and licking himselfe. So watching his best advantage to approach, having shot him, he chaseth him by his bloud and straine till he get him."

And there was more than the deer in the quarry, for hunting was a kind of courting, since the hunters who excelled had the favors of the women.

We are not permitted to know what, besides dress, diverted the Tidewater red women unless it were work and the compensations of child-bearing. The men, however, in their leisure played at games with a ball, in one of which they hit the ball with a kind of bat, and in another they kicked it and toed it for a goal. Yet the savages were not wholly lacking in good sportsmanship, for "They never strike up one another's heeles, as we doe, not accounting that praiseworthie to purchase a goale by such an advantage." The less active diverted themselves with a game "wherein they card and discard, and lay a stake, too," and so gambled away their beads, their bows, their clothing, and any loose chattels they had at hand. They likewise danced, and drank a liquor until they were "sick," and sang—whether in or out of liquor is unindicated—*erotica carmina,* bawdy songs; in a manner "tunable enough."

Wholly ignorant of letters, unable to read or to write, they nevertheless lived under an organized government, whose code, however, was embodied in custom and oral tradition. This government was made up of many districts or villages, each ruled over by a king or commander called a werowance, and all united under an emperor whose name, at the time of the first white settlement on this continent, was Powhatan.

His domain was almost identical with the extent of what is now familiarly known as Tidewater Virginia, with the exception of the peninsula called the Eastern Shore. He ruled from the James to the Potomac and over all the territory between from the rivers' mouths on the bay back to the falls. His capital, if so might be called his main place of residence, from which he ruled, was on the north shore of the York River about two-thirds its length from the bay.

Powhatan became master of his domain partly by inheritance and partly by conquest. He governed it by force of an extraordinarily tyrannic and ruthless nature. His punishments were swift and in their details ghastly. He held his subjects not merely in terror of death, but of the long barbarous cruelties which slowly culminated in it. He was obeyed not merely as a king but as a demigod as well.

The religion of the Indian was simple. It was based on fear. All things beyond their ken and control which could do them harm they worshiped. Hence, thunder, lightning, fire and water became the objects of their adoration, but as water put out fire they held it in the higher esteem. For God they worshiped a devil whom they called Okee, a supreme spirit of mischief and evil, capable of doing them the most harm and so inspiring their greatest fear.

For the practise of their religion they had rude buildings called temples, in which they raised images of Okee, and, in conformity with what such idols represented to them, they were "evil favouredly carved." They also had priests who presided in the temples and arrayed themselves in imitation of the Devil of Fear and so made themselves figures of grotesque hideousness. The arborlike, mat-covered temples, of which the largest recorded one was sixty feet long, were also the tombs of their mummied kings. What with the awesome idols and royal mummies in such a fane it is not surprising that only kings and priests entered it and that the humbler savage dared not even go up the river past it without casting copper, white beads or some other offering into the water.

On the whole, considering their primitive natures and the loose social system under which they carried on, the subjects of Powhatan seem not to have been an unreasonably warlike people. Smith noted that "they seldom make warre for land or goods, but for women or children, and principally for revenge." Probably the last was in retaliation against their arch-enemies, in the highlands beyond the falls, who seem to have given them their most restless days. The final decision as to going to war rested with Powhatan, but in his decisions the old gentleman leaned heavily on the advice of his priests and conjurers.

They were "inconstant in everything, but what feare con-
straineth them to keepe. Craftie, timorous, quick of apprehen-
sion, and very ingenuous . . . They are soon mounted to anger, and so malicious that they seldome forget an injury; they
seldome steale one from another lest their conjurers should
reveal it, and so they be pursued and punished. . . . Their
women are careful not to be suspected of dishonestie," to
which gallant Smith adds the illuminating clause, "without the
leave of their husbands."

Nowhere have I seen it stated, or even implied, that an
Indian had any sense of humor whatever. Much less are there
any flotsam or jetsam of anecdote indicating any levity or
light mood on the part of the noble red man. But how can it
be that he had none? Resembling his brother of every other
color in so many other ways it must have been that he, too,
sometimes had a twinkle in his tongue and a twinkle in his
eye, and occasionally enjoyed his joke, and perhaps actually
laughed.

But the whole tradition of the red man is sobriety—not
the sobriety of abstinence from the bottle but sobriety of abstinence from levity. One can well understand that the savage
in his painted awfulness, with war-whoop and tomahawk, was
no laughing matter to the white pioneer, but may not the
pioneer have sometimes been a laughing matter to the red man
and so lowered his reserve? The only joke he seems to have
appreciated was a ghastly joke, steeped in gore and dripping
blood; of which he was not least often the victim at the hands
of the ingenious executioners of his emperor.

What of the Indian remains in Tidewater? The population
of twenty thousand red men in 1607 has dwindled to eight
hundred twenty-two. This is astonishing, less by the shrink-

age in their number than by the fact that they are so many. On the banks of the waterways may still be found deposits of oyster shells, in advanced states of decay, which presumably indicate the locality of the aboriginal settlements. In some cases they coincide with the position of the Indian towns shown on Captain John Smith's map. Near the surface have been found fragments of pottery, chips of stone, and some scraps of stone implements. Museums treasure a few specimens of the native craftsmanship. But in its entirety this amounts to little. Gone are the canoes, the frail houses, the so-called temples, the graves of kings and commoners, and every vestige of their towns. They exist no more except in our acquaintance with them by virtue of Smith's extraordinary account of them, and the copyists of him, or, perhaps, in the ready imagination of a visitor to Powhatan's empire who has the grace to see with his mind's eye.

CHAPTER III

THE WHITE MAN COMES

Who Was the First White Man in Tidewater Virginia—Early Voyages—Conjectured Visits—Cabot and Vespucci, Verrazano, Avilés, Lane and Ecija—Meaning of Chesapeake—The Bay's Early Names—The *Sarah Constant,* the *Goodspeed* and the *Discovery*—First Permanent English Settlement in America—Explorations into the Wilderness—Captain John Smith—An English Knight's Son Follows an Indian King—Death of Harry Spelman—Bluff Samuel Argall—Fleet, the Trader—Who Was Edmond Heller?

GAIN the question presents itself, who were the first white men to visit Tidewater Virginia? Who were the first pale-faces to astonish this small world of red men, who little suspected that the newcomers brought the beginning of the end of their peaceful undisturbed occupation of the waters and the lands about them? This is but another way of asking, who were the first white men to sail into Chesapeake Bay?

The date of such first arrivals may have been 1498, only five years after the arrival of Christopher Columbus on this side of the Atlantic Ocean. In that year, or within a year of it, John Cabot, under commission from King Henry VII of England, sailed out of Bristol and reached land on this side of the ocean. He cruised south along the opening to the great bay. There is no authentic record that he entered it, though no one can say with certainty that he did not. However, one may with reasonable assurance say that Cabot was the first white man known to have passed this way with the opportunity to enter the capes.

44

These were empty seas in those days. Sails were infrequent-ly seen. Yet it is strangely but actually possible that Cabot, sailing south, might have encountered Amerigo Vespucci sail-ing north, for it was just at this time that the latter sailed up the coast from Florida to a point which by some is identified with Chesapeake Bay and by others with the Bay of St. Law-rence. It is even conjectured that Vespucci sailed into the Chesapeake. But conjecture is too poor a peg on which to hang certainty.

Of the subsequent twenty-six years the chronicles are silent. Then along came another Italian, Verrazano, in 1524. His whole expedition is the subject of controversy, but there are champions who believe in his exploit and believe, too, that he may have entered the bay. Two years after Verrazano, came the Spaniard, Ayallon, who entered quiet waters identified as Chesapeake Bay and made a settlement which he called San Miguel de Gualdape. There are those who say that the site of San Miguel was identical with that of Jamestown on the James.

Another thirty years. Then, in 1566, Menendez de Avilés, having established St. Augustine in Florida, dispatched an ex-pedition up the coast to "St. Mary Bay," and of its identity with the waters along which lie the lands of Tidewater Vir-ginia there seems to be no doubt. And this exploit confirms some previous Spanish explorer here—perhaps, Ayallon—for on this voyage the captain took with him "an Indian, brother of the Cacique of Axacan (whom the Dominicans had taken from that land and, carrying to Mexico, the Viceroy, Don Luis de Velasco, had him baptized, and gave him his name.)" Some historians have gone as far as to drag this Spanish ex-pedition up the inner waterways as far as Occoquan, on the west side of the Potomac River, based on an imagined analogy or identity between the words Axacan and Occoquan. Alexander Brown and J. G. Shea locate Axacan-Occoquan on the Rappahannock River. Robert Greenhow says that "Axacan comprised the lower part of the present state of North Carolina"! Such are the stumbling-blocks in the way of decision.

Certainly from this time at least the bay now called Chesapeake was, under some name, known to the European explorers and promoters. It was a pretty question into whose possession the prize should fall. As already noted, English interest had been aroused as early as 1498. In searching for a reason why King Henry VII, the reigning monarch at that time, did not act on Cabot's explorations and reports, and send English settlers, we find it in that king's ambition to marry his son, Prince Arthur, to Katherine, daughter of King Ferdinand and Queen Isabella, and in his consequent disinclination to create bad feeling by disturbing the Spanish in their gold-hunt in these new lands. That is at least one reason why the English did not find themselves established in Virginia for another hundred and nine years.

The Spanish came here again in 1570, 1571, 1573 and 1588; and as a result of the third of those voyages we have, in Barcia's words, what is probably the earliest surviving description of the bay and rivers of Tidewater. After locating "St. Mary's Bay" at thirty-seven and one-half degrees north, he says:

"It is three leagues wide and you enter it N.N.W.; within there are many rivers and harbors on both sides, where a vessel can enter; at the mouth, near the land, on the southern shore, there is nine to thirteen fathoms water; and on the north five to seven; two leagues outside at sea, the depth on the north and south is the same as inside, with more sand;

following the channel, nine to thirteen; inside the port, by fifteen or sixteen fathoms, he found spots where the lead did not touch bottom."

The bay seems actually to have been rediscovered to the English in 1585 by the visit there of Captain Lane, one of the Raleigh colony farther south in Carolina. He came into what later became known as Elizabeth River, "the country of the Chesepiooks," whose name the English later gave to the bay. Lane did not remain, and he left no settlement behind him at that time. The English seemed not to be seriously interested in the bay. There is record of only two ships there out of England in one hundred years. The Spanish, however, sent thither five expeditions in the twenty-two years between 1566 and 1588. And they persisted, however slowly it may seem at this distance.

Under orders from the King of Spain, Pedro de Ybarra, Governor of Florida, in June, 1609, sent Captain Francisco de Ecija, in the ship, *Asuncion de Christo,* to explore the coast as far north as forty-four degrees, thirty minutes latitude (where Maine now is) in order to "find out whether there are on said coast ports, settlements of people of different nationalities [that is, who were not Spaniards], who may have occupied such places without any authority, only wishing to take possession of them and there exercise their piracy; so that we may take steps to avoid the many troubles therefrom likely to arise to the great injury of God, our Lord, and of his Majesty the King."

The narrative of this voyage goes on to say that, on July twenty-fourth, "we came to the Bay of Axacan. When we were a short distance from its southern promontory [Cape Henry?] the man on the look-out spied a ship anchored in the Bay. As it was already night the Captain ordered us to anchor and forbear entering until another day." This ship seems to have created something of a panic among the Spaniards. They spent a sleepless night. They saw the ship inside the capes again at dawn. An Indian down the coast had told them of an English settlement in the bay. They believed they faced a hostile guard, and that "God, our Lord and His Majesty the King would be best served by our going back." Back they went. It was the last effort of the Spanish to extend their empire in the north. They were, indeed, too late. The English had arrived in the bay two years before, their settlement on the James was two years old, a government had been organized, and the actual development of Tidewater Virginia was under way. The Spaniards had seen an English ship.

The expedition that counted in the permanent settlement of Tidewater Virginia consisted of three ships: the *Sarah Constant,* the *Goodspeed* and the *Discovery*. The expedition was under the sole charge and command of Captain Christopher Newport. Of it Alexander Brown makes this observation: "The route [was the same] by which both *Christopher* Columbus (the bearer of the religion of Rome) and *Christopher* Newport (the bearer of the religion of England) brought their ships to these shores. . . . Both commanders bore the same name, which means 'bearing Christ,' an object of both. Both commanded three ships, came the same route, and connected with both there is an indefinite account of a mutiny at sea."

Newport's three ships crossed from England early in 1607; and on April twenty-sixth (new style May sixth) "about foure a clocke in the morning," wrote Percy, "wee descried the land of Virginia: the same day wee entered into the Bay of Chesapioc directly without any let or hindrance; there we landed and discovered a little way, but wee could finde nothing worth the speaking of, but faire meadowes and goodly tall trees, with such fresh-waters running through the woods, as I was almost ravished at the sight thereof."

The cape, round which they had entered, was named Henry "in honour of our most noble Prince. The shew of land there is white, hilly sand like unto the Downs and along the shores great plentie of Pines and Firres." A point which gave their ships protection was called Point Comfort because its harbor "put us in good comfort." They advanced up the river which seems to have been called the Powhatan or King's River and which they rechristened the James, after their reigning monarch, and selected for their site an island which they called Jamestown. On May fourteenth "we landed our men which were set to work about the fortifications and others some to watch and ward, as it was convenient." And this was why the Spanish under Ecija were by at least two years too late.

Of the name by which the Indians originally called the bay there is no record. As is already evident the earliest Europeans to sail thither called it by several names, before it was known by the name which now identifies it.

The first name by which it was known was *Bahia de Santa Maria* (St. Mary's Bay). It was so designated by the Spaniards in several documents, at least as early as 1526. Three-quarters of a century later they were calling it *Bahia del Xacan* (Axacan Bay). A third early name given it was *Madre de Aguas* or Mother of Waters. Stith, in his *First Discovery and Settlement of Virginia,* published in 1747, writes entertainingly of this:

"Some say that Chesapeake signified, in the *Indian* language, *The Mother of Waters;* implying, that it was the Parent and grand Reservoir of all the great Rivers within it. But this is a dark and uncertain Guess; especially considering the Unstableness and vast Mutibility of the Indian Tongues, and that nobody at present can pretend to understand their Language at that time. The best that I have met for this Derivation, is what a Gentleman of Credit once assured me, that in a very old *Spanish* Map, which he had seen, our Bay was laid down under the Name of *Madre des Acquas,* or some Expression to the like Purpose."

How right was Stith about the "Unstableness and vast Mutibility of the Indian Tongues" is overwhelmingly obvious when we begin to look into the origin and meaning of the bay's permanent and present name. This it took from the Chesapeake Indians who inhabited the shores of Elizabeth River, the first inlet inside the capes, now separating the cities of Norfolk and Portsmouth. Here are a few quotations on the subject given in the belief that they confirm good William Stith:

Heckewelder says: *"Chesapeake* corrupted from *Tschiswapeki,* or *K'tschischwapeeki,* compounded of *Kitschi,* signifying, highly salted, and *peek,* a body of standing water, a pond, a bay."

Trumbull agrees and adds: *"Chesapeake,*—written *Chesapeack, Chesupioca, Chissapiacke,* etc.,—is the equivalent of the Massachusetts *'K'che-seippog,'* Abnaki *'K'tsi-soubekou,* great saltwater, great sea or bay.' "

All of which Tooker says is "an error" and explains that the term applies to land and not at all to water: "The terminal generic *peek,* of Heckewelder, which denotes 'standing-water or water at rest, a pond,' would never have been used by an Indian to describe the turbulent waters of *Chesapeake* Bay. Neither does the term contain the radical for 'it is sour, or salt,' as used dialectically by the Indians of that section. Now the question arises, what are the phonetic elements, as embodied in its early notations? Hariot's map gives us *Chesepiooc*; Percy, *Che-supioc*; Smith, *Chis-siapi-acke*; *Che-sipi-acke*; 'Brooke of *Chi-sape-ack*'; 'we sayld up a narrow river up the country of the Chi-sape-ack'; etc., etc. The prefix *che* is undoubtedly, as Doctor Trumbull suggests, the equivalent of the Massachusetts *K'che*, 'great.' The second component *sepi, supi* or *sipi,* however, is not 'salt-water,' but the parallel of the Massachusetts and other Algonquin dialects *sepu,* or *seip,* 'a river,' which with its locative affix *ack,* 'land or country,' gives us a synthesis of *K'che-sepi-ack,* 'country on a great river.' " But the early English found the term so near the waters that they baptized them with it, and without regard to its meaning, if, indeed, any one but the early Indians and Doctor Tooker ever knew it.

Turning now to the original name of the lands of Tidewater the facts are fewer and less bewildering. To the Indians it was Atlanoughkomouch or Tsenahcommocah, meaning plantation, and Tooker found "the difference between them being due more perhaps to individual utterance than to any dialectal change." The English named their grant Virginia after their "Virgin" Queen, Elizabeth. And Tidewater has never been known by any other names.

The first letter home said:

"We are set down eighty miles within a River for breadth, sweetness of water, length navigable up into the country, deep and bold channell so stored with sturgeon and other sweet fish, as no man's fortune hath ever possessed the like. . . . The soil is most fruitfull, laden with good Oake, Ashe, Walnut tree, Poplar, Pine, sweet woods, Cedar, and others yet without names that yield gums pleasant as Frankincense and experienced amongst us for great vertue in healing green wounds and aches."

No sooner were the colonists entrenched at Jamestown than the explorations began. Newport took twenty-one others up the river with him, in a shallop provisioned for a voyage. They hoped to find the short-cut to the Pacific. What they found was the falls, and above them, an Indian town "of twelve houses pleasantly seated on a hill." This was the site of the present city of Richmond.

In Captain Newport's party was John Smith, a young adventurer who, after Newport's early return to England, made himself the head of the colonists. The first year Smith made "3. or 4. journies and discovered the people of Chickahamania," who gave their name to the Chickahominy River. On the last of them he was taken prisoner and his life was eventually saved by the dramatic act of Pocahontas, daughter of Powhatan. It was while he was in Powhatan's power that he was led a prisoner all over Powhatan's domain, a white man's first comprehensive journey through Tidewater: across the York, the Pianketank, the Rappahannock, even to the Potomac.

What Smith saw under these circumstances fired his eagerness to hunt the passage to the western sea farther up the bay. "As soon as corn was planted" the next spring, 1608, he set out on what was the first thorough exploration of the bay and Tidewater. Smith was accompanied by fourteen men, among them "Walter Russell, Doctor of Physicke," and the trip was made in "an open Barge neare three tuns burthen."

Dropping down to Cape Henry they "crossed the Bay to the Eastern Shore, and fell with the Isles called Smith's Isles, after our Captaines name." Rounding Cape Charles, they found "Accomack, the habitation of their Werowance, where we were kindly treated. This king was the comeliest, proper,

Adam Thoroughgood House

St. Paul's Church, Norfolk

GEORGE WASHINGTON

Bust by Houdon, made at Mount Vernon, left there by him, and the only
bust or statue of Washington made from life

civill Salvage we incountred. His Country is a pleasant fertile clay soyle, some small creekes; good Harbours for small Barks, but not for Ships."

Smith's party could talk with these Indians as they spoke the language of the Powhatans, "wherein they made such descriptions of the Bay, Isles, and rivers, that often did us exceeding pleasure." Cruising up the coast of the Eastern Shore they searched every inlet for harbors and habitations. Seeing many islands ahead they approached but were driven off by a storm. These they called Russell's Isles, after their physician no doubt, but now they are known as Watt and Tangier Islands.

After some adventures with weather as well as the Indians, they crossed to the western shore. The storms had shredded their sails, which they repaired with their shirts; they were exhausted by nearly a fortnight at the oars; and moreover their supply of bread spoiled "with wet so much that it was rotten (yet so good were their stomachs that they could digest it.)" Wherefore his men begged Smith to give up the expedition and return to Jamestown. To which Smith replied:

"Gentlemen, if you would remember the memorable history of Sir Ralph Layne, how his company importuned him to proceed in the discovery of Moratico, alleadging they had yet a dog, that being boyled with saxafras leaues, would richly feede them in their returnes; then what a shame would it be for you (that haue bin so suspitious of my tendernesse) to force me returne, with so much provision as we haue, and scarce able to say where we haue beene, nor yet heard of that we were sent to seeke? You cannot say but I haue shared with you in the worst which is past; and for what is to come, of lodging, dyet, or whatsoever, I am contented you allot the worst part to myselfe. As for your feares that I will lose my selfe in these unknowne large waters, or be swallowed up in some stormie gust; abandon these childish feares, for worse then is crept north slowly. The "relations" lay no emphasis even on trips into the adjacent York or Rappahannock. There were visits to Powhatan's capital on the Pamunkey, but as this was only twelve miles across the peninsula from Jamestown the visits were made by land rather than by the vastly longer water route. Even the Potomac was for another quarter of a century left to its Indians and its solitude. During that time of awaiting the first white settler only three conspicuous adventurers seem to have come into that then remote wilderness. They were Henry Spelman, Samuel Argall and Henry Fleet.

Young Spelman—he was only twenty-one years old when he adventured out of England—was the third son of the distinguished antiquary, Sir Henry Spelman, of Cougham, Norfolk. He was one of five hundred immigrants who reached Virginia in nine ships in the year 1609. In one of the Indian massacres, which took place soon after his arrival, he was the sole survivor, but he was made a prisoner by Powhatan. While in that monarch's custody, the King of the Potomacs came down to the Pamunkey on a visit to his Emperor. Between Harry Spelman and the northern Indian some sort of attachment developed. When the King set out for his home on the Potomac, Spelman followed him and remained with him several years. With such opportunities to become acquainted with the Indians and their resources he became a trader, and Captain John Smith declared he was "one of the best Interpreters in the Land."

Spelman's last trip into the Potomac was made in the *Tiger* in 1623, at a time when the Indians of all Tidewater were inflamed against the whites by a hostile condition which was really local about the James. He had brought his ship up within a few miles of the falls. While he was ashore with all but five of his ship's complement, some of the natives slipped off in their canoes and boarded his ship. To frighten the savages one of the sailors discharged "a peece of Ordnance" quite at random. The intruders were terrorized, abandoned their canoes and swam for the shore. The five sailors believed they had saved the day. They learned presently the direct effect of their aimless shot. There was a loud commotion among the Indians on shore. A man's head, a white man's head, was thrown over the bank. It was the head of the Potomac King's friend, Harry Spelman.

The historian of this incident declared that how he "was surprized or slaine is uncertaine," and tops off the tragedy of this first white full length figure who spent the best part of his life at the head of Tidewater, with this philosophic couplet:

"Thus things proceed and vary not a jot,
Whether we know them, or we know them not."

Sam Argall followed soon after Spelman. He was of another sort, shrewd and commanding, apparently at times quite unscrupulous. Yet he was a valiant explorer all over the north Atlantic, named Delaware Bay for his patron, was knighted eventually and was nominated governor of Virginia, but the minutes of the London Company tell how signally he failed of election. His most picturesque exploit in Tidewater establishes the interesting fact that King Powhatan's daughter, Pocahontas, was somewhat of a traveler in her own country. It happened on a trading trip which Argall made into the Potomac in April, 1613, and which he described in a letter sent to England in the June following:

"While I was on this businesse I was told by certaine Indians, my friends, that the Great Powhatan's Daughter Pokahuntis was with the King Patowomeck, whether I presently repaired, resolving to possesse myselfe of her by any stratagem that I could use, for the ransoming of so many Englishmen as were prisoners with Powhatan: as also to get such armes and tooles, as hee, and other Indians had got by murther and stealing from others of our Nation, with some quantatie of Corne, for the Colonies reliefe. So soone as I came to an anchor before the Towne, I manned my Boate and sent on shoare, for the King of Pastancy and Ensigne Swift (whom I had left as a pledge of our love and truce, the Voyage before) who presently came and brought my pledge with him: whom after I had received, I brake the matter to this King, and told him, that if he did not betray Pokohuntis into my hands; we would be no longer brothers nor friends. Hee alleaged, that if hee should undertake this businesse, then Powhatan would make warrs upon him and his people; but upon my promise, that I would joyne with him against him, hee repaired presently to his brother, the great King of Patowomeck, who being made acquainted with the matter, called his Counsell together: and after some few houres deliberation, concluded rather to deliver her into my hands, then lose my friendship: so presently, he betrayed her into my Boat, wherein I carried her aboord my ship. This done, an Indian was dispatched to Powhatan, to let him know, that I had taken his Daughter: and if he would send hom the Englishmen (whom he had detained in slaverie, with such armes and tooles, as the Indians had gotten, and stolne) and also a great quantitie of Corne, that then, he should have his daughter restored, otherwise not. This newes much grieved this great King, yet, without delay, he returned the messenger with this answer. That he desired me to use his daughter well, and bring my ship into his River, and there he would give mee my demands: which being performed, I should deliver him his Daughter, and we should be friends.

"Having received this answere, I presently departed from Patowomeck, being the 13. of Aprill and repayred with all speed to Sir T. Gates, to know of him upon what condition he would conclude this peace, and what he would demand: to whom I also delivered my prisoner, towards whose ransome within few days, this King sent home seven of our men, who seemed to be very joyfull for thet they were freed from the slavery and feare of cruell murther, which they daily before lived in. They brought also three pieces, one broad Axe, and a long Whip-Saw, and one Canoe of Corne. I beeing quit of my prisoner, went forward with the Frigat which I had left at Point Comfort, and finished her."

Harry Fleet was not so picturesque as the romantic Spelman, nor so commanding as the broad-gage Argall. But he came to the Potomac almost as early as they and remained much longer, long enough to see the first settlers here, and to be their friend and interpreter.

He had three ships trading in upper Tidewater, and for years his sails were the only regular and dependable ones the Indians knew. Periodically he bought and took away hides, beaver fur, corn and tobacco, and periodically he brought and sold "beads, bells, hatchets, knives, coats, shirts, Scottish stockings and broadcloth. . . . The women desire bells and some kind of beads."

Fleet's first voyage into the headwaters of Tidewater Virginia was made with Harry Spelman in the *Tiger,* when that young nobleman was butchered by the Indians. He was one of the twenty-one who accompanied Spelman on shore. His life was spared, however, though he was held a prisoner for several years. Eventually he was ransomed and resumed his roving life.

Spelman and Fleet each left a brief "relation." One of the most interesting items in Fleet's narrative is his description of the neighborhood where he was made captive, and it is obvious from it that the spot was near the site of the present Federal Capital:

"This place without question is the most pleasant and healthful in all this country, and most convenient for habitation, the air temperate in summer, and not violent in winter. It aboundeth in all manner of fish. The Indians in one night will commonly catch thirty sturgeons in a place where the river is not above three fathom broad. And as for deer, buffaloes, bears, turkeys, the woods do swarm with them, and the soil is exceedingly fertile, but above this place the country is rocky and mountainous like Cannida. The 27th of June I manned my shallop, and went up with the flood, the tide rising four feet, at this place. We had not rowed above three miles, but we might hear the Falls to roar, about six miles distant."

There was one other shadowy figure on the shores of the Potomac who was forgotten until Moncure D. Conway found, on Potomac Run, a tombstone on which was this inscription:

HERE LIES INTERED
THE BODY OF EDMOND
HELDER PRECTIONER IN
PHYSICK AND CHYRURGE
RY. BORN IN BEDFORDE
SHIRE OBIIT MARCH 11
1618. S ATATIS SUA Y6

He was prompted to his search by a rumor which persisted during the middle of the last century that "one of the Pall Bears of William Shakespeare" was buried in Fredericksburg. He found nothing to sustain that rumor, but in a wider flung search he did find the new world's oldest English epitaph.

And who was Doctor Helder? And how came he to the Potomac? That "prectioner in physick and chyrurgery" must at least have known Spelman and Argall and Fleet.

After Spelman and Argall and Fleet made known the farther reaches of Virginia's Tidewater the dream of a short passage that way to India faded, the colonists came and found a good substitute for the riches of India on the shores and in the waters of these rivers, and gradually civilization crept over them, conquering them up to the falls, and the wilderness was no more for ever.

CHAPTER IV

TIDEWATER YIELDS TO CIVILIZATION

John Smith's Companies and the First Supplies—Stagnant Tide of Population—Illness, Starving Time and Massacre—The Land Beckons the Settlers—How Civilization Crept up the Rivers—The Indian Recedes—Indian Names and English Names on Tidewater's Map—The Social Fabric—Servants and Slaves—Accumulating Land—Rise of the Great Plantations—Genesis of the Home—Priceless Nails—An Almost Townless Territory.

HE settlement of a new country is always an exciting event. There are few romances equal to man's coming into a wilderness, conquering it and making it serve him. The settlement of Tidewater Virginia is of peculiar interest because it is the first chapter in the English settlement on the American continent. Other English came into Massachusetts Bay and began their settlement at Plymouth in 1620, thirteen years after Powhatan's people reported the arrival of the three "great ships"—they were small enough comparatively and actually—with the colonists at the island to be called Jamestown. France, about the waters of the St. Lawrence to the north, and Spain, on the peninsula of Florida in the south, had prior footholds on the continent, but it was the English strain which was to prevail and to determine the character of the Republic which they began.

When Captain Christopher Newport sailed back to England on the fifteenth of June, 1607, he left behind him, isolated, surrounded by the savages, a total of one hundred colonists.

The Council numbered six of whom five bore the title of captain. In addition, forty-eight were listed as "gentlemen," including one preacher and one surgeon; there were four "carpenters," twelve "laborers," a blacksmith, a sailor, a barber, a bricklayer, a mason, a tailor, a drummer, another surgeon, four "boys," and "divers others to the number of one hundred."

The next year arrived two "supplies." The first included thirty-two "gentlemen," twenty-one "laborers," six tailors, two apothecaries, a jeweler, two refiners, two goldsmiths, a gunsmith, a perfumer, another surgeon, a cooper, a blacksmith, a "tobacco pipe-maker," and "divers others to the number of one hundred twenty."

The second supply included "gentlemen," "tradesmen," "labourers," "boys" to the number of seventy, among whom were "Mistresse Forrest, and Anne Burras, her maide" and "eight Dutch men and Poles." These three groups of settlers brought the total population up to about two hundred ninety-five before the end of 1608. This entire population came out of England, but in that year John Smith wrote home of "a marriage between John Laydon and Anne Burras; which was the first marriage we had in Virginia," and so no doubt there was a beginning of a domestic "supply." But only one hundred seven births are reported in Virginia between 1609 and 1625.

At first, haste was made slowly. The people were not acclimatized. There were massacres by the Indians, and there were "famines." By John Rolfe's count there were in Virginia only three hundred fifty white people in 1616. Fourteen hundred forty immigrants out of England are accounted for up to the end of 1619, yet it is estimated that the total population at that time was but nine hundred.

THE SPREAD OF POPULATION

It is variously estimated that there were between twelve hundred fifty and twenty-two hundred people settled in Virginia, probably much nearer the former than the latter figure, when the *Mayflower* reached Plymouth in December, 1620. Five thousand additional men, women and children arrived up to February, 1625. Nevertheless, the census of 1634 tells a bitter story of hardship, illness and Indian troubles, for, in spite of the continued supply, it lists but forty-nine hundred fourteen whites of all classes; less than there were nine years before. If we look ahead by larger periods the outlook is more heartening for by 1649 this population had trebled itself to fifteen thousand, and in 1666 there were forty thousand settlers in Tidewater.

How were these people distributed over the land? At first, for self-protection from the Indians, they all settled on the island of Jamestown. Soon after they took up the land adjacent. So gradually they spread up and down the James, although there was early settlement near the mouth of the bay inside both the capes.

There is another record, besides the census, which helps to gage the speed and direction of the rising tide of population in Tidewater. Up to 1619 the colony had been governed by a council appointed in England by the London Company. The people themselves actually had no say. In that year the franchise was granted to the Virginians with the right of holding a General Assembly. Then and so, for the first time in America, appeared representative government. Lists of the representatives, with the counties they represented, survive in part, and they help to time the spread of population along the various rivers.

The lists of representatives for the first ten years show none who did not live on the James River. Whatever population there was elsewhere it was too sparse and scattered to warrant votes. Then in 1629 Accomac was given a voice, though it was not heard that year. A note after the list of burgesses said: "For the Easterne Shoare noe burgesses did appear." But it was heard from when there was fighting to be done, as was witnessed by a list of the colony's military resources in which the Eastern Shore was credited with "4 coats of mail" in a total of two hundred seventy-six; "21 armors" in three hundred eighty-four; and "3 swords" in four hundred four. Three years later, in 1632, representatives of "Yorke" came to Jamestown, doubtless by the short-cut across the peninsula.

Whoever were the hardy pioneers who ventured farther up Tidewater, along the nearer Pamunkey and Mattapony Rivers where the Indians were now conscious of their difficult defensive if not yet at bay, or above the "frontiers" on the Rappahannock or the Potomac, they were too few or too busy to be represented in the Assembly for yet another dozen years.

The remote settlers did not, however, always readily seek representation. Jamestown left them alone to fight their own battles with primitive nature and the resentful Indians. It was when the seat of government on the James became conscious of the assets of these remoter settlers, and began to tax them, that they became concerned with representation, in order to have a voice in how their taxes were laid and how they were spent. That at least was one of the reasons why in 1645 burgesses appeared in the Assembly to speak and vote for the new county of Northumberland, when that county included all the land between the Rappahannock and the Potomac, then and since known as the Northern Neck, and was without limitation as to its western boundary. The appearance of these northern members in the House of Burgesses, seems to indicate that the population jumped suddenly from one end of Tidewater to the other. Singularly, the south bank of the Potomac was not first settled by the "supplies" which came into the James. The wilderness here first attracted to it English colonists from Maryland, across the river, colonists who became disaffected with the Catholic rule at St. Mary's.

Between the James and the Northern Neck settlement had actually gone slowly. Not until 1651-52 were new counties being heard in the Assembly. At that time members from Gloucester, at the mouth of the York, and Lancaster, broken off from the Rappahannock side of Northumberland County, were seated. The advance of population up the Potomac was manifested again only three years later, when the upper end of the Northern Neck was erected into a county called Westmoreland and its representatives sat with the other burgesses for the first time.

A notable thing happened in the House of Burgesses of 1666. Hitherto it had appeared a close little corporation of James River planters. There were a few others, but they were, even collectively, out-voted by the James. Then in this year of 1666 the balance of power, for the first time since the foundation of the Assembly forty-seven years before, passed from the group representing the James River. The population had spread thickly enough elsewhere to send, for the first time, enough burgesses to out-vote the older group. It began to look as if Tidewater were thoroughly self-conscious; it had become of age. Virginia then really became Tidewater Virginia and no longer merely the banks of the James River. In the list for 1666 it is interesting to find for Westmoreland, the name of "Colonel John Washington."

With the rising tide of white population there was a concurrent ebb in the red population. Though still a menace from the outskirts, they were a hopeless minority in the population of the Tidewater country itself. In a census for the year 1669, a census which included Westmoreland County, then the most remote frontier of Tidewater, the county farthest from Jamestown, there were listed only seven hundred twenty-five Indians. They retired to make another stand beyond the falls, nearer the foot-hills of the mountains. The Indian, "sullenly and reluctantly yielding step by step to the onward crush of a stronger civilization" is indeed one of the pathetic spectacles of history.

The Indians departed, but they left their names all over the map of Tidewater. At the same time the newly arrived English made their definite impression with the names they put on the same map. And the distribution of Indian names and English names here presents a fact worth noting. Although the principal rivers, with the exception of the James and the York, bear Indian names,—the Appomattox, the Chickahominy, the Pamunkey, the Mattapony, the Pianketank, the Rappahannock and the Potomac,—none of the counties in Tidewater have Indian names with the exception of Nansemond and Accomac. The county names reflect the Virginians' English origin and their allegiance to the British sovereign and royal family, as in Princess Anne, Prince George, Elizabeth City, James City, Charles City, King William, King and Queen, Caroline, and King George; the settlers' allegiance to home counties and other localities in England, as in Norfolk, Isle of Wight, Surry, Warwick, York, New Kent, Gloucester, Middlesex, Northampton, Richmond, Lancaster, Northumberland, Westmoreland and Stafford.

The settlers who came and developed this country represented all sorts and conditions of men. Among them, however, were scarcely any other than English. Though they came classed as gentlemen, yeomen, mechanics and servants, they came under such circumstances that a social system grew up which divided itself sharply between master and slave.

The master class was made up of all who came with at least the means to pay their own passage and establish themselves after they arrived, generally on the land. Members of this class were in some cases younger sons of aristocratic English families; in not a few cases they were men of title; others were soldiers or the sons and kinsmen of merchants; but the representation from the mercantile class was not so numerous as that which included those descended from the gentry. It is often pointed out that in the time of the civil wars in England great numbers of "Cavaliers" came out to Virginia. This is true, but, though this immigration undoubtedly included a high proportion of gentry, it should be remembered that in the sense here used cavalier did not refer to a social class merely but to a political party as well.

The slave class was at first made up wholly of whites. The importation of the African did not assume proportions of importance until about 1670. The black was an involuntary slave. The white entered voluntarily upon what was practically slavery. The black was generally a slave for life, the white only during a period for which he had bound himself. He was not called a slave but a "servant" and generally came out of the laboring class of England, or, perhaps, was some one from a slightly higher social level, adventurous, eager to strike out in the highly touted new world, but without the means for passage over the ocean, much less for the acquirement of land,

and so bound himself freely under an indenture for a fixed period. This slave or "servant" class later received some recruits from England's exportation of convicts into her colonies and from the system of kidnaping and exportation. There was little free labor. But once the white servant had worked out his indenture, he generally moved up into the farming class, and it has been remarked that, as a class, "They led the van in the first stage of the majestic march of the race, which did not halt until the shores of the Pacific had been reached."

The land of Tidewater was at first claimed by the English sovereign as absolutely as if it had been his own by ancestral heritage. No right of the Indian to soil he had occupied indefinitely was even considered, much less allowed. The Assembly did later, however, whether prompted by fear, pity, justice, or all three, give the Indian consideration and often protected him in his title to the land. But the Indian could not accommodate himself to civilization, and its approach drove him involuntarily back toward a larger field in which to subsist on the natural product of forest and stream, and the remnant of the natives left on the land gradually diminished by death and decreasing birth-rates.

Title to the land vested, by grant from the sovereign, in the London Company. Acting as its regents the governor and council conveyed title to the settler. Each shareholder in the company was entitled to one hundred acres, from which arose on the James that sometimes remaining place-name of "hundred." Only one-third of the shareholders in the company actually came out to Tidewater. The others sold their shares in England or sent their agents out to sell their shares for them in Virginia.

Meritorious service of various kinds was another basis for

BLANDFORD CHURCH, PETERSBURG

SHIRLEY ON THE JAMES

WESTOVER ON THE JAMES, THE HOME OF WILLIAM BYRD II

awarding a portion of the soil. Soon a grant of one hundred acres was made to every planter who at his own cost came to the colony. But by far the most important means of land acquisition was the "head right." Under this law every one who transported an immigrant oversea to the new colony was given fifty acres. There was no limit to the number of immigrants he might transport, and as labor was the great need of the planter, he gladly added to his land by yielding to the imperative necessity to import the hands to cultivate it. In the operation of this practise we find one of the first evidences of the vast plantations which prevailed in Tidewater, for it is of record that during the four years between 1618 and 1623, grants of land were made to forty-four different individuals each of whom had transported to the colony at least one hundred persons at his own expense. This meant that each of these forty-four individuals received a grant of five thousand acres. These were, however, the rare exceptions to a more general rule of the existence of only one hundred or a few hundred acres in each holding.

This head right, as a source of land acquisition, was in force only south of the Northern Neck. Between the Rappahannock and Potomac Rivers the system of purchase was in operation. The price was five shillings for every one hundred acres in a tract under six hundred acres, and ten shillings for each one hundred acres in a tract of more than six hundred acres. This system produced vastly larger estates than the head right and explains the "baronial" holdings along the Rappahannock and the Potomac, where, for instance, Nicholas Hayward held a unit of thirty thousand acres, and William Fitzhugh at one time owned, though not wholly contiguous, a total of forty-five thousand acres.

thus providing a fireplace for each of the four main rooms. I have heard it said that colonial titles in Tidewater were sometimes founded on the number of the planters' chimneys; that if he had two chimneys on his house he was called Major, but if his house boasted four chimneys then he was called Colonel. The saying leaves us to conjecture the title of the owner of a house of eight chimneys, such, for instance, as Stratford.

It is true that all the houses of the first half of the seventeenth century, that is to say built between 1607 and 1650, have disappeared, with the probable exception of the Adam Thoroughgood house on Lynnhaven Bay, Smith's Fort on the James and the Packer house on Eastern Shore; nevertheless, and in connection with them, traces and documents and credible tradition of others, make possible a good general idea of the evolution of early domestic buildings.

When the early house developed beyond the log stage, for some time it took on one general type with few and modest variations. It was generally rectangular on its ground plan. Generally, too, there was a hallway from door to door through the center of its shorter dimension. In modest houses there was only one room on each side of this hall; in the more pretentious houses of increased depth there were two rooms on each side of it. But the hall itself, though frequently called "the passage," was often ten or more feet wide, and as it drew a refreshing current of air through from door to door, it was in warm weather the most comfortable and frequented, as it was the most commodious, room in the house.

When the space under the slopes of the roof of such a house was divided into rooms, then windows appeared high up on either side of the chimney ends and the roof slopes were pierced awarding a portion of the soil. Soon a grant of one hundred acres was made to every planter who at his own cost came to the colony. But by far the most important means of land acquisition was the "head right." Under this law every one who transported an immigrant oversea to the new colony was given fifty acres. There was no limit to the number of immigrants he might transport, and as labor was the great need of the planter, he gladly added to his land by yielding to the imperative necessity to import the hands to cultivate it. In the operation of this practise we find one of the first evidences of the vast plantations which prevailed in Tidewater, for it is of record that during the four years between 1618 and 1623, grants of land were made to forty-four different individuals each of whom had transported to the colony at least one hundred persons at his own expense. This meant that each of these forty-four individuals received a grant of five thousand acres. These were, however, the rare exceptions to a more general rule of the existence of only one hundred or a few hundred acres in each holding.

This head right, as a source of land acquisition, was in force only south of the Northern Neck. Between the Rappahannock and Potomac Rivers the system of purchase was in operation. The price was five shillings for every one hundred acres in a tract under six hundred acres, and ten shillings for each one hundred acres in a tract of more than six hundred acres. This system produced vastly larger estates than the head right and explains the "baronial" holdings along the Rappahannock and the Potomac, where, for instance, Nicholas Hayward held a unit of thirty thousand acres, and William Fitzhugh at one time owned, though not wholly contiguous, a total of forty-five thousand acres.

There was a great deal of cheating done by some of the large landholders. By law they were required to "build a house upon the ground acquired, improve and plant the soil and keep a good stock of cattle and hogs." Many of these wealthy men merely erected a small bark hut and turned two or three hogs loose near it. At most they would clear an acre and make a planting of corn for one year. The abuse prevented poorer people from acquiring desirable land, and there was at one time a serious migration of Tidewater settlers to Carolina and other places on account of it.

Among the glories of Tidewater Virginia to-day are the numerous surviving colonial mansions, monuments of the domestic and social life along the rivers before the Revolution. Many of the great houses which have their place in history, either as the homes of celebrated characters or as the scenes of historic events, have disappeared, taken in the toll of Time, the elements, fire or decay, which the shattered fortunes of the families to whom they belonged were unequal to staying. Nevertheless the survivals, most of them in excellent condition, are so numerous that Tidewater is not matched elsewhere in the number and beauty of its storied colonial mansions. The development of architecture in this historic region is therefore scarcely less interesting than the story of the sweep of the human tide across its lands and waters.

Newport's company in the *Sarah Constant,* the *Goodspeed* and the *Discovery* arrived at Jamestown without any building material whatever. Axes and saws they brought, and abundant pine and cedar they found in the endless forests. Their first houses must have been the rudest of one-room shacks, hastily put together of green plank, immediate victims of the warping and shrinking and rotting inevitably induced by alternate heat,

70

cold and damp. Such shanties were succeeded by the scarcely less primitive log cabin, with the bark on and the chinks filled with mud or with clay. This became a new type. It was called "the Virginia house," and it has been acknowledged as the earliest form of colonial architecture. Long after a more refined type of house had appeared along the earlier settled James, the log cabin still appeared as the vanguard of architecture farther and farther out in the wilderness; at first on the York and Pamunkey, later on the Pianketank, then on the Rappahannock and Potomac. There was, however, one early embellishment to the log cabin, if it may be called so pretentiously. That was the high palisades of serried young trees, making of each man's house his fort, if not quite his castle.

Logs eventually gave way to clapboards and later to bricks. Clay was abundant in Tidewater so that buildings of brick became popular, affording better protection against weather during a longer life and with less need of repair. But whether of log, clapboard or brick, one of the early features of every house was an outside brick chimney carrying off the smoke out of a deep and broad fireplace. This fireplace was the colonist's domestic altar, the source of most of his physical consolations. Its sacred fire warmed him and cooked his food for him. About it hung the brass and copper and pewter of the domestic rites. On its hob the vessels sent forth appetizing odors of stews and brews. In its ashes nestled the veritable manna of the Virginia pioneer: the little rolls of corn pone, which for centuries have been a type of pioneer southern cooking.

With the growth of the size of the houses, the chimney at one end of the house was matched by a second at the other end. Soon after, two chimneys rose at each end of the house, thus providing a fireplace for each of the four main rooms. I have heard it said that colonial titles in Tidewater were sometimes founded on the number of the planters' chimneys; that if he had two chimneys on his house he was called Major, but if his house boasted four chimneys then he was called Colonel. The saying leaves us to conjecture the title of the owner of a house of eight chimneys, such, for instance, as Stratford.

It is true that all the houses of the first half of the seventeenth century, that is to say built between 1607 and 1650, have disappeared, with the probable exception of the Adam Thoroughgood house on Lynnhaven Bay, Smith's Fort on the James and the Packer house on Eastern Shore; nevertheless, and in connection with them, traces and documents and credible tradition of others, make possible a good general idea of the evolution of early domestic buildings.

When the early house developed beyond the log stage, for some time it took on one general type with few and modest variations. It was generally rectangular on its ground plan. Generally, too, there was a hallway from door to door through the center of its shorter dimension. In modest houses there was only one room on each side of this hall; in the more pretentious houses of increased depth there were two rooms on each side of it. But the hall itself, though frequently called "the passage," was often ten or more feet wide, and as it drew a refreshing current of air through from door to door, it was in warm weather the most comfortable and frequented, as it was the most commodious, room in the house.

When the space under the slopes of the roof of such a house was divided into rooms, then windows appeared high up on either side of the chimney ends and the roof slopes were pierced to take on the projecting dormer-windows. These developed later, as in the instance of stately old Bewdley in Lancaster County, into two banks of dormers, one rising above the other. Then, too, the stairway was introduced, at first and almost universally in the passage, but eventually this room, so precious in domestic ease and comfort, was often left uninterrupted, and one of the side rooms was sacrificed in part, and in a dark well the steep steps rose up in what was sometimes referred to as the "hidden stairway."

Houses took other shapes than that of the rigid quadrangle. According to their form—more often produced by the position in which additions were put on than by a preconcerted ground plan—they were called, alphabetically, a "T" house, an "L" house or an "H" house. Later the wing appeared at the end, then at both ends, then set off from the main house by connecting curtains, but by that time a century of development had set its stamp and there began to appear great places which we may see to-day or know by tradition.

A feature of nearly all houses, however humble they may have been, was the covered stoop, or porch, or portico, made necessary by the heat of summer. But the great columns now seen farther inland were not a feature of colonial Tidewater houses. They appeared after the Revolution under the influence of Thomas Jefferson's classic taste as an architect.

In this country without minerals, nails were scarce. Such nails as the pioneers had were imported from England, and they were accounted so precious that it is said that some settlers, when they sold their lands to take up other lands at a distance, would burn their cabins in order to salvage the nails in it, so as to carry them along and use them in the construction of their next home. In the total absence of any large nails, the larger timbers were held together by pegs. This method prevailed well into the last century. It is rarely that a Tidewater house of the colonial period does not reveal wooden pins in the joinings of the timbers supporting its floors and its roof.

There is a pleasing but improbable tradition that the bricks of this-and-that chimney and in this-and-that house or church in Tidewater were brought from England. But such importations were few, non-significant by the records and by the logic of the situation. Nearly everywhere in Tidewater there are deposits of excellent brick clay. Such building material was literally "cheap as dirt." On the other hand the ships out of England were small, and in them every inch of space was needed for the stowage of manufactured articles of every character, for the water-mills, for the workshops, for the operation of the plantation, the equipment of the houses, for the clothing of the settlers, the adornment of their wives, and for every particle of luxury they enjoyed.

The fiction of "bricks from England" probably had its origin not in the fact of the place where the bricks were made but in the trade phrases "Dutch brick" and "English brick." These terms referred to sizes. The Dutch brick was small, the English brick was large. Though the patterns of the English brick, of which Tidewater chimneys and houses and churches were made, may have come from England, they were the product of clay kilns and workmen on this side of the Atlantic.

Reference has been made to Thomas Jefferson's influence on American architecture. He was in fact one of the first, if not actually the first great American architect, and he exercised a great and too little appreciated effect on the taste of the designers of public and private buildings. In his *Notes on*

Virginia, revised by him before its publication in Paris in 1784, he made, however, a singularly severe indictment of Tidewater architecture.

"The genius of architecture," he said, "seems to have shed its maledictions over this land. . . . The first principles of the art are unknown, and there exists scarcely a model among us sufficiently chaste to give an idea of them."

This was written when the last of the colonial mansions had been built. It seems a somewhat ill-considered criticism to make of a region, well known to him, in which stood Westover, Shirley, Brandon, Chatham, Rosewell, Mount Airy, Stratford, Carter's Grove, Gunston Hall, Nomini Hall, and others relatively as excellent and beautiful in their interior as well as exterior design and workmanship.

Inquiry into the date of the building of these great mansions reveals the period of Tidewater's finest bloom, when, having graduated from a wilderness to a prosperous agricultural region, it eventually became celebrated for its culture and cultural manifestations. Stratford as it stands to-day rose soon after 1729 on the ruins of an earlier house which was destroyed by fire in that year. Rosewell dates from 1725; Westover, 1730; Chatham, 1740; Carter's Grove, 1751; Gunston Hall, 1755; and Mount Airy, 1758. Precise dating of other great colonial mansions here is not always possible, but it may be assumed that most of them rose in that great building period which gave Virginia its finest specimens of domestic architecture, between 1725 and 1760.

Tidewater Virginia was from the beginning agricultural. Its wealth came out of the soil. Its professional men, politicians and statesmen came from the planter class. Cities and towns were few. No civic community was considerable until the nineteenth century. The settlement had begun with a town, to be sure—Jamestown—but the population was held there largely as a matter of mutual self-protection against the Indians. The exigencies of another kind of self-preservation soon distributed that population over the land. The people had to live, they had to live from the product of the soil, so they had to go out and settle on it. They had no use for a town except as a seat of government. To-day even the county-seats in Tidewater consist of little more than a court-house.

Each plantation, each large plantation at least, became in effect a town. It was self-sufficient. About or near the "great house" were gathered the quarters of the servants and the building wherein nearly all the manufacturing and repairing necessary to the life of the inhabitants was carried on. Anything further was purchased in England and delivered by ship direct at the plantation landing. The parish church stood apart in a field or in a forest clearing, central to the neighborhood it served. There were no post-offices because in colonial days there was no postal system. Letters were carried privately, by favor.

Nevertheless the masters of the colony, from the first, had a fixed idea that cities were necessary to it. So they legislated cities. But only a shred of such towns remains. Jamestown has gone. Henricopolis of Sir Thomas Dale, though in five years presenting a more substantial aspect than Jamestown, actually fell into hopeless ruin immediately after that time. The surviving names of counties on the James—Charles City, James City, Elizabeth City—stand for no survival, and merely witness the irresistible conquest of economic laws.

In 1662 a law was passed ordering that four towns be built to serve as ports of entry: one on the York, one on the Rappahannock, one on the Potomac, and one on the Eastern Shore. Soon after Culpepper's arrival in 1680 a more extensive program of town building was ordered, and the following places were selected: Varina in Henrico County, Flower de Hundred in Charles City, Smith's Fort in Surry, Patesfield in Isle of Wight, Huff's Point in Nansemond, Mouth of Deep Creek in Warwick, the Jervise plantation in Elizabeth City, the Wise plantation in lower Norfolk, the Read plantation in York, the Brick house in New Kent, Tyndall's Point in Gloucester, the Wormeley plantation in Middlesex, Hobb's Hole in Rappahannock, Peace Point in Stafford, Corotoman in Lancaster, Chickakony in Northumberland, Calvert's Neck in Accomac and King's Creek in Northampton. Another such law was passed in 1691. But actually little that was tangible came of such legislation.

The little capital had a reason for existence. When it was destroyed by fire in 1698, the seat of government was transferred from Jamestown a few miles inland to the Middle Plantation, and Williamsburg came into being there. That community has survived but always as a comparatively small economic factor. Greater forces than artificial legislation were needed to determine the time and the place where the Tidewater cities would rise.

As the pioneers trekked westward the heads of navigation at the falls on the principal rivers became cargo transfer points. Hence, at these points, warehouses appeared, about which later rose stores and dwellings, then churches and schools, and the other details of towns and cities. That was the reason of the rise of Richmond at the falls of the James; of Fredericksburg at the falls of the Rappahannock; and of the ports of Alexandria and Georgetown near the falls of the Potomac. The development of steam land transportation made inevitable the rise of Norfolk and its surrounding cities at the mouth of the James, for the great ocean carriers could not go to the falls so conveniently and economically as the railways could bring the freight of the hinterland to the great oceanside docks.

These cities, it should be noted, are all on the edge of Tidewater Virginia. At heart it is townless, still a land of plantations, and in this respect at least little changed during the three hundred years of its history. Its chief glory, apart from its traditions and its line of eminent characters, remains its natural beauty, its water stretches and its storied churches and plantation mansions. In many of its aspects it is still colonial. In feature and in fact it is the Old Virginia whose people and houses and history lend so much glamour to that name.

CHAPTER V

THE GOLDEN AGE

Kinship with Friendly Waters—The Self-Sufficient Plantation—The Great House, Outbuildings and Quarters—Tidal Water-Mills—When Tobacco Was the Only Cash—Self-Perpetuating Labor—Trade with England— The Ships' Captains—Interior of the Plantation Houses—Feeding the Fireplaces—Painters, Portraits, Books and Plate—The Planter and His Lady—Old-Time Hospitality—Larks of the Colonial Youngsters—Games, Music and Dancing—A Six-Day Dance—Fox-Hunting—Horse-Racing— Cock-Fighting—At the Play—Colonial Churches.

Y THE middle of the eighteenth century all the water-front and other desirable land in Tidewater had been taken up and developed. The extreme of population, within the limitations of domestic and economic life as led there, seemed to have been reached. Immigrants swept into the bay and up the rivers, but now they did not pause there, not even at the several falls. They pressed on into the "new forests," on to the high lands, on toward the mountains. Tidewater Virginia had not only developed, but life there had begun to ripen, to become mellow.

The conflicts with the Indian were a thing of the past. The wolves, which in pioneer days had harassed the folds and pastures, had retired with the red man toward the mountains to harass another generation of settlers in a newer land. There were no more famines or "starving times." As the climate was now understood, and the population now reproduced itself instead of depending on the "supply" of unacclimated immigrants, there was no more of the distress of "seasoning time."

79

As a result of one hundred years of pioneering, of the development and improvement of the land, of the settled order of economic life, of the consequent accumulation of wealth and of its liberal expenditure, the plantation as a finished product is perhaps best observed as it was at that time.

In journeying about Tidewater to-day what one sees of the past, other than the immediate past, is in general the survival of the fifty years preceding the Revolution. There are houses and churches dating back into the seventeenth century, but only enough to emphasize their uniqueness and not enough to give their own accent to the outlook.

And so the interest in the vanished life that was led in and about and between these survivals attaches to the plantation life of the half-century before the declaration and achievement of our independence.

The planter always built his house in sight of the water. On the lower rivers where the land rises only a few feet above the water and then stretches back with an almost unvarying level to the next river, he put his house near the riverside, and often his gardens and hedges led directly to the shore where the landing stood. Thus stand the houses on Eastern Shore, on the James and the York and even some of those on the Rappahannock and the Potomac. But some forty miles above the mouths of the last two rivers, the elevation of the terrain varies and there the houses were erected on the higher outlook which varied in its distance from the waterside, though the distance seldom exceeded half a mile.

In either case the prospect from the front door presents that incomparable and inexplicable beauty produced by the union of land and water. Land alone seldom presents an outlook of activity. Water nearly always seems alive. Every breath of the wind stirs its surface to a smile. It catches the reflection of moving clouds and so doubles the infinite variety of the flying islands of the sky. But no reach in Tidewater is ever left long with only its natural woods and beauties. Seldom a stretch but sails etch their light lines in the offing and, diminished by distance, wing their flight across the blue waters like butterflies vivaciously idle.

The house itself rarely stood alone. It generally had no "back" but two "fronts"—the river-front, where the family maintained its out-of-door privacy, and the approach front, where the drive terminated in a circle edged with box and where visitors were made welcome. This naturally drove the outbuildings beyond the "sides" of the house. There, at one end one found the well-house, the summer kitchen, the ice-house, the house-servants' quarters, the tailor shop, the smoke-house, the loom- or spinning-house, and houses devoted to other domestic activities related to the interior of the "big house," or controlled by the mistress of it. These small build-ings generally clustered in a detached group a little way from the big house. At the opposite end, at an equal distance in a similarly detached group, were the coach-house, the stables and barns, the wheelwright, blacksmith shop, the carpenter shop, and the quarters of the servants who attended to these and other activities related to out-of-door life.

Often these outbuildings were screened or "planted out" by shrubbery so that, though not always invisible from the big house, they were almost inconspicuous. There were, of course, occasional exceptions to so general a rule. At Mount Vernon they were nicely placed on little streets that gave the unit of domestic buildings the effect of a village which in fact it was. Both Stratford and Nomini Hall stood in the center of a square at the four corners of which rose identical contributory out-buildings which housed all such domestic activities.

The cabins of the field-hands, called the "quarters," were at a distance from the big house, generally out of sight of it. Often they were distributed over the plantation so that those charged with the care of certain fields lived near them. Though such quarters were out of sight their position was often re-vealed by wisps of smoke, rising over the bushes or trees, from the fireplaces where the kettles boiled or the pone lay buried in the ashes; or by the shrill play of the piccaninnies, or by the seldom modulated scolding of the black women, or by the shouting of the interminable gospel hymns, those "spirituals" which were wafted across the fields as often under the blatant broiling noonday sun as in the quiet of the evening.

Somewhere on the waterside of nearly every plantation was the mill where the planter ground corn-meal for batter bread and pone, white flour for beaten biscuit and waffles and cakes, and mash for the year's supply of hard liquor. In Westmore-land County there were twenty-three grist-mills within a ra-dius of twelve miles, with a capacity of thirty thousand bushels yearly "which quantity is sufficient to furnish bread for 2,000 persons one whole year, estimating fifteen bushels to each, the common allowance for negroes, who are not fed with animal food."

Such mills were of two kinds, windmills and water-mills. The water-mills were also of two kinds, those whose wheels were turned by water flowing over them and those whose wheels were turned by water flowing under them. The over-flowing waters came from the picturesque ponds which, curi-ously, were not fed by running streams. In the flat reaches of Tidewater there were few streams with gravity fall, and so these ponds were mere reservoirs of rain water, gathered as it fell, and stored, and used sparingly. The underflowing waters were the briny waters of the inlet forced past the wheels by the tide, and the supply of power for such a wheel was unfailing and practically continual in one direction or the other, as the tides ebbed and flowed.

The main source of the planter's wealth was the tobacco raised on his plantation. Tobacco was not merely the main source of the planter's fortune, it was very nearly the only source. Just before the Revolution the proportionate values of the five principal exports, in English pounds sterling, for a given period were:

Tobacco	768,000
Indian Corn	30,000
Wheat	40,000
Deer and other skins	25,000
Iron	35,000

The tobacco exportation alone was worth more than five times as much as all the others combined.

The foundation of the planter's economic operations was cheap labor as expressed in negro slavery. Money invested in the purchase of a black man bought also the solution of his owner's labor problem; it obviated rehire, as possession extended over the lifetime of the slave, and it brought natural increment as it possessed the owner also of all the offspring of his slave. Once a man had a force of slaves equal to the needs of his plantation his labor problem seemed not only solved temporarily, it seemed solved for all time, for the supply, which involved only a moderate investment, was self-perpetuating.

Such a compact and practically self-sustaining unit was the plantation with its self-perpetuating labor supply; with its own little village of carpenters, blacksmiths, weavers and other manufacturing artizans; and with its own supply of cereals, meats, fish, dairy products, that the absence of villages and towns from their region is easily understood.

Though there were no local towns to supply luxuries, nevertheless the planter and his family did live, in varying degrees, in luxury. The luxuries all came from England by those ships which came directly to each planter's landing. During the winter such a ship had taken off the year's crop of tobacco to be sold in England. It came back again loaded with luxuries which the planter could not produce on his own estate. It brought silk, velvets, ribbons, laces, wigs, shoes, hats, bonnets, jewelry, silverware for the table, books, furniture, harness, coaches even, and field machinery. Although the planter distilled his own liquors, for the big house and for the quarters, his wines came from oversea, ordered by the "pipe," a variety for every course and every occasion, appraised and selected by vintage.

One can scarcely over-estimate the place occupied in the life of the planter by the captains of the ships which battled the Atlantic and then sailed quietly up the river inlets to the protected landings. To him they were not merely mariners, they were the planter's only contact with his English agent, and frequently the captains themselves shopped for him in London and Bristol; they had dresses dyed, watches fixed, old wigs made over, old swords exchanged for more fashionable rapiers, coats of arms authenticated at the college of heraldry and drawn and colored and framed; they carried letters and presents back and forth; they were even in a sense the first

BRANDON ON THE JAMES

St. John's Church, Richmond

White House of the Confederacy, Richmond

editors, for they gathered the news of court, exchange, Parliament, family and friend, and edited it according to its relation to the planter at each of the various landings, and retailed it when it was the earliest approach to a personal gazette.

Such captains, however, at times a godsend, were at other times a sore trial, for their real business was the rough travail of the sea and seamen, and they were at times so utterly lacking not only in capacity for these nice conveniences but even for the proper handling of the vitally important papers in connection with the transport and sale of the tobacco that they exasperated the planter to protests which fell just short of the profanity which was no doubt in his heart.

In such a mood William Byrd wrote, in 1736, that the sea captains of whom he was having experience "are commonly men of no aspiring Genius, and their understanding rises little higher than Instinct, when they go out of their Element. They are most of them airant Sea Calves, and the Tritons that swim under, are just as wise as these that sail upon it. The most that they can be taught to do, is, some times to deliver a letter, and if they have superior Parts, they may be instructed perhaps to call for an answer. One may as soon tutor a Monkey to speak, or a French-woman to hold her Tongue, as to bring a skipper to higher Flights of Reason."

Such a common fellow certainly was not Captain Dobby of the *Susannah* and the *Beaufort,* who was one of the intimates of Councilor Carter's family at Nomini Hall on the Potomac. He bobbs up frequently in Fithian's diary:

"At five this Evening, Ben, *Prissey* & I rode out on Horse back for exercise; before we returned Captain *Dobby,* of the ship *Susannah,* an agreeable, sensible, polite Gentleman came & 'Squire Lee. . . .

"Breakfasted with us Captain *Dobby* & Mr. Taylor, their conversation promiscuous [and one wonders on what subjects and to what degree]. . . .

"Captain *Dobby* dines with us; he is a man of much Spirit and Humour; A great Mimick. . . . He acquainted us that at Hobbe's Hole this Day is a Boat-Race on the River Rappahannock . . . and that in the Evening there is a great Ball to be given—I believe both the *Rowers & dancers,* as well *Ladies* as *Gentlemen* will perspire freely—or in plain English that they will soak in Sweat! The Captain invited us on Board his Ship next Tuesday to Dine with him & wish them a pleasant Passage as the Ship is to Sail the day following."

The whole family from Nomini Hall joined the party on Captain Dobby's ship for the Regatta, Fithian recording: "The Beaufort is a stately Ship; Captain Dobby had an Awning from the Stern over the Quarter quite to the Mizen-Mast, which made great Room, kept off the Sun, & yet was open on each Side to give the Air a free passage. At three we had on Board about 45 Ladies, and about 60 Gentlemen besides the Ships Crew & Waiters Servants &c. We were not thronged at all." One regrets to be told that hospitable Captain Dobby's entry lost in the race.

"There were six ships riding in the Harbour and a number of Schooners & smaller Vessels."

Ships and sails seem always to have been in sight in Tidewater. Apart from the "Schooners & smaller Vessels" in the local river trade and doing the small chores between landings, there were in the middle of the eighteenth century three hundred thirty ships and three thousand sailors in the tobacco trade alone between Virginia and England.

Whatever may have been the artistic shortcomings of the exterior of some of the colonial houses, from the remains of the survivals it would seem that few of them lacked impressive interior features. There may have been no architects in Tide-water, but there was no dearth of "joiners" and carvers. They had learned their trade in England and transmitted good patterns and deft craftsmanship to their apprentices, generation after generation.

In the passage, the drawing-room and the dining-room of the better houses, the walls were less often plastered and papered than paneled in pine or oak or mahogany. And where the walls met the ceiling there was often a bravely carved cornice. This, it seems, was not oftener true of the larger houses than the small houses.

What seems to have been universally lacking from the colonial house were plumbing, hence bathrooms, and built-in clothes closets. The sole supply of fresh water was the well, and the only system of running water in the house was, as Vaughan Kester said, "a nigger with a bucket." It seems not to have occurred to the designers to build in closets. Their places were taken by cumbersome wardrobes and clothes-presses, often of handsome wood and design, which stood against the walls of the bedrooms.

There was, however, no dearth of fireplaces. Generally there was one in every room. In the total absence of furnaces and stoves, they were the only means of heating the houses. The erecting of flues was the colonial builder's masterpiece, his best understood art. Heat was abundant in Tidewater. Nature supplied it in summer. The apparently inexhaustible woodland of pine and oak and hickory supplied it in winter. Though there was abundant wood and abundant labor it must have been no mean job to keep the fireplaces of one of the mansions supplied in severe weather. Fithian gives a hint of how surprisingly extensive was the operation at Nomini Hall. During a snowy and icy January period he wrote:

"Mr. Carter has a Cart & three pair of Oxen which every Day bring in four Loads of Wood, Sunday excepted, & yet these very severe Days we have none to spare; And indeed I do not wonder, for in the *Great House, School* House, Kitchen &. there are twenty-Eight steady fires! & most of these are very large!"

In its furnishings the planter's house much resembled the country houses in England of the same period. It could not be otherwise. His carpets, cabinets, tables, chairs, curtains and whatever art objects there were in evidence, came oversea from the same market as the supply for the English homes.

In his effort to hang his walls with pictures he was often at a disadvantage. Such colonials as went to England either as youths to college or later in life on business and to travel, had themselves "limned" by the better artists there. Warner Lewis, of Warner Hall in Gloucester, and Councilor Carter, of Nomini Hall in Westmoreland, were painted by Sir Joshua Reynolds. Other great eighteenth-century artists, including Sir Peter Lely and Sir Godfrey Kneller, painted the Virginians. As the women of the planter's family rarely made the crossing there are fewer English portraits of women than of men up to the second quarter of the eighteenth century. The wife and daughters and sons of Edward Jaqualaine, of Jamestown, however, were all in England, and the portraits of all of them were there painted by "an artist of the greatest merit" Mr. Jaqualaine could find. The wives of "King" Carter, of Corotoman, and William Fitzhugh were, it is believed, also painted in England. Up to about 1700 there were no significant painters in Tidewater. About 1736 Charles Bridges came to Virginia and subsequently painted many portraits. Among the portrait painters reported here by Robert Sully were "Durand, Manly and Woolaston—the first tolerable, the second execrable, and the third very good." But Peale, Thomas Sully and Sharples also painted in Virginia, and Hesselius painted in upper Tidewater year after year. The planters were often not more eager in having their own portraits than in having paintings of their favorite racing horses; and whenever possible they had their coat of arms emblazoned, framed and hung on the paneled over-mantel.

Considering the distance from the English supply and the fact that there were no domestic publishers and few domestic booksellers, it is astonishing how many private libraries of considerable size were built up here. Very few of the inventories of estates are without the mention of books. The longer lists were left by Ralph Wormeley, Robert Carter, William Byrd, Richard Lee and George Washington. The largest of these, Byrd's library at Westover, consisted of "near 4000 Volumes, in all Languages and Faculties, contained in 23 double Presses of black Walnut. . . . Great Part of the Books in elegant Bindings, and of the best Editions, and a considerable number of them very Scarce." Among the Virginia bookplates named in Dexter's work on the subject are fifty-two which can be safely asserted to be colonial. Others have been added. The list is, of course, practically a limited directory of the families along the shores of Tidewater.

The planter was a kind of feudal lord over his house, his family, his plantation and his "people" as the black servants were familiarly called. He was, himself, in some cases, however, ruled over by his wife. But whether she ruled her lord or not, the planter's wife was mistress in their house and in all the little adjacent houses where the activities contributed to the domestic situation. As a rule she understood the domestic arts and kept an understanding control over the house service, the dairy, the jellying and preserving, the weaving, the curing of the hams which in Tidewater reached its highest art at Smithfield, and the attention needed by the sick on any part of the plantation. Although she kept the control, the activities were generally left to others.

So, too, with her spouse. He was an administrator, not a dirt-farmer. His soft palms rarely knew contact with an implement. He rose between the hours of six and nine, early or late according, it would seem, to his wealth, and in summer at least gave the new day the benediction of a mint julep. Then he rode forth over his acres on the daily inspection of his fields which were so many and extended to such remote edges in the greater estates that the owner of such a one took his "farms" in turn, day after day, until he had made the round of all of them.

The planter's table was large, his supply abundant. It had to be, for the families were extensive and hospitality was unbounded. In addition to the parents and children there were usually at table an otherwise homeless relative or two and the resident tutor of the children. The size of the plantations made considerable the distance between them. This, in connection with the wretched roads, discouraged school building and made classes in the home quite general.

These same conditions made a fine art of hospitality. Inns and ordinaries were few and existed only for the stranger or for the commercial traveler. Others en route went from one private house to another, and they never suffered for any lack of welcome. The code of courtesy imposed this on the host, no matter what the inconvenience. It was often abused, but it was never refused. Fitzhugh, of Chatham, opposite Fredericksburg on the Rappahannock, found his seat, on the main north and south highway, so disadvantageous, that hospitality was breaking his fortune and actually drove him from his home. He built himself another house, Ravensworth, in a then remote inland part of Fairfax County and enjoyed economic retirement. Much later, in another part of Virginia, Thomas Jefferson, overwhelmed by visitors at Monticello, built himself a second house, Poplar Forest, a hundred miles away from his permanent home, and there took refuge from the burdens of hospitality three or four times a year.

There was a constant interchange of visits between the homes. No invitations were awaited or were necessary. People drove in, sent their horses to the stables and their portmanteaux into the big house, and remained by the week. Young people would go from house to house, so remaining absent from their own homes by the month. Such a "tour" was that of Miss Lucinda Lee who kept a journal of one such journey for the information of a friend. Our information of life in a Tidewater colonial house is enriched by her entries. The pages slip gaily by when, turning over one, we look through its sprightly candor upon this frank and veracious incident of a colonial night:

"I must tell you of our frolic after we went in our room last night. We took it into our heads to want to eat; well, we had a large dish of bacon and beaf; after that a bowl of Sago Cream and after that, an apple pye. While we were eating the apple pye in bed—God bless you! Making a great noise—in came Mr. Washington [a relative of the General's] dressed in Hannah's short gown and peticoat, and seazed me and kissed me twenty times, in spite of all the resistance I could make;

and then Cousin Molly. Hannah soon followed, dress'd in his coat. They joined us in eating the apple pye, and then went out. After this we took it into our heads to want to eat oysters. We got up, put on our rappers, and went down to the Seller tc get them; do you think Mr. Washington did not follow us and scear us just to death. We went up tho, and eat our oysters. We slept in the old Lady's room, too, and she sat laughing fit to kill herself. She is a charming old lady—you would be delighted with her."

Such girls and such larks are representative of colonial life on Tidewater plantations. Such girls grew into graceful womanhood. Without losing their penchant for pleasures they knew how to be serious and to face the more formidable demands of life with character. They were the mothers of those generations of Virginia statesmen and soldiers who led in directing the course of the revolt against England, in framing the Constitution and in establishing the young Republic.

Such larks are suggestive of the easy, pleasure-loving, hospitable life of the planters and their families and friends. The mild climate invited leisure. The distances between the great houses, and the deliberateness of communication which was based on travel by sail or by coach, made mere "calling" impractical. In its place one finds the visit usually extended to "spending the day." A neighbor often lived miles away, and a neighborhood roughly comprised all the plantations within a day's ride. Informality in arrival and remaining found at least one explanation in the frequent intermarriage among a comparatively few families. Tidewater was a region of "cousins." Such cousins seemed at home everywhere. They gave life a gracious informality.

At the races and fairs and in the taverns, gambling was openly and generally indulged in. The Tidewater colonial bet on any contest, from cards and dice and horses and nine-pins, to games called "cross and pile," "putt," "hazard," "seven and eleven," and "pass and no pass." Gambling was no mere popular amusement, it was fashionable. Card-playing was just as popular, and the men, at least, often seasoned it with "stakes." Entries in old memorandum books show the exchange of considerable sums. President John Blair, of the honorable Council, recorded that he lost £17.3 to Mr. Thomas Swann, but he won £17.3 of Mr. Sackville Brewer, £19.7 of William Byrd at Westover and £192.8.6 of this same young gentleman at Williamsburg. This young Byrd's father said of him, however, that he gambled "as a fashionable amusement merely—avarice being a passion alien to his breast." Colonel Landon Carter, apparently out of patience with the gambling debts of his sons, exclaimed in his diary: "Burn me, if I pay anything more for such sport."

Among the more innocent home games which cropped up by name in addition to the traditional English kissing and forfeit games, were "grind the bottle," "blind man's base," "hide the thimble," "buttons, to get pawns for redemption" and "break the Pope's neck," with the "leaders" in the last game supported by the rest of the company as "friars."

Music for its own sake played no considerable part in the domestic life. Not only were there no schools of music, but it was difficult even to find a teacher. It seems not improbable that Landon Carter, of Sabine Hall, exaggerated the musical situation in Williamsburg when he complained in his diary: "I hear from every house a constant tuting may be listened to from one instrument or another." Yet there were instances of fiddles, hautboys, French horns, flutes, virginals, spinets and harpsichords. General Washington played the

flute to Nellie Custis' accompaniment on the harpsichord.
What precisely may have been a "treble" and a "hand organ"?
One James Lucas, of York, "did break an instrument of
Mr. Charles Hansford called a Treble which cost the said
Hansford one pound eight shillings." The *Virginia Gazette,*
for September 17, 1767, contained this advertisement:

"A very neat Hand Organ, in a mahogany case, with a gilt
front, which plays sixteen tunes, on two barrels; it has four
stops. . . . The first cost was £16 sterling, and the lady being
dead it came in for, . . . it may be had on very reasonable
terms."

The one house in which music seems to have had a dignified
and important place was Nomini Hall. Fithian, in his diary,
frequently refers to the music in Councilor Carter's family:

"Miss Nancy is beginning on the *Guitar*. . . .
"We returned in the evening and found Mr. Carter & Miss
Nancy practising Music, one on the Forte-Piano, and the
other on the Guitar. . . .
"Spent most of the Day at the Great House hearing the
various Instruments of Music. . . .
"When we returned about Candle-light, we found Mrs.
Carter in the yard seeing to the Roosting of her Poultry; and
the Colonel in the Parlour tuning his Guitar. . . .
"Harriot is bold, fearless, noisey and lawless; always merry,
almost never displeased; She seems to have a Heart easily
moved by the force of Music; She has learned many Tunes
& can strike any Note, or succession of Notes perfectly with
the Flute or Harpsichord, and is never wearied with the Sound
of Music. . . .
"The Colonel at Dinner gave Ben & I a piece of Music to
prepare on our Flutes, in which he is to perform the thorough
Bass. . . .
"Mr. *Carter* is practicing this evening on the *Guittar*. He
begins with the *Trumpet Minuet*. He has a good ear for Music; a vastly delicate Taste, and keeps good Instruments, he
has here at Home a *Harpsichord, Forte-Piano, Harmonica,*

Guittar & *German* Flutes . . . he is infatigable in the Practice. . . .

"The Colonel showed me after Dinner a new Invention, which is to be sure his own, for tuning his *Harpsichord* & *Forte-Piano*: it is a number of *Whistles,* of various sizes so as to sound all the Notes in one Octave."

Among the musical books and compositions in the library at Nomini Hall, according to Fithian, were *"Alexanders Feasts, or the Power of Music; an Ode in Honour of St. Cecaelia, by Dryden, set to music by Handel; Malcolm on Music; Handels Operas for Flute; Book of Italian Music,* and **17** Volumes of Music, by various Authors."

Rather than being cultivated for its own sake instrumental music was the handmaiden of singing and dancing. Sentimental young men and women were the chief exponents of instrumentally accompanied song, for the negroes, though even more continuously vocal, whether in the field or about the cabin door at evening or at camp-meeting, generally sang their folk-songs and spirituals without accompaniment. However, the negro servants made the music for the white folks to dance to, and the advertisements for the sale or recovery of slaves often made such references to their music as: "he can play on the violin," "he took his fiddle with him," and "he played exceedingly well on the banger and generally carries one with him." One such notice read: "To be sold a young healthy negro fellow who has been used to wait on a gentleman and plays extremely well on the French horn."

Of all the social diversions in the home none equaled dancing. Sometimes it was a stately minuet, sometimes the saraband or gavotte, but inevitably a party finally romped into the Sir Roger de Coverley which here became so completely adopted that it came to be known only as the Virginia reel. The young people seem to have been only a little more enthusiastic about dancing than their seniors. General Washington was especially fond of "stepping to a tune," and on one occasion he remained on the floor with Mrs. Nathanael Greene dancing continuously for three hours.

In the course of a house-party dancing often continued by day and by night for several days, the company reenforced by others from neighboring plantations who drove or sailed over for a day or two or three. Richard Lee, of Lee Hall in Westmoreland, gave such a ball when "the company left the ball quite wearied out" after six days although their host "intreated them to stay the proposed time."

While the planter did little manual work, it would seem that he took equally little exercise other than his daily ride of inspection over his estate. Indeed the only athletic sport in which he indulged was fox-hunting. There are numerous references in diaries and letters indicating the enthusiasm for this sport. It was another tie-back to the English strain which dominated this region. This sport was, indeed, the favored occasion for the gathering together of a number of gentlemen who, on fine mounts, behind a yelping pack of hounds, to the accompaniment of "wild hallos" and hunting horns, would follow the fox across the fields and through the woods, over fences and hedges and ditches, hour after hour, and then finish with a lively hunt supper at a house belonging to one of the party.

Up to the Revolution Tidewater was the breeding-spot of thoroughbred horses par excellence on this side the Atlantic. The strain was English. Importation of fine stock from England was kept up until the break with the mother country, although a little previous to that time and perhaps anticipating it, in Fredericksburg, in 1765, there was a race for horses "which have no mixture of English or foreign blood" indicating an effort to develop the native animal.

The Tidewater gentleman took his exercise in fox-hunting, and had only a breeder's and owner's relation to racing. He not only provided the entries in a race, but he did the betting. This seems to have been his exclusive privilege, for in one of the very early official references to this sport, in a court order of York County, in 1767, it is set out that:

"James Bullocke, a Taylor, haveing made a race for his mare to runn w'th a horse belonging to Mr. Mathew Slader for two thousand pounds of tobacco and caske, it being contrary to Law for a Labourer to make a race, being a sport only for Gentlemen, is fined for the same one hundred pounds of tobacco and caske."

The neighborhood about Richmond and on the peninsula between the Rappahannock and the Potomac became the best developed racing regions. As early as 1700 there were already in the latter district at least three race courses in Northumberland County alone. But there is some confusion as to what actually in each instance a "course" was, for it certainly was not always an oval track. One of the most popular early forms of racing in Tidewater was over "race paths," short straightaways. This developed the popular "quarter race," so characteristic of Tidewater, which was a contest between two horses only to run one-quarter of a mile straight out.

At first the races were held in what were called the "old-field tracks." From these developed the popular track at Williamsburg where the racing season was a feature of the entire tidal region, and eventually, by the middle of the eighteenth century, the sport developed many jockey clubs, not least famous among them being the jockey clubs of Fredericksburg, Dumfries and Alexandria, where the then Colonel George Washington was a frequent visitor during "the meet," hobnobbing with other turfmen, judging the fine points of the entries, laying his occasional wager, and participating in the exhilarating enthusiasm of the race.

Cock-fighting had its place among the diversions. It was a much more democratic sport than racing. It was indeed especially the sport of the negroes. But youth generally went in for it, and there are evidences that at times it had the dignified attention of the gentles. Washington noted in his diary in 1752: "A Great Main of Cocks was fought in Yorktown between Gloucester and York for 5 pistoles each battle and 100 ye odd. I left with Colo. Lewis before it was decided."

Three years later the *Virginia Gazette* reported a "Great Cock Match" between Gloucester and New Kent, and remarked that "some James River cocks that fell on the New Kent side distinguished themselves in a very extraordinary manner."

The same gazette, in 1768, contained this advertisement for a cock-fight at Sussex Court-House on April fourth: "A Match of Cocks, between the Brunswick and Sussex Gentlemen to show 30 cocks a side, for 5 1. a battle, and 50 1. the odd. At night there will be a ball, for the reception of the Ladies and Gentlemen."

The most brilliant annual feature of colonial life here was the period of the sitting of the House of Burgesses at Williamsburg. The Assembly attracted the leading planters from the James to the Potomac. Some of them maintained townhouses here. The "season" at the little capital was the one touch of urban cosmopolitan life which Tidewater provided.

THE FIRST AMERICAN PLAYHOUSE

It centered about the Palace of the Royal Governor and when the strain between the Burgesses and the Governor was not too tense took its tone from the entertainments there. In addition to dinners and balls, the races and other entertainments, this little "season" presented one of the few opportunities which the planters had to enjoy the diversions of the theater.

Here, in Williamsburg, in the second decade of the eighteenth century, was built the first playhouse to be erected in America. Thereafter English actors, visiting the colonies, came here, and they and American actors from Philadelphia and New York acted the farces and comedies and tragedies which attained success on the London stage.

But there is a record of a theatrical performance of "a play commonly called ye Beare & ye Cubb," having been given in Accomac in 1665, fifty-one years before the erection of the Williamsburg theater and thirty-eight years before the first recorded dramatic entertainment in New York.

Having established their fame in Virginia by playing their repertoire in Williamsburg, the actors would then appear in Norfolk, Petersburg, Hobb's Hole (now Tappahannock on the Rappahannock), Fredericksburg, possibly Dumfries and Alexandria.

From such accounts of dining and dancing, gambling and racing, cock-fighting and the theater, it might be assumed that the people of Tidewater were godless and unregenerate. The contrary is the fact. They were deeply devoted to their church. Excesses in all these diversions existed and, as such, offended the people, who, nevertheless, saw nothing incongruous between a pleasant happy social order and the ideals of a Christian character.

The churches of Tidewater are among its most interesting historic survivals, for they were built out of love and respect, well and strong, and in some instances the combination of their own lines and proportions with the "mantling over" of the weathers of the centuries, produced specimens of appealing beauty. These churches are never large. Their style was the creation generally of the domestic builder. Always they survive in brick, because stone was not used, and because such frame buildings as rose long ago fell victims to time and the elements.

Life in the old houses along the shores of the rivers and the bay was indeed pleasant and gay, and it is gone. But it left behind it memories and characters which have enriched our whole national life. As it was based on ease and elegance, it attained grace and distinction. It was frequently colorful and often romantic, and in instances it may have indulged some of the excesses of its mode. But it produced a gallery of public figures whose character has ever since been a source of admiration and whose attainments have not ceased to excite astonishment.

Having considered, in general terms prescribed by limited space, how the white man came here and what he found, how the wilderness retreated before civilization, and how eventually the planters lived, the way is somewhat cleared to coast the shores of Tidewater and see with rather more particularity the places where the conspicuous figures lived and other localities which history and romance have distinguished with their touch.

COUNCILOR ROBERT CARTER
Painted by Sir Joshua Reynolds

WILLIAM BYRD II
From the painting by Sir Godfrey
Kneller

PATRICK HENRY

RICHARD HENRY LEE

RICHMOND IN 1838
From a painting of the period

STATE-HOUSE, RICHMOND, TO-DAY
The center building was designed by Thomas Jefferson. The wings are
more recent

CHAPTER VI

NORFOLK'S NEIGHBORHOOD

A City Walled with Ships—Lynnhaven Bay—Good Adam Thorough-
good—His Wife and "Goody" Layton—Early Penalties—A Suggestion
of Shakespeare—Grace Sherwood, the Witch—Blackbeard, the Pirate—
A Bloody Head at the Bowsprit—Home of the Chesapeakes—Poplar Hall
—Old St. Paul's—The Longest Bridge in the World—Hampton Roads—
An Echo of the Black Man's Curfew.

HE triangle which is Tidewater Virginia is to-
day marked at its three angles by three notable
cities. At the eastern angle of its base, where
the Atlantic meets the Chesapeake, is Norfolk.
At the western angle of this base, where tidal James terminates at its falls, is Richmond. At its apex is Washington, the
Federal Capital.

Norfolk and Richmond are relatively of the same size. Norfolk is, however, a more significant city than its own figures
show. It is the nucleus of a great interlocking commercial unit
made up of Portsmouth opposite it on the Elizabeth River,
of Newport News and Hampton just across Hampton Roads,
and of other contiguous communities. It is the true daughter
of the Chesapeake, for it draws its nourishment from the
mother bay. Though the number of its human integers does
not place Norfolk near the top of a list of our populous centers, nevertheless the water-borne exports do entitle it to a
privileged place among the eight leading ports of the entire
Republic.

Like Carcassonne, Norfolk is a walled city. Unlike Car-

101

cassonne, but like Rhodes, it is a walled city by the sea. But unlike either of those picturesque products of the remote past, Norfolk's walls are not built of stone; their ramparts are undefended. The sea-walls of Norfolk are piers and docks. Its ramparts are the hulls of great ocean carriers. Its towers and turrets are masts and funnels. It is a wholly modern product and exemplar.

The city is crowded on to a peninsula between the tortuous inlets called the La Fayette River and the Elizabeth River. But, beyond these waters, shipping, industry and habitations extend out with diminishing density for miles. Railways interlace the flat hinterland. Eastward along the ocean the white surf rolls up to a long line of cottages and caravansaries for seaside pleasure-seekers.

If that were all there is to Norfolk and its neighborhood its story might be told with a rubber stamp, for such features are characteristic of other neighborhoods in many other directions. One might come here and see only a city throbbing with the conventionalities of commerce, rimmed with ships and throwing out across its flat environs streamers of white cement or glistening thin metals alive with creeping carriers. But the real lure of the place is found in other landmarks. Clustered behind Cape Henry are interests, historic and romantic, of which only fragmentary sign-posts are in evidence. But they give this corner an attraction which it has not either of nature or of its modern life. On its white sand-dunes are written other stories.

"There is but one entrance by Sea into this Country," wrote Captain John Smith more than three hundred years ago, "and that is at the mouth of a verie goodly Bay, the widenesse whereof is neere eighteene or twentie miles. The Cape on the

South side is called Cape Henrie, in honour of our most Noble Prince. The shew of the Land there is a white Hilly sand like unto the Downes, and along the shoares great plentie of Pines and Firres."

When the ships of the English settlers entered at dawn on that "six and twentieth day of Aprill" in 1607, one of Smith's companions saw "faire meddowes and goodly tall Trees, with such Fresh waters running through the woods, as I was almost ravished at the first sight thereof . . . we got good store of Mussels and Oysters, which lay on the ground as thick as Stones: we opened some, and found in many of them Pearles." When he ate them he found them "large and delicate in taste." This was the birth of the fame of the Lynnhaven oysters. But not yet was Lynnhaven christened. That waited a few other years on the coming of Adam Thoroughgood.

That gentleman's name has carried across the centuries in a halo of high regard. He is still spoken of as "good Adam Thoroughgood." Here, near the bay of famous oysters to which he gave its name, still stands Thoroughgood house, contesting with the dwelling called Smith's Fort, up the James opposite Jamestown Island, the distinction of being the oldest house in Virginia "whose date can be positively identified."

Adam came here a boy of fifteen, in the year 1621, in the ship *Charles*. Although two brothers in England were knights, one of them in the suite of the Duke of Buckingham, Adam came over a "servant." He became one of the rich men of the colony and so gave an early example of how, in the new world of equal opportunity, a man moves only within a sphere of his own limitations. His English home was Lynn. For it he gave to the inlet, where Percy and his party had relished their first taste of the native oysters, the name of Lynnhaven Bay. Beside its waters rose his house, and it has had such care, inspired perhaps by the tradition of good Adam Thoroughgood, that to-day it is a robust survival of the earliest days here. It is a small brick box with walls three feet in thickness, supported at each end by a broad pyramided chimney, and with second-story rooms peeping out of the steep roof sides through banks of dormer-windows. Its wainscoting reaches the ceiling, and the lovely old red pine thereof has never known paint.

It is not surprising that Adam left behind him a widow of character. "Madam Sarah Thoroughgood" they called her because she was a woman of position, in distinction to the quaint title "Goody" which attached to humbler females. Still fresh, across the long interval, comes the altercation between Madam Thoroughgood and Goody Layton. The latter complained that no one could get a bill out of the former's late husband.

"Goody Layton, could you never get yours?"

She was forced to admit she could, and Madam Thoroughgood dared her to produce one who could not. Whereat Goody Layton "turned about with a scornful manner," but her only answer was "Pish!"

"Goody Layton," retorted Madam Thoroughgood, "you must not think to put it off with a 'pish' for if you have wronged him you must answer for it, for though he be dead I am here in his behalf to right him."

Which she forthwith proceeded to do, swearing a warrant against Goody Layton who was required the next Sunday morning, after the first lesson at morning prayer in the parish church, in the presence of the court and the people, to ask Madam Sarah Thoroughgood's pardon.

Other evidences of the stern mettle of Sarah's character came later when she had become the wife of Captain John

Gookin. They are preserved in the records of the General Court which sat at Jamestown, where, on October 8, 1644, the following judgment was rendered:

"Whereas, it appeareth to the Court by the confession of James Lapham, that he hath in a most bestial and uncivil manner, by most scandalous and false suggestions, defamed Sarah, the daughter of Captain Adam Thoroughgood, deceased, to her great disparagement and defamation.

"It is therefore ordered that the said Lapham shall receive fifty lashes, at the mulberry tree, well applied to his naked back, and stand committed til he put in security for his good behavior.

"Whereas it appeareth to the Court, that John Farnehough hath in a most scandalous manner defamed the daughter of Mrs. Gookin, to her discredit though most vilely and falsely suggested.

"It is therefore ordered, that the said Farnehough shall publicly in the parish church at Lynn Haven, in the time of divine service, ask the said Mrs. Gookin, and her children's forgiveness, put in security for good behavior, and pay unto the said Mrs. Gookin eight hundred and fifteen pounds of tobacco for her charges herein expended."

This Lynnhaven Bay reeks of romance. But it is not the romance of fiction. It is stranger than fiction because allied to fact. On the way to its rambling reaches one passes Lawson Hall, too new it would seem to have a tradition. But it rises on the foundation of other houses built long ago on the same spot. The very name Lawson dates back to Virginia's beginnings for the land on which the present modern dwelling stands is part of what was a Crown grant in 1607 to Sir Thomas Lawson. Seeking to find if Sir Thomas ever came to Tidewater Virginia, we learn something vastly more interesting. It is said that he sailed in the ship of Sir George Summers which was shipwrecked off Bermuda, an incident popularly believed to have provided William Shakespeare with the background of the plot of *The Tempest;* and so it is pleasant to imagine the first owner of this estate as, under the alias of a Neapolitan name, having been the companion of Ferdinand on Prospero's magic island.

Along the deeply indented shores of Lynnhaven and its estuaries one's interest tingles at the sound of the names attaching to the localities. London Bridge Creek hints of where home was to early comers here, and Wolfsnare Creek carries the suggestion of tragic struggle, both conjectural. But Witch Duck Point, Pirate's Fort and Blackbeard's Hill in spite of their weird words carry to the realm of actual and robustious fact.

Witch Duck Point reminds that here, behind the sand-dunes of Princess Anne, Virginia, like Massachusetts, had her witches. The best authenticated of them was one Grace Sherwood. There were Puritans, too, here among the early settlers, but though Grace's neighbors behaved Salem-wise, it is not known that the Puritans were among them.

Rosemary abounds about Lynnhaven. One is told that this witch brought the fragrant shrub "in an eggshell" out of England to Princess Anne. But less lovely accusations than this were made by her contemporaries. Jane Gisburne said she had cast a spell and blighted her crop of cotton. Elisabeth Barnes accused her of having assumed the appearance of a black cat and so having visited the Barnes home, jumping over the accuser's bed, driving and whipping her, and then having left by a key-hole or a crack in the door, though that detail was uncertain to the unnerved Elisabeth. Grace sued for such slander and got little for her pains. On another occasion Elisabeth, wife of Luke Hill, attacked and beat and barbarously damaged Grace. Brought to the bar by her victim's demands for fifty pounds' damages, she said that Grace had bewitched her and she would not stand for it, but, though probably not greatly to the "witch's" satisfaction, she did have to stand for a fine of twenty shillings.

Seeking revenge for the loss of her twenty shillings, Elisabeth Hill next hailed Grace Sherwood to court as a witch. The proof, according to the witch-lore of those days, would, it was believed, be found in the marks on her body, abrasions or warts or moles, the accredited signs of her contract with the devil. The magistrates delivered her body to be examined by twelve dames, whose forewoman was none other than that Elisabeth Barnes whose privacy she had invaded in the guise of the pugnacious black cat! Grace must have seen the verdict foreordained in her old enemy's eye. Almost inevitably it would seem, she was found guilty. But she could not have been deemed very guilty for, after much referring of the case back and forth for a sentence, she was condemned to a ducking off the point which ever since has been Witch Duck Point.

Such a ducking was not more a penalty than a test. The "witch" was "stripped naked and cross bound, the right thumb to the left toe, and the left thumb to the right toe," and so cast into the water. The strange theory was that if she swam to security she was favored of the devil and so was self-convicted. The alternative was no less strange, for, if the bound victim sank and so proved her innocence, it was to what proper compensation?

Grace was led to the water's edge; she was stripped and bound; and she was cast to her fate. But she did not sink; she did not drown. She lived another thirty-five years, a self-convicted "witch." If anything came of it the subsequent surviving court records are silent. She seems to have been allowed to live those years unmolested and to have died in peace. So much is fact, but about Grace Sherwood have grown up legends and tales, repeated here to this day in the wide stretches behind Cape Henry, as genuine a bit of folk-lore as one will find anywhere in America.

Pirate's Fort and Blackbeard's Hill remind that here, too, Virginia had her trouble with the buccaneers, among whom no other gave the ship-owners and captains so much concern as Edward Teach, known to history and fiction as Blackbeard. Here on Lynnhaven Bay bristle the names which suggest the operations of this bloody miscreant, but somehow the conjecture is lacking in documentation. His presence here on the dunes, his ship snugly at anchor in the little bay off the mouth of the greater bay, would have given him a superb lookout, matchlessly secure, to observe a passing vessel and pounce upon it. Perhaps he did. Who shall say he did not?

There is lore of Blackbeard elsewhere in Tidewater. It is said that he buried "a great treasure" near Stratford Hall on the Potomac, and on those same shores, when "conditions" are right, there are nights when "Blackbeard's gun" is still heard, if one is so minded.

What we know with certainty, however, is that the ships entering the inlets of North Carolina were his chief victims. The planters and mariners of that colony found themselves not only victims of the pirate but of their own venal governor who winked at facts and shared the pirate's spoil; and so they appealed to Virginia to come to their relief. Two sloops, in command of Lieutenant Maynard, were sent to beard Blackbeard in his retreat in Okerecock Inlet. The battle was bloody and to a terrible finish. But when Maynard sailed homeward round Cape Henry, if there were any lookout there that day, on what is now Blackbeard's Hill, he might have seen dangling at the ship's bowsprit the black and bloody head of the last famous marauder of these waters.

Maynard brought the imprisoned remnant of the pirate crew manacled in the hold of his victorious sloop. To Williamsburg they went and soon were hung by the neck on thirteen gibbets. Teach's head—was the famous black beard still parted at the chin and withdrawn below each ear and tied behind as was his wont?—was set upon a pole, and posted at the mouth of Hampton River where it angles on the James behind Old Point Comfort. Tradition says the head so stood for years, a warning to other pirates. Tradition, always glib, though sometimes careless, also says that Blackbeard's skull was fashioned into a cup and is still preserved in Tidewater; without revealing where.

Back again in crowded, busy, modern Norfolk these real things all seem unreal. Nothing seems actual except the tangible prosaic present. Yet through the shrieking of ship sirens and hurrying auto horns one may discern even here some few hostages of similarly real romance.

That same Elizabeth River, whose name honors the Virgin Queen honored by Virginia's name, and whose dark oily waters set Norfolk and Portsmouth face to face across them, contributes its basic facts. Strip its shores of ships, docks, warehouses and all the modernities that clutter and conceal its soil, and there may be found the land of the Indians who called themselves the "Chesapeacks." Every vestige of them is gone; but their memory will survive as long as the great bay bears their name.

The shores are not so easily stripped, however. Yet among the modernities may be found a few smiling ancients of another day. On the Norfolk side, at the water's edge of Broad Creek, is Poplar Hall, a simple, roomy, venerable brick house, on land entered by Hoggard, the immigrant, in the middle of the seventeenth century, and ever since, spanning seven generations, it has remained in the Hoggard family.

When, during the Revolution, Lord Dunmore made his attack on Norfolk and secured a footing in the town, the citizens, "to remove the obstructions to the view, and to the execution of the balls from our cannon, and in order also, to deprive the enemy of quarters and provisions," bravely put it to the torch. Out of the wreck of the burned city at least one venerable building remained, and stands to-day, ivy-clad in the midst of its shady burial-yard, the church whose adjective of age is lovingly made part of its name—old St. Paul's. It is credited as dating at least to 1739.

In the ashes of that great fire, over a century and a half ago, it sometimes seems as if all memory of local history were consumed. The new city rose, a modern practical engine of commerce. The atmosphere here is not, as elsewhere in Tidewater, made romantic with the lavender of long ago. The talk is not of the past; it is of the present and to-morrow.

With pride is shown the great connecting bow of bridges and highways, more than twenty-five miles long, which carry motor traffic from Norfolk to Fortress Monroe just over the Roads. First it strikes out across the Elizabeth River, through the lesser city of Portsmouth, a city dedicated, it would seem, to the ships and sailors of the navy. Next the highway crosses the Nansemond River whose tide carries up a little way to old Suffolk, "the peanut capital," littler and lazier and wider margined than energetic Norfolk, and giving the commonplace a fillip by reminding that it antedates the great port and in the middle of the eighteenth century had its own boom when buildings were needed faster than brick could be found and it achieved a fame as a city of wooden chimneys.

Onward this land and water highway leads over the flats to the James where another vast bridge, this one the longest in the world, reaches across five and a half miles of water to the ship-building city of Newport News. Thence, its way is eastward along the north shore of Hampton Roads, through quieter Hampton with its own historic old church, a little city whose proud claim it is to be the oldest English-speaking settlement in continuous existence in the United States, and so onward to the great defensive guns of Fortress Monroe.

Here is respite and peace again on the tip of Old Point Comfort, dedicated to so many generations of navy frolic. But inside this vast horseshoe of cement and steel the present pulsates as it does in all great modern harbors. Everywhere in perspective diminishing to obscurity, are ships: ships tied up at docks, ships anchored in the broads, great ones belching clouds of smoke as they move forward with cautious majesty, little ones chugging hectically as they dash puppy-wise among them. And in their presence the talk is only of facts and figures and prophecy.

It is Hampton Roads. It is the depot and distributing center for its own and its great hinterland's products. Coal leads in quantity, and trailing after are cotton, tobacco, fruit, vegetables and sea-food. Not least are peanuts, for Southside Virginia is the peanut garden of America. In the sea-food industry over eight thousand motor-boats are licensed to handle the oysters, clams, crabs and fish which abound hereabout. And with a gesture, one is told that so deep are all these waters to the very land and so indefinitely lengthy the shore-lines in the adjacent estuaries that, in spite of any imagined multiplication, marine commerce will never outgrow this basin.

If at evening one's mind is not too dizzy with figures, as the air trembles with a distant gun, some one may remember that tradition still survives here. It is the "nine o'clock gun" fired nightly at the Portsmouth Navy Yard, a survival of slavery days when negroes were not allowed on the streets after nine P. M. It is the echo of the black man's curfew.

At such an hour the darkness tempers the sharper lines, and silver mists draw in the distances, and through them only a little imagination is needed to perceive the great procession of the ghosts of historic craft that have passed across these waters. There are the Spanish galleons searching for El Dorado but turning back as three gallant little English ships pass on to their moorings up the James. A whole century of tobacco bearers sail back and forth through the silent night. Other English ships come, with serried flanks of significant portholes; and soon De Grasse, leading his French fleet toward the York. Next *Old Ironsides* sails past from the Severn to the sea, bravely to play the prelude of a second war with Mother England. Then just here approach and meet and battle the newly strange flat ironclads, one the *Monitor* and the other the *Merrimac,* and doom the ages-old cycle of the wooden fighting ship in opening the modern era of the metal hull. They disappear before the white armada of the self-conscious young nation sailing forth to gird the globe. Last of all the epic hosts of transports and convoys, surprising all the world though themselves most, as outward and across the ocean they bear help and hope to war-worn allies struggling heroically on to peace. These Roads have been the stage of major scenes of every act of our national naval drama.

CHAPTER VII

THE JAMES RIVER

Land of Sky and Water—Oldest Protestant Church in America—Home of a Famous Ham—A Colonial Gentleman's Coach—Bacon's Castle—Carter's Grove—Jamestown of Three Hundred Years Ago, and Now—Virginia's Oldest Brick House—The Royal Governor's Country Palace—"Lady Berkeley Peep'd"—Teddington and Claremont—The Two Brandons—Homes of "Tippecanoe and Tyler Too"—Flower de Hundred—Westover and the Byrds—Berkeley and the Harrisons—A Bride Who Would Not Obey—Appomattox River and Petersburg—Curles of the James—Shirley—Turkey Island and the Randolphs—Nathaniel Bacon's Home.

HE James, among all Virginia's rivers, is her chief pride, but all America has copartnership in its contribution to our national strain and story. On it, in the first year of their arrival in the new world, Newport's party set up the first permanent English settlement in the western hemisphere. Here, soon after, they established the first English legislative assembly on this side of the Atlantic. Here the shores on both sides of the river were the homes of the first settlers in America and from them descended the families which make up so large a part of that strain which Virginians have called their "blood royal." Virginia's earliest and latest capitals are on its banks. The first wars of the English in America were fought here with the Indians. The next generation of English became conscious Americans when Bacon led them along the river in rebellion against the Crown Governor. A century later British ships and troops campaigned here against the Revolutionists.

After nearly another century the warring states locked in battle along its banks. Small wonder then that no pilgrim, bearing any fragments of this river's history in his scrip, can sail up its waters without a thrill of expectation.

Along the forty miles from Hampton Roads to Jamestown the James is often more than four miles wide and only twice, then briefly, is it less than two. The seeker for scenic beauties will be disappointed. A few long, low, horizontal lines draw the narrow belt of land which separates sky and water. The land lies so flat that the dome of blue seems to rise almost at the river's sides. Man's world seems only water here, and the low threadlike banks, sometimes lightly pink with raw earth and sometimes darkly green with trees and brush, is its rim.

During these first reaches above the river's mouth, where the shores are far apart, fortunately the interests on land are comparatively meager. It is above Jamestown, as the water-way narrows and the shores come closer together, that the objects of interest multiply. The lower reaches, however, are not without their points.

It is in passing up between Newport News Point and Candy Island, the crowded agitated Roads dipping below the horizon behind, that one begins to feel the James. Here in the flat far-reaching spaces again "Nature her custom holds." Again the individual emerges from the crowds and from a complex environment. A bird in flight becomes an exciting incident. The break of the wake of the boat is low sweet music.

If the eye is eased, there, nevertheless, are wraiths of history hovering above every acre in the distance, for here were the homes of the first-comers and of the first "supplies" of 1607 and the few years soon after. The names significant of England's earliest days of pioneering in the new world are preserved here almost exclusively in the names of counties, districts, points, creeks, bays and islands, even as the name of the river itself dates its entrance into English history under its first English king who was called James.

If the flat lands of the Isle of Wight County on the south were to rise into ever so sparing hillocks, on one of them might be seen the little brick church of St. Luke, an ancient edifice sometimes called Smithfield Church, with its Gothic walls and square tower showing just a trace of Renaissance. It has been standing here since 1632, and it is the oldest Protestant church in the new world, older even than the fragments of the church-tower at Jamestown. St. Luke's too was long in decay, and before its restoration it was occupied during the earlier years of the nineteenth century by a sect called the O'Kelleyites.

The oldest communion silver in America is farther back at St. John's Church at Hampton. One of its pieces, a cup, bears the inscription, "The Communion Cupp for St. Mary's Church in Smith's Hundred in Virginia" and the date 1617.

Near old St. Luke's, up Pagan Creek, is Smithfield, so named after Arthur Smith, an early owner of the site, but given a fame all its own by the hams which originated there and bear its name, one of the gourmet's priceless treasures. The explanation of the curing process is locked up in silence. The experts meet inquiry with enigmatic smiles. Or when mere hearsay ventures it is for one to date the secret back to the feeding of the hog on peanuts, for another to advance it to the method of smoking and the choice of particular wood, while yet others claim the peculiar virtue in this ham comes from the rubbing in of peanut oil during the smoking process.

In the neighborhood of Smithfield in colonial days lived

"Colonel Parker" and, whatever else he was or did, he was at least a gentleman who rode "behind two postillions" in a worthy vehicle whose description survives in an order on London for it:

". . . a new handsome Post Chaise, the Body neatly carved and run with raised Beads and scroles, the roof and upper pannells covered with neats leather Mtted [?] Japaned and highly polished, with plated mouldings round do. and head plates, painted Prince of Wales Ruffs with arms and crests neatly painted in large handsome mantles [mantlings] on the doore pannels and the Body highly varnished, the inside lin'd with superfine light col'd cloth and trimmed with raised Casoy laces, the sides stuf'd and quilted, best polished plate glasses, mahogany shutters, with plated frames, do. plated handles to the doors, double folding inside steps neat wainscoted trunk under the seat and a carpet to the bottom, a handsome perch carriage and wheels suitable to the body, the perch plated on both sides with iron to make it appear light, hind foot board fixed between the beds, the Carriage neatly carved and runn with Town made German Steele springs, strong Iron axle trees with broad screw'd plate nutts to the ends, wrought Iron pipe boxes and collars. Platform Budget before covered with neat leather Wilted and Japaned, the carriage and wheels painted light yellow, the Iron works picked out with Corpean [?], Springs stript [striped?] and oil varnished, the Body hung with a set of neat leather braces made up with whole plated buckles and loops, the whole of the best material and executed in the most workmanlike manner."

As the river turns north it is extended to its widest by Burwell Bay on the left. Inland from its banks is a seventeenth-century brick dwelling called Bacon's Castle. As a castle it is not imposing, but in the early days here the term "castle" did not carry the imputation of any architectural importance. It and the term "fort" were somewhat synonymous and interchangeable, and any fortified building might have been called a castle. "Castle Duties," for instance, were duties paid by ships as a kind of toll for the fort at "Poynt Comfort."

Bacon's Castle is believed to have received that name because the house was fortified and held by Nathaniel Bacon in the Rebellion of 1676.

Standing north, to make the sharp point on the left, one sees ahead on one of the highest bluffs of the lower river, the Georgian house known as Carter's Grove, supported by its detached brick wings, and framed in the green of trees whose venerable tops rise high above it.

Its interior is one of the most complete survivals from colonial days. The walls of the wide hall and the adjacent rooms are paneled to the ceiling, and cornices deep and broad top the paneling. The stairway is especially fine, rising behind a broad arch which divides the hall, its banisters carved, and still bearing Tarleton's cipher in the gashes made by the sabers of his men when these British raiders swept through Virginia in 1781. The builder, in 1751, was Carter Burwell who named his home for his mother who was the daughter of Robert "King" Carter, of Corotoman, at the mouth of the Rappahannock.

The turn round the point is made, and just ahead is the island which is the site of old Jamestown. So low it lies that land and water seem at the same level. So frail it was that much of its historic soil now lies below the water. A seawall has been built to defend the precious remnant against the further erosion of the river.

Here on May thirteenth, in 1607, Christopher Newport brought the *Sarah Constant,* the *Goodspeed* and the *Discovery;* but not to anchor, for he found the water then so deep offshore that the ships came alongside the banks and were tied to the trees. Coming ashore the colonists stretched a sail cloth overhead to protect themselves from the late spring sun and gave thanks for their safe arrival.

One can not help wondering if among them at this Thanksgiving service, or detained on ship, was one particular "adventurer," ironically out of favor at the moment but destined to become the salvation of the colony and to make himself its first great figure. At that thrilling moment, daring and resourceful but difficult, Captain John Smith was a prisoner.

It was a day of gratitude and hope, but by the end of the summer sixty of the party succumbed to the malaria of the swampy spot, to the unhealthy drinking water, and to the arrows and tomahawks of the Indians. The "supply" of one hundred colonists who came the January following found thirty-eight only of the original one hundred five. Fire added its discouragement to the efforts to build a town. Added to the distress of winter was the tragedy of the "starvation time." Eventually the supplies of food gave out and the remnant of the survivors was reduced to roots and herbs for sustenance.

The end seemed to have arrived after three years. In June, 1610, the remaining colonists abandoned Jamestown and embarked for England. Scarcely were they round the first bend in the river, and out of sight of the island, when they sighted other ships approaching with the new Governor, Lord de la Warre, and his supply, and with a new store of provisions aboard. He induced them to return. On the fresh start then made was founded the real building and brief life of Jamestown as a city.

In 1619 the first English legislative assembly met at Jamestown. On the ruins of the several early efforts at a church, one of which was "a homely thing like a barn . . . roofed with grass and earth," about 1640 they built another of brick, the remnants of whose tower is suggestive of the older tower of St. Luke's near Smithfield except that this Jamestown tower has defensive apertures behind which stood the town's defenders and through which they shot at the enemy. It is a unique example in America of a fortress church. A few other buildings were constructed of brick, but the town never achieved distinction. It was the seat of government, not more. The colonists scattered themselves up and down the James and other Tidewater rivers and made their homes away from the capital. Tobacco was money, and they could not all raise tobacco on the island.

Physical disasters pursued the fated city. Three times it was devastated by fire, the second time in 1676 during Bacon's Rebellion. The century was old, but not ended, when finally, after more than ninety years of heroic struggle against natural and ungovernable odds, the mistake of its situation was admitted, and, in 1699, the House of Burgesses met there for the last time in the course of a session which decreed the removal of the capital seven miles north, to a locality called the Middle Plantation, a little more than half-way across the peninsula to the River York. William of Nassau, Prince of Orange, was on the throne of England at the time, and for their sovereign the colonists named their new capital Williamsburg.

Abandoned Jamestown then began its period of decay. Singularly at almost the same time another of the colonial capitals entered upon a similar drama of obliteration. Near the mouth of the Potomac stood St. Mary's City, seat of government of Lord Baltimore's colony of Maryland. Between 1634 and 1696 it became a considerable city, much larger than ever Jamestown was, and boasted at least eighty brick buildings.

Then, in that latter year, the government was moved to the banks of the Severn where it still sits in Annapolis. The end of each of these earliest neighboring colonial capitals was strikingly similar. The annihilation of St. Mary's was absolute. Not a building remains, not even a trace of one.

Jamestown survives in some few ruins, however, which have been carefully preserved. Above ground rise only the picturesque remnants of the broken church-tower, and about it some fragments of sculptured tombstones. One of these bears the Ludwell arms and was erected over the grave of Philip Ludwell's wife, the widow of Sir William Berkeley who ruled here thirty years as royal governor, and thanked God there were no printing presses in America, and hanged more men for participating in Bacon's Rebellion than King Charles executed for the beheading of his royal father. Another of the tombs has been clutched in the claws of the roots of a giant sycamore, which wrenched it to fragments. But in these remnants one may read the mutilated epitaph of Sarah, daughter of Colonel Benjamin Harrison, of whom some particulars later, on the occasion of her marriage to the commissary, James Blair, "some time minister of this parish," who founded William and Mary College. Elsewhere on the island, at the level of the earth, are some brick foundations. Other such foundations extend out under the water of the river which long ago engulfed a part of the town's site.

In addition to the protective sea-wall a number of other embellishments now stand where the city stood. In general they were placed here about 1907 to mark the three hundredth anniversary of the arrival of the first colonists. Looking out over the water is a statue of Captain John Smith. Not far away is a statue of Powhatan's daughter, Pocahontas, the Indian girl who saved Smith's life, was baptized here into the Christian faith, and was married to English John Rolfe. Close to the church enclosure another monument celebrates the first General Assembly of 1619 under Governor Sir George Yeardley. This governor is further commemorated here in Yeardley House, a brick rest house and museum which was built and presented by the National Society of the Daughters of the American Revolution in 1907, was later partly destroyed by a storm and was rebuilt from a bequest by Mary Custis Lee.

Inside the church enclosure and behind the ivy-covered tower, which remains its ruined self without any effort having been made to repair the decay of time in it, rises the church itself, a modern building and a present from the national membership of the Colonial Dames of America to the Association for the Preservation of Virginia Antiquities, in whose ownership and care the site of Jamestown and many other historic monuments in Tidewater now stand.

We find here the foundations of three of the five churches erected by the Jamestown colonists. Here are the cobblestones which supported the wooden superstructure in which met the first legislative assembly of any one of the thirteen original colonies. This was not, however, the scene of Pocahontas' baptism as made famous by Chapman's painting in the National Capitol. The site of the little chapel of that event lies with the rest of the submerged city under the waters of the James.

Just opposite Jamestown Island the shore begins to take on a rolling character almost for the first time above its mouth. In addition to length and breadth there is now a relieving sense of rise, and of broken horizon line undulating a pleasant trifle. The north side of the river remains low and flat a little farther. In these first rises opposite the site of the ancient capital a creek reaches in through the low fold of the land. It is Gray's

Creek, at first named Rolfe's, and on the east of its entry on
the river John Smith's map showed "The New Fort," built
probably in 1608 or 1609. The fort was designed to command
the river and probably to serve as a place of retreat if the
Indians should successfully attack Jamestown. Later this became known as Smith Fort and now the land is called the
Smith Fort Farm. On it, about two miles up the creek, stands
the oldest brick house in Virginia of whose age there is docu-
mentary evidence.

Old Warren House

It is known as the Warren house. Its length is fifty feet
and it rises one story and a half high. In the Surry records
there is a deposition which says the house was begun in 1651.
The land on which it stands was originally presented by the
Indian King to Thomas Rolfe, the son of John Rolfe and Pocahontas, and he sold it to Thomas Warren who gave the place
his name and whose descendants still flourish in Surry.

The western point on this creek is known as Swann's Point.
On it in 1677 the commissioners sent over by King Charles II
to examine into the cause of Bacon's Rebellion held their
court.

Passing this point one is soon in view, on the same side of the river, of a little brick house supported by four chimneys and displaying five dormer-windows. The place is called Four Mile Tree and takes its interest from its burying-ground in which is one of the oldest tombstones in Virginia with a legible inscription. It stands over the grave of Alice, wife of Colonel George Jordan, Attorney-General of the colony in 1670, but it states that she died in 1650. The inscription reads:

"Here Lyeth Buried The Body of Alice Myles daughter of John Myles of Branton, neare Herreford, Gent. and late wife of Mr. George Jordan in Virginia who Departed this Life the 7th of January 1650.

    Reader, her dust is here Inclosed
    Who was of witt and grace composed
    Her life was Vertuous during breath
    But highly Glorious in her death."

The five-mile stretch of shore from Jamestown to the mouth of the Chickahominy River was the southern boundary of an estate of three thousand acres laid out in 1619 for the use of the Royal Governor and known as The Governor's Land. The house stood far back from the James on some higher ground. The estate was called Green Spring.

The house was built by Sir William Berkeley in 1643. From the traditions of it, it may be believed that few other mansions more splendid were raised in colonial America or that any other official lived in such state as that maintained here by "The Tyrant Governor."

He kept open house for the cavalier refugees who fled to Virginia from the Puritan Commonwealth in England. Green Spring was Nathaniel Bacon's last stop before he marched on Jamestown where Berkeley was entrenched. After Bacon destroyed the state-house it was here at the Governor's country place that the next meeting of the General Assembly took place.

Sir William's widow married a Ludwell, but she retained her title and even on her tombstone she was inscribed as Lady Berkeley. But this is not the last we hear of her. Green Spring passed through the Ludwells to the Lees.

When Governor Berkeley was preparing to return to England a visit of courtesy was paid him here by the very commissioners who sat across the river on Swann's Point in their investigation of his "reign." When they left the house they found Sir William's coach at the door ready to convey them back to the river landing. At the moment when the King's representatives were about to drive away the "Postillion that used to Ryde" was boldly put to one side by a strange man who mounted in the other's place. When they reached their boat the commissioners found to their astonishment, and perhaps to their horror, that the strange postilion who had driven them away from the Governor's mansion was no other than the common hangman who "put the Halters about the Prisoners' Necks in Court when they were to make their submission."

The blame for this insult was placed less on the Governor and several of his councilors who witnessed it without interfering than on Lady Berkeley who "went into Her Chamber, and peep'd through a broken quarrell of the Glass, to observe how the Show look'd." Her Ladyship may not have felt equal to masking her malicious satisfaction in the gruesome insult, or she may have relished indulging it.

For over one hundred years the ruins of a brick house, in which William Ludwell Lee lived last, have been believed to be the ruins of Governor Berkeley's country Palace. But, buried, forgotten and unknown, the foundations of the original buildings have recently been discovered three hundred and fifty feet nearer the James in the peaceful lawn which stretches out before the visible ruins. The discovery dispels the long puzzling discrepancies between the modest ruins of the Lee mansion in comparison with the traditional splendor of Berkeley's Palace with its thirty bedrooms capable of receiving forty or fifty guests whom the proud old Governor would entertain in honoring his commission from his King.

The Green Spring foundations, which are now thought to be completely unearthed, show that the structure had a length of one hundred sixty feet and a breadth of fifty-two feet, in certain portions. Nothing of its height has yet been demonstrated, but it is known that the salons on the first floor were all connected by a gallery ten feet wide and the length of the building. The walls were thirty inches thick.

The excavations have shown that walls curved away from each end of the Palace and enclosed a great lawn which dropped away in terraces. At the end of these walls stood detached brick houses. Two of them still stand. One is believed to have served as a guard-house. The other house still protects the green spring for which the place took its name, mentioned by one of the early chroniclers, Reverend John Clayton, as "a fine green spring, whose waters are so cold that 'tis dangerous drinking thereof in summer time."

In addition to the Lee ruins, the guard-house and the old spring-house, there still stands adjacent to them the old jail erected by Berkeley when Green Spring was the summer capital of so large a part of the North American continent. This building, which has been put to many amiable uses since Sir William's day, was used by him to detain those who offended the laws of the colony and the interests of his King, and in his later years, those who offended his own personal whims. It was in this jail that the Governor held many of those captured at the close of Bacon's Rebellion, and here took place at least three of the twenty-six hangings with which Berkeley satisfied his thirst for vengeance at the close of the rebellion. This staunch, plain, weather-beaten brick structure is still equipped with its stout iron bars. In 1677 one Henry Good, of Jamestown, complained that the Green Spring jailer had refused to loose him from this building when his term expired until he, Good, presented the jailer with a cow and a calf.

The Chickahominy, which meanders out of the James just beyond Green Spring, north and then westward toward the Piedmont, is one of the lesser tidal rivers of Virginia. On its banks John Smith was taken prisoner in 1607 by Opechancanough, brother of Powhatan. He was led all over Tidewater, even to the Potomac, as an evidence of an Indian triumph. Finally he was brought to Powhatan's court on the banks of the York River and there prepared for execution. At that moment happened one of the most celebrated incidents of the great adventurer's career, for two great stones having been brought before the Emperor, the savages dragged Smith to them and "thereon laid his head and being ready with their clubs to beate out his braines, Pocahontas, the King's dearest daughter, when no entreaty could prevaile, got his head in her arms, and laid her owne upon his to save him from death: whereat the Emperor was contented he should live to make him hatchets and her bells, beads, and copper."

This old river flowed modestly and uneventfully through the background of the chronicles for more than two hundred fifty years when suddenly its banks became alive with the armies of the warring states, and the operations there had an important effect on the issue of the war.

The first projecting land beyond the mouth of the Chickahominy is Dancing Point—a gay name for the gruesome tradition attaching to it. It was not ankle-play but arms-play which carries its name in the chronicles. On Dancing Point, in 1619, Edward Stallinge is said to have met Captain William Eppes in a duel and to have died from the thrust of his rapier. Contrary to a romantic tradition duels were rare in the early period in Tidewater. Only two are known actually to have been fought before the Revolution.

Beyond the Chickahominy the James narrows perceptibly behind Sandy Point and Claremont Wharf. Here on the right, sitting back about forty yards from the bright yellow beach, is the low house known as Teddington. Its appearance seems to indicate frame construction. Actually it has massive brick walls which are masked over with weather-boards. This was known in colonial days as a "stock brick building." The estate belonged to the Lightfoot family from the date of the erection of the house in 1717 until 1852 when it passed to the Baylors. Until comparatively recently Teddington consisted of one holding of five thousand acres. Now it is divided into five farms, belonging to five different owners. The lines of the old formal garden, once a glory of Teddington, have disappeared, but its box trees are still rated among the finer ones on the James. The burial-ground reveals an assembly of old tombs on which are chiseled the coats of arms of the Lightfoots and Steptoes above long recitals of virtues and character among which one finds inevitably "Loyalty to his King and Affection to his Country," the twin civic virtues of the planter, until 1776.

Across the river stands Claremont, screened by the trees with just a tip of the red roof visible. This estate of twelve thousand acres remained in the Allen family from 1649 to 1875. They had the largest holdings of land in this part of Tidewater. One of this family, before the Civil War, owned between thirty and forty thousand acres on the James.

Among the romantic details of the construction of the old houses in Tidewater is that of "the bricked pit built in the center of the fire place, in which all the family money and jewels were put. An iron plate fitted over this safety box and ashes were raked over it and a fire was built over them when the coming of the Indians was feared"; and another is that of "the house where, when scraping the window paneling, a loose panel accidentally disclosed century old flint locks in their hiding place." Such tales have been told of Claremont, and here, at least, are the pit in the fireplace and the flint-lock hiding-place in the secret panel behind the folding shutters. It has, also, its brick walled underground passage to the river.

Among the frequent visitors to Claremont was Edgar Allan Poe, and it is a tradition of the Allen family that this house entertained every president of the United States from Washington to Buchanan. This, however, is said of other great houses here. The most picturesque legend which attaches to Claremont is that of the first owner and says that "two brothers, Allen and Eric Guelph, princes of the house of Hanover, were rivals for the love of a high-born English lady. Eric was successful in his suit, but on his wedding night was fatally stabbed by his brother Arthur [sic], who then fled from England . . . changed his name to Arthur Allen" under which name he reached Tidewater Virginia and took up the grant of Claremont.

After Claremont the river turns north again for a few miles, its short interrupted reaches making it seem more a lake than a river, and one travels ten miles to achieve the four-mile width of the intervening peninsula. This peninsula was granted first to John Martin, one of those who came over in 1607 with Christopher Newport and John Smith. Its earliest name was Martin's Brandon, and Brandon has been a part of its name ever since. On it are two of the most famous houses of the James, Brandon (sometimes referred to as Lower Brandon) and Upper Brandon.

Martin's Brandon changed hands several times in the course of the first century of its settlement. One of its owners was Richard Quiney, a brother of the Thomas Quiney who married Judith, daughter of William Shakespeare, and another was the husband of Ellen Saddler whose niece was the wife of John Harvard, founder of Harvard College. But in 1720 it passed into the hands of the Harrison family whose descendants have owned it during the subsequent two hundred years.

The Harrisons were conspicuous in both the colony and the commonwealth in every generation. By marriage with the Carters, the Fitzhughs, the Carys, the Randolphs and Byrds, they became "cousins" to most of the aristocrats of Virginia. The Harrison family of Virginia and the Adams family of Massachusetts each enjoys the unique distinction of having furnished two members of its name to the Presidency of the United States: John Adams and his son, John Quincy Adams, and William Henry Harrison and his grandson, Benjamin Harrison.

Brandon came by inheritance, in the middle of the eighteenth century, to Benjamin Harrison, the third of that name in Virginia. The Harrisons seemed to outlive their wives. This

Benjamin was the husband of two. The first was Anne Randolph, of Wilton, who gave him no children. The second was Evelyn Taylor Byrd, niece of the celebrated Evelyn, of Westover, who gave him two sons. Benjamin Harrison divided the great estate for the first time by his will which gave the eastern side of the peninsula to his eldest son, George Evelyn Harrison, for there stood and still stands the ancestral seat, Brandon; and the western side to his second son, William Byrd Harrison, who built Upper Brandon on it.

Brandon is a veritable English country house with its square, two-story, brick central building connected by an enclosed one-story brick passage at each end with square, two-story, brick wings. In every aspect it reflects dignity and comfort: outside, by its lovely setting of giant old trees and its relation to the river, and inside, by its spacious rooms and their arrangement and embellishment.

The house sits back about one thousand feet from the shore on a level of land not twenty feet above the water. It is not always easily seen from the river. Forests mask it on both sides, and before it is a screen of garden trees with a narrow central alley up which one may, however, catch a glimpse of the white columns and cornice of the portico. The garden, extending two hundred feet from the riverside toward the house, is divided into two parallel ranks of four square gardens each. The grassy walk between leads to the low "fall," or terrace, cleared and grassed in a huge rectangle over one hundred feet deep and extending beyond the ends of the long house. It is edged by formal box walks. The vast combination of formal landscaping and planting, in connection with the environment of towering forest trees, presents a unique and unforgetable effect.

The house, for years and until it passed out of the ownership of the family, was adorned inside by the accumulation of over two hundred years of family treasure. In spite of the beauty of the storied old silver and the distinction of the rich old furniture, it was the collection of portraits which was unique. These represented not only the Harrisons, of Brandon, but also that other preeminent James River family of colonial days, the Byrds, of Westover. The Westover portraits were brought to Brandon by Evelyn Taylor Byrd, daughter of the third William Byrd, of Westover, when she married Benjamin Harrison. In addition to West, the elder Peale and other eminent early American artists, the Brandon collection represents the best English portrait painters of the eighteenth century, including canvases by Sir Godfrey Kneller, Sir Thomas Lawrence and Sir Peter Lely.

On the panels, which reach from the floor to the ceiling of the great dining-room, hung William Byrd's own collection of the portraits of his English friends, which included Sir Robert Southwell; the Earls of Orrery, Albermarle and Egremont; Sir Charles Wager, First Lord of the Admiralty; Charles Montagu, Earl of Halifax; John, second Duke of Argyle, in a steel corselet and a crimson mantle; Sir Wilfred Lawson; and Robert Walpole, Earl of Oxford.

Among these worthies in their full-bottomed wigs, corselets, velvet cloaks and laces, there was one other portrait which commanded attention. It displayed a man of keen thin visage under a three-cornered hat, who was merely Mr. Waltho, for many years clerk of the Virginia House of Burgesses. He presented his own portrait to Colonel Byrd, "requesting that it should be hung among his peers, for whom he might show his republican contempt by wearing his hat in their presence." The gift was accepted and was placed over the door, "in token" says Charles Coleman, "that the clerk of the House of Burgesses finds the company too good for his keeping and is in the act of leaving."

Upper Brandon is the junior of the other house by a full century. Like the older Brandon it is built on a large scale, with similar central building, and with passages connecting it with the large, square, two-story wings. It stands in full view from the river just beyond its turn round the point of the peninsula of old Martin's Brandon.

Just above the narrowest point on the river here, and as yet the banks had not approached so near each other, on the east side, is an old estate called by its original Indian name, Weyanoke. Here Newport and Smith in their explorations up the river in 1607 found seated the Queen of Weyanoke, an Indian ruler subordinate only to Powhatan. The roomy frame house, on the site of an earlier dwelling, dates from 1740. Weyanoke stands at one corner of a triangle at the two other corners of which are the two homes of John Tyler, tenth President of the United States: Greenway and Sherwood Forest.

Greenway is north and inland a little way. The President's father described it as "a genteel well-furnished dwelling-house, containing six rooms, all wainscoted, chair-board high." Here John Tyler was born and here he lived a great part of his life before he was elected president. At the close of his administration he came back to his native Charles City County, bought an estate of twelve hundred acres, and built the home of his later years. This stands at the other angle of the Weyanoke triangle, on the bank of the James, just opposite the Brandon estates. Its central building is two and a half stories high, flanked by wings of one and a half stories. Beyond these

WILLIAM AND MARY COLLEGE, WILLIAMSBURG
With the statue of Lord Botetourt in the foreground

CHANCELLOR WYTHE'S HOUSE, WILLIAMSBURG

PEYTON RANDOLPH'S HOUSE, WILLIAMSBURG

are long enclosed colonnades, attached to yet another story-and-a-half building at each end of the low lengthy dwelling. It is upward of three hundred feet in length and is the longest connected dwelling-house in Tidewater.

President Tyler showed himself a man of some sense of humor. When he was outlawed by the Whig party he likened himself to Robin Hood. When he bought this tract and built this house he had the comparison in mind and called his estate Sherwood Forest.

His favorite companion here was an old horse, called General, who had served him many years. When finally General died, he was buried at Sherwood Forest, and his appreciative master wrote this epitaph and put it on a wooden slab at the head of the grave:

"Here lieth the bones of my old horse, General, who served his master faithfully for twenty-seven years, and never blundered but once—would that his master could say the same."

The next plantation west on the south side of the James, opposite Weyanoke and just behind sharp Windmill Point whose name reminds that here stood a windmill so early that local lore claims it as the first such erected in the colonies, is Flower de Hundred, another "hundred" among those which appeared in the first maps and papers of the Jamestown colony. The use of the word "hundred" as a territorial division carried over from England, where such divisions were town or tithing, the hundred, and the shire or county. As its name implies, the town or tithing was composed of ten families, the hundred was composed of ten times ten; and the county of an indefinite number of hundreds. The English names were introduced into Tidewater without regard for numerical exactitude. The hundred was merely a territorial unit for judicial, military and political purposes.

The spelling of the word "Flower de," used as the name of this hundred, has been subject to many variations, though the form used here is the one now most generally accepted. The uncertainty of the spelling reflected an uncertainty as to the origin of the name of this plantation. A plausible explanation is offered by N. P. Dunn, who, in citing how it was patented in 1618, by Sir George Yeardley, points out that Sir George named it for the family name of his wife, Lady Temperence Flowerdew.

The year after its patent Flower de Hundred was represented in the first American representative assembly by Lady Temperence's nephew and by John Jefferson, earliest named American ancestor of Thomas Jefferson. It changed owners often in its first years, and in 1636 it passed into the hands of William Barker, mariner, a picturesque old sea-dog, who sailed in the ship called *Ye Merchant's Hope* and was of the group to found the parish whose old brick church, a few miles inland and built as early as 1657, still bears his ship's name.

Flower de Hundred was the scene of General Grant's crossing of the James, in June, 1864, one hundred thirty thousand strong. The old estate has, moreover, been made the scene of three published romances. In spite of the distinguished history of this land the most venerable portion of the house now standing on it is only a little over one hundred years old.

Adjoining Flower de Hundred on the west is Maycocks. The house greets the passer on the river, but the interest here is in the man behind the name, rather than in the house. This name, which has survived the changes of more than three hundred years, was given the plantation by its first owner,

Samuel Maycock, who came to Tidewater about 1618 and settled here on the James. He was a graduate of Cambridge University and became a member of Sir George Yeardley's council, and here he was killed in the Indian massacre of 1622. At Maycocks we find one of the earliest personal connecting links between Tidewater Virginia and Massachusetts, for among those massacred here, in 1622, was a certain Edward Lister who had come over from England to Plymouth in the *Mayflower* in 1620, only two years before his death.

Opposite is Ducking Stool Point, a name which is sufficiently suggestive of the very early practises in the corrective efforts to keep the ungodly in "the straight and narrow," or, failing that, in "deep water." Next it, and superbly placed by the waterside, is another of the James's most famous seats, the home of the Byrds, Westover.

The first of the Byrds to sail out from England was William who arrived with his wife in 1674 and settled "up at the Falls" where he built himself a house he called Belvedere. Fourteen years later he bought from Theodorick Bland the estate even then called Westover, behind Ducking Stool Point. The year of his arrival from England his son was born and christened William after him; and this Byrd, second William in America, built Westover house about 1730.

William Byrd II must have been a man of extraordinary charm and accomplishment, for the tradition of his happy gifts, supported by much sound and permanent evidence, has kept him a live and vibrant figure. Not merely on account of his own personal character and attainments, but also as the builder of Westover and the father of the romantic Evelyn Byrd, he has been the most significant figure in the distinction which has attached to the Bryd family in America.

"In the young master at Westover were met such an unusual number of happy gifts, so well improved by cultivation," said Lancaster, "that he was dubbed the 'Black Swan' of Virginia. He was not only born to 'an ample fortune'—as his epitaph informs us—but with a brilliant mind, a courageous spirit and a kindly disposition. Besides he was handsome, graceful and fascinating. He was liberally educated abroad, where he travelled much and was in the best society. He was in demand everywhere, for he was at once the most elegant of gentlemen and the best of good fellows. He was a man of many resources, with a special leaning toward literature, and collected at Westover the finest library in colonial times in America. He did not write for publication, but left diaries which have been printed under the title of 'The Westover Manuscripts' and are models of pure English—fresh, sparkling and picturesque. He took an active part in public affairs, and filled many important offices—among them that of President of 'his Majesty's Council.' "

His character is probably reflected in his house which is at once spacious, graceful, decorative and sound even now after the vicissitudes of nearly two centuries and of several wars. Benedict Arnold, sailing up the James in 1781 in command of British troops, stopped at Westover on his way to attack Richmond. During the War between the States it was the scene of military activities which left it badly scarred though not quite a ruin. It has since been restored to a fine expression of its original beauty.

The approach to Westover is almost equally effective whether one comes to it by its water landing and across the green carpet stretched to the great front door on its "river front," or to its "land front" through the ornate iron gates which bear the Byrd coat of arms guarded by two eagles perched on the flanking columns.

The heyday of life at Westover was undoubtedly during the years of the young womanhood of William II's five daughters.

He married twice, and the marital connections of himself and his children assemble again not a few of the leading family names of Tidewater, as when the Harrisons, of Brandon, or almost any other family gave themselves in marriage. Tidewater aristocracy was a close corporation. It is renewed evidence why on a certain social stratum Virginians find all Virginians to be "cousins."

He first married Lucy, daughter of Colonel Daniel Parke, who was the Duke of Marlborough's aide-de-camp, and for his second wife, Maria Taylor, of Kensington. Their children were Evelyn, Wilhelmina, Anne, Maria, William and Jane. Wilhelmina was married to Thomas Chamberlayne; Anne to Charles Carter, of Cleve; Maria to Landon Carter, of Sabine Hall; and Jane to John Page, of North End. Their brother's first wife was Elisabeth Carter, of Shirley, and his second was Mary Willing, of Philadelphia.

Evelyn Byrd became one of the romantic traditions of the Tidewater country. She was a belle and a beauty, as is shown in her portrait by Sir Godfrey Kneller which hung on the walls of Brandon, and the artist must have been as proud of it as he was of his portrait of Beatrix Esmond before whose youthful charm, Thackeray tells us, Madame Bernstein sat and meditated so grimly in her old age.

Mistress Evelyn went to England when but eighteen, and there she was exceedingly popular in all circles. When she was presented at court the King, George I, struck by her loveliness, is said to have allowed himself the levity of a pun, remarking his pleasure that his colonies could furnish such "beautiful Byrds." The old King was safely wed to his Queen Sophia, but not so the bachelor Charles Mordaunt, Earl of Peterborough. He wooed the young Virginian beauty, and he won her. Her father, however, disapproved, intervened and hurried her back oversea to the James. Here tradition steps in to remark sentimentally that "she gradually faded away and, at the age of twenty-seven, died a spinster, of a broken heart." There were at least the elements of good romance here, for the fair Evelyn did quit the scene early, enduring only seven years whatever heartbreak her father's discipline occasioned, and she was so far true to her lover that she never married any other. Her practical father gave, however, a more practical explanation of her spinsterhood, when in writing to the Earl of Orrery he said that the only reason he knew why his daughter Evelyn remained an "antique Virgin" was that "Either our young Fellows are not smart eno' for her, or she seems too smart for them."

It is not surprising to find this gay gentleman in the same mood even in the face of death. But there his wit met its match, and he doubtless relished the encounter. Among his acquaintances was Mr. Patrick Coutts, a rich Scot, who lived and owned a ferry at Richmond. They both became ill at the same time. Believing that he could not survive long, Colonel Byrd posted a courier off to tell Coutts not to hurry his end but to wait for him. Though actually he was dying, Coutts had the strength to say:

"Tell Colonel Byrd that when Patrick Coutts makes up his mind to die, he waits for no mon."

Adjoining Westover is Berkeley, "cradle of the Harrisons." Though settled early in the days of the English on the James it came to the Harrison family only at the end of the seventeenth century. From it they spread across the James to Brandon and to other places in Tidewater, and all over America. Among the distinguished characters born in this house were

Benjamin Harrison, signer of the Declaration of Independence, and William Henry Harrison, the hero of Tippecanoe and ninth president of the United States. Berkeley is in Charles City County as is Greenway, so that this county has the almost unique distinction of having been the birthplace of two presidents. Another and its wholly unique distinction is in having provided a political party with both its presidential and vice-presidential candidate in the same election, which was the case when the Whigs nominated William Henry Harrison and John Tyler in the campaign which they made famous by the slogan "Tippecanoe and Tyler too!" While "Tippecanoe's" grandson, Benjamin Harrison, was president of the United States, he visited this seat of his ancestors.

The house stands back a quarter of a mile from the water. It is a large, rectangular, brick dwelling, whose fine original lines are somewhat obscured by a modern porch which completely surrounds it. Two other, detached, rectangular buildings flank it at its ends. The interior is made distinguished by its admirably proportioned rooms, including a large arched hall, by its carved mantels and by its unusually fine cornices.

The Harrisons were conspicuous in the colonial records even before this old house was built though not before there was a Benjamin Harrison on the James. One such Benjamin had a daughter, Sarah, who seems to have been as much doubted by her lover as coveted by him. So when she told him she would marry him, he was a little skeptical, perhaps with the sight of a string of other beaux in the offing, and he exacted of her, and secured, this curious written promise:

"These are to Certifye all persons in Ye World that I, Sarah Harrison, Daughter of Mr. Benja. Harrison, do & am fully resolved & by these present do oblige myself (& cordially pro̶mise) to Wm. Roscow never to marry or contract Marriage with any man (during his life) only himself. To confirm these presents, I the above said Sarah Harrison do call the Almighty God to witness & so help me God. Amen.

(Signed) "SARAH HARRISON."

This was duly recorded "Aprull ye 28, 1687," and one can almost smell the orange blossoms and hear the wedding-bells. But, alas for the constancy of these spirited Virginia girls, in spite of Sarah's full resolve, her cordial promise and her call upon the Deity to witness, the early orange blossoms and wedding-bells were not for her hopeful William. Two months after subscribing to that paper Sarah scrapped her promise and gave herself to Dr. James Blair, who became the founder of William and Mary College.

Perhaps, if the discarded William Roscow attended that ceremony, he had a measure of satisfaction in having escaped a woman who was not only so fickle but so wilful as she then and there proved herself. When, in the course of the marriage ritual, Mr. Smith, the parson, asked her to repeat the promise to obey her husband, she replied *"No* obey." A second time he repeated the formula for her promise, but the second time she replied with added emphasis, *"No obey."* When a third effort only brought the same result, "the g'd Mr. Smith went on with the rest of the ceremony." It is this Sarah Harrison Blair whose mutilated tomb survives in the raised clutch of the sycamore on Jamestown Island.

Bishop Meade recalled that the rector of the Harrisons' church, Westover, once "offered to be the bearer of a challenge from Benjamin Harrison, of Berkeley, to Benjamin Harrison, of Brandon, assuring the former, as his friend, that the conduct of the latter justified such notice. But," he added, "Mr. Harrison, of Berkeley, was not persuaded by him."

A FASCINATING WIDOW

The wharf at Berkeley is known as Harrison's Landing. As such it has identification in the operations between the Federals and Confederates during the Civil War. General McClellan used the mansion as his headquarters after Malvern Hill, his army was encamped for miles along this river bank, and when he left he embarked his troops from Harrison's Landing.

A mile or two above Berkeley is the estate known as the Forest, where Thomas Jefferson courted Martha Wayles with his music, won her, married her and carried her off to the Piedmont, first mistress of his Monticello.

The next projection of land round which the river bends is Jordan's Point where once lived the too fascinating widow, Cicely Jordan, whose history recalls another instance of the striking difficulties which the James River men had in holding their sweethearts to their promises. This headstrong lady provided the unique instance of a woman being sued by a man for breach of promise. When her husband died he left her so comfortably provided with worldly goods that thereby, in addition to her other charms, she became quite irresistible to Captain William Farrar, kinsman of the Deputy Treasurer of the colony, and also to the Reverend Greville Pooley, minister of the parish; and apparently they were equally irresistible to her, for she engaged herself to both! The parson sued. Though he lost his case and had to sign a formal release of the Widow Cicely, binding himself in the sum of five hundred pounds "never to have any claim, right or title to her," the Governor and council of the colony were so stirred by the extraordinary incident that they issued a solemn proclamation against a woman engaging herself to more than one man at a time. And there is not in Virginia any known record that this edict has ever been revoked.

A few miles beyond Jordan's Point the south bank of the James opens for the entry of the Appomattox River. It is tidal only twelve miles toward the little but venerable city of Petersburg. About it clusters many interesting memories.

On its east bank, where it angles on the James, is City Point, once, and from the early days of the colony, called Eppes' Point. Here in 1635, had come Francis Eppes, a member of his Majesty's Council, and he gave his name to the point and to the island just across the James, and here he built the first house on the higher land back of the point. It was torn down after standing more than a century, and its timbers were used in building, in part at least, the present house, put here in 1751. The estate is called Appomattox, and it has been the home of the Eppes family continually for nearly three hundred years, a record for Virginia, and probably for America as well.

The mouth of the Appomattox became famous in the Civil War during the seige of Petersburg, as General Grant's headquarters, and here, at City Point, Lincoln came for consultation with his generalissimo, a few days before the evacuation of Richmond. During the late World War the magic city of Hopewell sprang up here for the manufacture of ammunition, and though its emergency purpose has passed it survives at peaceful occupations. But the neighborhood has lost and will probably never know again that pastoral charm which endeared it to three centuries of Eppes. Once Appomattox house commanded the neighborhood. Now, holding its own within itself, it otherwise is lost, and has to be hunted.

Up this little river is another ancient Eppes place, called Eppington. A son of this branch of the family, John Wayles Eppes, married Maria Jefferson, the younger daughter of

Thomas Jefferson, at Monticello, and later sat in the United States Senate. Along the same shore, at Cawson's, John Randolph, of Roanoke, was born when this was the seat of his maternal grandfather, Theodorick Bland. The years of this Randolph's boyhood, however, were passed at Matoax, a few miles farther on, near Petersburg.

Colonel Byrd wrote in his journal, of a trip which he made in 1733: "When we got home, we laid the foundation of two Citys,—one at Shocco's, to be called Richmond, and the other at the Point [Peter's Point] of the Appamattuck River, to be called Petersburgh. Thus we did not build Castles only but also Citys in the Air." The planters had no great belief in their genuine need of towns. These two air-cities, however, came to earth and became enduring and famous. The city of Appomattox survives under the name of Petersburg.

The ivy mantled walls of old Blandford Church, in Petersburg, are the repository of many of most treasured local associations. It stands on high ground among generations of tombs. Shortly after the Revolution it fell into decay and was used only as a mortuary chapel for the final prayers over those who were buried around it. More recently restoring hands have been laid on it and it has been dedicated to a new service as a Confederate Memorial Hall.

Associated with historic memories of Petersburg are two Bolling houses, Bollingbrook and Centre Hall. The former was made the headquarters of the English General, Phillips, when the British troops first occupied Petersburg in April, 1781. When they returned in May, General Phillips resumed his residence there. This time he was ill. At the moment the Americans, under Lafayette, were cannonading the city, and the situation was so severe that for safety the sick General was taken into the cellar. We still hear his plaint as one cannon-ball tore directly through the house above his head: "Why will they not let me die in peace?" He found his peace, in death here, a few days afterward.

Near Petersburg are Battersea of the Banister family, Mannsfield with connections in many Tidewater families, and Violet Banks, a skeleton of its former splendor and disappearing gradually in the rising tide of city growths about it.

Between Hampton Roads and Jamestown the James has both breadth and long watery reaches ahead. Between Jamestown and the mouth of the Appomattox it narrows somewhat and begins gently to curve. After the Appomattox it becomes a narrow tidal stream and begins actually to curl. These bends are often called the Curles of the River, and in olden times this section was also often called The Corkscrew. So nearly completely circular are some of these "curles" that to go the six miles from City Point to Farrar's Island the river takes a sinuous course of sixteen miles.

On the first "curle," just after the river sweeps round Eppes' Island, Shirley comes in sight. Those who know little else of the James have heard at least of Brandon, Westover and Shirley. It is the loftiest house on the river, rising three full stories, its third story hipped and presenting a spectacular array of eighteen high dormer-windows. Above them tower the chimneys, and the roof tapers to an apex on which is a massive pine-cone. The height of Shirley is accentuated by the absence of wings either attached or detached. It stands alone. It is said that it once had wings, advanced beyond its axis and connected with it by curved passages, forming an open forecourt somewhat after the pattern of Mount Airy on the Rappahannock and Mount Vernon on the Potomac.

The building is of brick laid, like its other great contemporaries, in Flemish bond of alternately glazed black headers and dull pink broadsides which give the walls solidity, distinction and a rich beauty. The reception-rooms carry heavy cornices over walls entirely paneled, and the carved doorways and mantels are equaled in few other colonial houses. Here, too, the collections of books, plate, furniture and portraits remain almost intact, representative of an accumulation over many generations, for Shirley was built by a Carter and has been owned and lived in only by Carter-born. Shirley has never been on the market.

Yet the origin of Shirley house is unknown. Like many other Tidewater domestic place names, the name here antedates the surviving house. Before this mansion is known to have been here the estate was known to the records as Shirley. It was granted to one Colonel Edward Hill in 1660. He and his son, the second Colonel Edward Hill, of Shirley, were men of the first importance in the colony. The father was a member of the House of Burgesses, of which he was sometimes speaker, and also of his Majesty's Council. The son was "one of his Majesty's honourable Council of State, Colonel and Commander-in-chief of the Counties of Charles City and Surry, Judge of his Majesty's high Court of Admiralty, and sometime Treasurer of Virginia."

He lies buried at Shirley, and whether one looks upon his tomb's massive marble, engraved with the Hill coat of arms, or upon him in his portrait still hanging on the walls of Shirley, handsome and aristocratic, in crimson velvet and lace, with flowing peruke, one can not help believing that Shirley is the house he would have built. He died in the year 1700, and if he raised the present house then it could be the oldest of the major colonial mansions on the James.

His daughter, Elisabeth, became the wife of the Honorable John Carter II, eldest son of "King" Carter, of Corotoman at the mouth of the Rappahannock, and by this marriage Shirley passed into the Carter family. Near the portraits of these two hangs also that of their son, Charles Carter, whose two wives bore him twenty-three children. One of these, Anne, became the wife of General "Lighthorse Harry" Lee and the mother of General Robert E. Lee.

A little way from Shirley is Malvern Hill, an estate with a long pedigree, a battle-scarred record, and a charming small new house replacing the colonial mansion which was destroyed by fire about 1905. During the Revolution General Lafayette camped here with his troops; in the second war with England it was the camping-ground of the Virginia Militia; and in the War between the States, Generals Lee and McClellan here fought the bloody battle of July 1, 1862. That nightfall saw the old place bathed in the blood of more than seven thousand dead, and in return it christened the conflict with its own name as the Battle of Malvern Hill.

The stretch of shore opposite the peninsula, sometimes called Turkey Bend and at other times Presquile, is known as Turkey Island, and it was the original seat of the Randolphs in Virginia. William Randolph, of Warwickshire, was the immigrant in 1660. This patriarch, by the seven sons and two daughters all born on this estate, was the common ancestor of Peyton, John and Edmund Randolph, all attorneys-general; Chief Justice John Marshall; John Randolph, of Roanoke; President Thomas Jefferson; Richard and Theodorick Bland; Stith, the historian; Richard Henry Lee and his five almost equally celebrated brothers; General "Lighthorse Harry" Lee and General Robert E. Lee.

The house was destroyed during the War between the

States. It was a landmark on the river for generations. From its dome, and from the birds that sailed about and settled there, it was familiarly called "the bird cage." Of all this vast estate not one rod belongs now to one of the Randolph blood.

Here in the midst of the "curles" on the north side, was the home of Nathaniel Bacon, the younger, who in 1676 led the Tidewater colonists in rebellion against the arbitrary Governor, Sir William Berkeley. The first peninsula on this side made by the inconstant course of the river, takes its name from the nickname of the water, and for hundreds of years has been known as Curle's Neck. Whatever house may have looked over the river in colonial times, it is now dominated by a massive modern brick mansion. Farther along on the same side is the site of Varina, which tradition says was the home of John Rolfe and his Indian-bride, Pocahontas. The last of these peninsulas in the "curles," and made an island artificially by a canal across the few hundred feet of its narrow neck, is the site of much early planning and expectation on the part of the earliest English settlers.

This canal was formerly a primitive ditch for shallop, pinnace and canoe, cut here in 1611, and then and ever since called Dutch Gap. Here, in that year, came the Royal Governor of the colony, Sir Thomas Dale, with a magnificent project for making the artificial island the site of the great capital of the new English world. It was to be called Henrico or Henricopolis after the eldest son of King James I whose name had already been given to the cape at the other end of Tidewater.

Here, on foundations of brick made on the spot by brickmakers from England, and set in three streets, rose the houses of the city of so many expectations. The settlement was made secure by five blockhouses commanding the river. Behind their palisades the guards clanked their noisy vigil back and forth in old coats of mail and steel armor which had seen service on the battle-fields of Europe and had for years been rusting in the Tower of London, when they were polished up and sent out to protect Dale's men against the Indians' arrows and tomahawks. Here, in 1618, the authorities proposed to build a university. Ten thousand acres of land were set aside for it. Money was collected for it, amounting to the equivalent of one hundred thousand dollars. Not only was the Royal Governor behind the enterprise, but it was backed also by the distinguished characters of "the Company in England." Suddenly broke the great catastrophe which nearly wiped out the permanent first English colony in America. On Good Friday morning, 1622, the Indians rose and began the direful massacres. That put an end to capital and university here, and both tumbled into an oblivion which has little troubled any one since passing the desolate site of their projectors' hopes.

Two sentinels of a brighter memory of colonial days in Tidewater still stand on the last straight stretch of the James before its tidal waters are halted by the falls. They face each other across its narrowed waters. On the east side stands Wilton and on the west side stands Ampthill. They are somewhat similar solid rectangular brick buildings, set among giant old trees. Ampthill has two square wings, solid as itself, set on the axis of the "big house" but unattached to it.

Wilton was built by the third of the William Randolphs, and it still carries the evidence of the solidity and distinction which characterized so many of the houses erected in Tidewater in the middle of the eighteenth century. Young Thomas Jefferson, with one eye on the law and the other on the young

OLD BRUTON CHURCH, WILLIAMSBURG

INTERIOR OF OLD BRUTON CHURCH, WILLIAMSBURG
The canopied "pew" of the Royal Governors may be seen on the left of
the chancel

INTERIOR OF POHICK CHURCH
Washington was a vestryman of Pohick, and the Mount Vernon pews
are the two pews immediately in front of the chancel

ladies, was an admirer of the builder's daughter, Anne, a belle of many beaux. "Ben Harrison has gone courting to Wilton," he wrote in one of his early gossipy letters. This Ben was Benjamin Harrison, heir and later master of Brandon. His courting was effective and one day Anne rode away from Wilton as his bride, and began her reign as mistress of Brandon.

Ampthill opposite was originally a Cary home. It was built in 1732 by Henry Cary who superintended also the building of the state-house and the Governor's Palace in Williamsburg and the rebuilding of William and Mary College after its destruction by fire. His son, Archibald Cary, who from his force and determination was known as "Old Iron" of Ampthill, added a particular luster to his family and to his state by his service as chairman of the committee of the Virginia Convention of 1776 which directed the Virginia members sitting in the Continental Congress to agitate and vote for entire independence of Great Britain. When later the government was established and he took his place in the Senate, and there was talk of setting up a dictatorship with Patrick Henry, though without his knowledge or consent, as dictator, he came face to face with Henry's half-brother, and said to him:

"Sir, I am told your brother wishes to be dictator. Tell him from me, that the day of his appointment shall be the day of his death, for he shall find my dagger in his heart before the sunset of that day."

For these last seven miles of the James, before the rocks and rapids stay the farther rise of its tide, the river reaches north a direct shaft of dark water, driving into the heart of suddenly precipitous hills. Lying along the flanks of these hills, and creeping over their summits, high above the union of "freshes" and brine, is Richmond.

CHAPTER VIII

RICHMOND ON ITS HISTORIC HILLS

An Embarrassment of Names—Byrd Founds the City—Patrick Henry in Old St. John's—"Liberty or Death"—Benedict Arnold Burns Richmond—Winning the Constitution—James Madison and George Mason Lead Opposing Forces—Jefferson, Architect of the Capitol—Chief Justice John Marshall—Trial of Aaron Burr—Poe and *The Raven*—Capital of the Confederacy—Remembering the Worth of the Worthies.

ICHMOND is a scant two hundred years old, yet we read: "Richmond is a comparatively modern town." It is a little arresting to find Henry Howe thus pulling the metropolis of the James up by its historic roots. But the Collector wrote this nearly a century ago, and he wrote with one eye, no doubt, on his tables. They would have told him that, although, as already seen, Richmond and Petersburg were twins at birth, when Richmond was not yet, already Belhaven was a community on the upper Potomac awaiting rechristening as Alexandria; the city of Williamsburg had been the colony's capital for thirty-four years; Norfolk had been incorporated a town fifty years before in an earlier century; Fredericksburg had had civic being for sixty-two years; and Jamestown, one hundred twenty-six years old, had been abandoned to decay, disintegrate and fall into the waters of the James.

History, however, had been busy with the spot where Richmond stands, ever since the first year the English settled on the James. On an early June day in 1607, when Captain Newport, Captain John Smith, Master Gabriel Archer and the

Honorable George Percy had been at Jamestown but three weeks, they and others to the number of twenty-one, sailed farther up the river to discover whether this might be the passage to India.

After six days they arrived at an Indian town called Powhatan "consisting of some twelve houses, pleasantly seated on a hill; before it three fertile Isles," and "to this place the river is navigable; but higher up within a myle, by reason of the Rockes and Isles, there is not passage for a small Boat, this they call the Falles."

Seeing that the waterway to the western ocean did not lead this way, Newport sailed back to Jamestown; but not before he had set up a cross on one of the little islands "with this inscription, Jacobus Rex, 1607, and his own name belowe." After a prayer, the little band proclaimed their King James king of this new land; and the "great showte" that went up, in Archer's account of it, echoes across more than three centuries.

The Indians at the falls did not see the strange white man again before another two years. Then, in 1609, Captain Smith sent a brother of Lord de la Warre, "Capteyne Francis West, with one hundrethe and fortye men upp to the falles wth sixe monthes victewells to inhabitt there." The fort they built was christened Fort "Lawares," in Percy's spelling of Delaware; but by other accounts it was called West Fort and changed soon to None Such, because they had seen "no place so strong, so pleasant and delightful in Virginia." Soon wounded stragglers dribbled back to Jamestown with such reports that Smith hastened to the harassed settlement. There was a quarrel with West, but when Smith started to sail down-river again West came humbly aboard his ship with his remnant, and there was an end of the first settlement "at the falles."

There seemed to have been no constancy whatever about naming this spot. When, a little later, in 1639, a settlement had been made on the river, only four or five miles below the falls, it was called World's End, and when, in 1644, a new defense was ordered constructed at the falls, it was called Fort Charles. But Fort Charles, and all that went with it, was, by an act passed two years later, offered to any one who would settle opposite on the low arable acres on the south side of the river, and they "so undertaking shall have and enjoy the houseing belonging to the said ffort for the use of timber, or by burning them for the nailes."

Nevertheless the English clung tenaciously to so strategic a military and commercial point as this at Tidewater's end, and though lacking details of the interval, we know they were again settled there a few years later, because about 1654, the Indians under Tottopottomoy there defeated the whites in the bloodiest battle in the history of the colony up to that time. The fame of it reached England and Tottopottomoy was immortalized as "mighty" by Butler in his *Hudibras*. Such attacks by the Indians continued in varying degrees of intensity well into the new century.

The skies cleared with the coming of the first of the Byrds here. Fortune seemed always to smile on any Byrd's appearance. The first William came directly from England to the falls to join an uncle already struggling to found a plantation, and remained as his heir. He established a significant and permanent activity. The way, to be sure, had been somewhat long and bloodily prepared for him.

He built himself a house with the pleasant name of Belvedere. He became a prosperous merchant, importing extensively from England, and his caravans of woodmen and traders extended his traffic inland into the wilderness over a "Trading Path" more than four hundred miles long. They took "in" tools and merchandise and medicine, everything "from goods to be sold by the yard to pills by the box;" sugar, rum and molasses from Barbadoes; "white servants" indentured out of England; black slaves bartered by the Dutch out of Africa; and they brought "out" furs to ship back, with tobacco from the plantations, to the factors in England. And any one watching the chrysalis of Richmond will note that at this time it was known both as Byrd's Warehouse and as Schockoc's after the creek of that name running by it.

Here, on the hill above the waterside warehouse, in his father's Belvedere, was born the second William Byrd. Later his father bought Westover plantation, and after his father's death he built the great mansion which survives there. But in the midst of a full and brilliant life at Westover he found time to carry on the valuable trading at the warehouse and occasionally to write in his diary, one quotation from which will bring this cultured and witty son of the eighteenth century vividly near, and the site of Richmond, too, for he was writing there in September, 1732:

"For the Pleasure of the good Company of Mrs. Byrd, and her little Governour, my Son, I went about half way to the Falls in the Chariot. There we halted, not far from a purling Stream, and upon the Stump of a propagate Oak picket the Bones of a piece of Roast Beef. By the Spirit which that gave me, I was the better able to part with the dear Companions of my Travels, and to perform the rest of my Journey on Horseback by myself. I reacht Shaccoa's before 2 a'clock, and crost the River to the Mills. I had the Grief to find them both stand as still for the want of water, as a dead Woman's Tongue, for want of Breath. It had rain'd so little for many Weeks above the Falls, that the Naides had hardly Water enough left to wash their Faces. However, as we ought to turn all our Misfortunes to the best Advantage, I directed Mr. Booker, my first Minister there, to make use of the lowness of the water for blowing up the Rocks at the Mouth of the Canal. . . .

"The Water now flow'd out of the River so slowly, that the Miller was oblig'd to pond it up in the Canal, by setting open the Floodgates at the Mouth, and shutting those close at the Mill. By this contrivance, he was able at any time to grind two or three Bushels, either for his choice Customers, or for the use of my Plantations. Then I walkt to the place where they broke the Flax, which is wrought with much greater ease than the Hemp, and is much better for Spinning. From thence I paid a Visit to the Weaver, who needed a little of Minerva's Inspiration to make the most of a piece of fine Cloth. Then I lookt in upon my Caledonian Spinster, who was mended more in her looks than in her Humour. However, she promised much, tho' at the same time intended to perform little. She is too high-Spirited for Mr. Booker, who hates to have his sweet Temper ruffled, and will rather suffer matters to go a little wrong sometimes, than give his righteous Spirit any uneasiness. He is very honest, and would make an admirable Overseer where Servants will do as they are bid. But Eye-Servants, who want abundance of overlooking, are not so proper to be committed to his Care. . . .

"We walkt from one End of the Island to the other, being about half a Mile in length, and found the Soil very good, and too high for any Flood, less than that of Deucalion, to do the least damage. There is a very wild prospect both upward and downward, the River being full of Rocks, over which the Stream tumbled with a Murmur, loud enough to drown the Notes of a Scolding Wife. This Island would make an agreeable Hermitage for any good Christian, who had a mind to retire from the World."

The next year, as another entry from his diary has already indicated, he presided at Richmond's birth, locating it along the very hill where he himself had been born. If he protested that he "did not build castles only, but cities in the air," he was nevertheless prophetic enough to foresee Richmond "a large city." When the streets of the checker-board were named the plan disclosed an early, perhaps the earliest, use of numerals for the streets in one direction and of the letters of the alphabet for the streets crossing them. One is always reluctant to leave the company of this able and delightful gentleman, but the century marched on.

By 1775 Richmond had spread from the waterside up and over at least one of its hills. That one was also the pedestal of Colonel Byrd's Belvedere, and it took the name of Church Hill from a little white frame church, named for St. John, which rose at the crest behind its own high square tower. The colonies had all been growing, but growing not least in self-consciousness and in vibrant indignation at the short-sightedness of the mother country. Here on a late March day of that year the nascent Revolution received what it had lacked and needed, a slogan.

The Virginians had gathered themselves in convention at Richmond to discuss and, if possible, to decide for themselves at least, the question of any further loyalty to a king and Parliament which kept them in political and economic slavery, and there were whispered suggestions of arming and fighting and freedom. The only assembly room in town large enough to hold them was little St. John's on the hill. With the grass newly green and the trees feathery with the promise of summer shade, the first men of the colony took their places in the church's square high-backed pews. Among them were men whose names were later to be written indelibly on the national roster: a tall auburn-haired young man from the Piedmont, named Thomas Jefferson, who the next year would write a Declaration of Independence; Benjamin Harrison, Carter Braxton and Richard Henry Lee who would pledge their life and all in signing it; George Mason who would write a Constitution for Virginia, the commonwealth; Chancellor Wythe, one of the fathers of American jurisprudence; Edmund Pendleton, Archibald Cary, Richard Bland, and the Potomac planter, George Washington.

Among this company was one named Patrick Henry, his head aflame with a red wig and his shoulders bending as if carrying more years than his forty-five. Already he was, when he rose to speak, accustomed to command attention. On the question of arming the colonists he was a radical. The soothing, temporizing friends of such a peace as the colonies labored under drew his fire. On this occasion he surpassed his own reputation for audacity and eloquence, and ended his impassioned speech with the historic peroration:

"Gentlemen may cry peace! peace!—but there is no peace! The war is actually begun! The next gale that sweeps from the north will bring to our ears the clash of resounding arms! Our brethren are already in the field! . . . Is life so dear, or peace so sweet, as to be purchased at the price of chains and slavery! Forbid it, God Almighty! I know not what course others may take; but as for me, give me liberty or give me death!"

He had not merely moved his hearers. In the last seven words the Revolution had received the needed slogan. They spread like wildfire; they were on every one's lips; the young nation about to be born trembled and thrilled with their repetition. It was for such an outburst as that on the spring morning in St. John's that Henry came to be remembered as the Tongue of the Revolution.

After some years of war, Williamsburg, in the lowlands between the James and the York, and not many miles from the bay, was considered dangerously accessible to the enemy and for this reason the capital was removed to Richmond, in 1779.

Even Richmond, one hundred twenty miles from the sea, did not prove to be wholly safe. The British fleet sailed up the James in January, 1781, and disembarked troops to the number of fifteen hundred at Westover. Thence, with the traitor, Benedict Arnold, in command, they marched up to the new capital. Governor Thomas Jefferson ordered all possible removable public property out of the city to a place of safety. Arnold entered without opposition. He remained twenty-four hours, during which he caused some public and some private property, as well as stores of tobacco, to be burned, and returned down-river. That was Richmond's only experience of fighting during the Revolution.

A few years later it saw one of the notable scenes in the formation of the new nation. It was in 1788. The war had been won; freedom from England had been secured. The organization of the Republic was struggling toward attainment. The key to the future lay with a constitution. Over it a bitter battle had been waging in every one of the thirteen new states. Some of them had ratified it, but the issue of its life and character hung in the balance and eventually the deciding vote lay with Virginia. And over the same issue the Virginians found themselves sharply, bitterly divided.

The critical convention opened one early summer day in 1788. Edmund Pendleton, friend of the Constitution, was chosen to preside. Others, like-minded, were Chancellor Wythe, Edmund Randolph, George Nicholas, James Innes, "Lighthorse Harry" Lee and John Marshall. The captain of this host was physically the smallest man among them, James

Madison, with a voice no larger than his person, dandified in his dress, with a trim-fitting suit of buff and blue, immaculate linen ruffled at the bosom and at the wristbands, his hair queued, powdered on top and tied at the back with a neatly bowed ribbon.

The leaders arrayed against these and the ratification were Benjamin Harrison, the giant of Berkeley; scholarly John Tyler; young James Monroe; swarthy, white-haired George Mason, down from his seat on the Potomac; and Patrick Henry whose tongue was dreaded by any who found themselves exposed to its lash. Two other Virginians were absent this time. Jefferson was against ratification, but he was on his diplomatic mission in France. Washington was known to be heartily in support of it, but with more than an inkling of the rôle which he would play if the Constitution were adopted, he remained tactfully in retirement at Mount Vernon.

The battle lasted for three weeks. The eyes and ears of the young nation were strained toward Richmond. It was the greatest debate ever held over the Constitution and it has been singled out as one of the greatest parliamentary debates of history. At last friends of the Constitution won. As a result, Virginia voted for ratification, the deadlock was thus broken, the Constitution was adopted and gave the Republic life.

Meanwhile Jefferson in France had been absent on an excursion into the southern part of that country and even over the line as far into Italy as Milan. Architecture was his avocation. What his destination was when he turned back has always been in doubt. Palladio, however, was his artistic master, and it is not unreasonable to believe he was on his way to Vicenza, the incomparable out-of-door museum of that architectural artist. What he actually did see, that is pertinent to this story, was a certain temple left by the Romans at Nimes. From that city he wrote the Countess di Tesse:

"Here I am, Madame, gazing whole hours at the Maison Quarrée, like a lover at his mistress."

To Madison he wrote of it:

"It is one of the most beautiful, if not the most beautiful and precious morsel of architecture left us by antiquity."

He had recently received a letter from Virginia asking him to draw plans for the required new Capitol building and he made the Maison Quarrée at Nîmes his model; drew plans, preserving its exterior esthetic features and skilfully adapting its interior to legislative chambers and offices; and from these plans of his rose the state's white Capitol which, based on the rosy glow of the pink brick of other buildings about and beneath it, stood on the highest hill, its pediment and columned portico, when seen from a distance, suggesting another Parthenon above another Athens.

At the time that the Capitol rose Richmond had but three hundred houses. But even then its distinction was less in its chattels than in the character of its people. Paulding described the residents of Richmond as "a race of most ancient and respectable planters, having estates in the country, who chose it for their residence for the sake of social enjoyment. They formed a society now seldom to be met with in any of our cities. A society of people not exclusively monopolized by money-making pursuits, but of liberal education, liberal habits of thinking and acting; and possessing both leisure and inclination to cultivate those feelings, and pursue those objects which exalt our nature, rather than increase our fortune."

That was written of Richmond when it was about to enter

upon nearly a century of uninterrupted peace. It was prophetic of the trend of life there through all that period, and the effect of it is one of the city's most significant survivals to-day. During that long interval of peace at least three figures of national import appeared in Virginia's capital city: a jurist, an alleged traitor and a poet.

The jurist was John Marshall. He came to the city a young man of thirty, with his bride, and throughout a long life it was his home, in spite of interruptions which during thirty-five years took him to Washington to sit in the Supreme Court of which he became its most famous and esteemed chief justice. His home was a center. His appearance on the streets is the subject of anecdotes which now verge toward legends.

Tales of his dinners to the members of the Richmond bar, assembled often to the number of thirty about his own dining-table, are still charged with their toasts and stories and hearty laughter. For years he led Richmond's curiously distinguished Quoit Club, where, surrounded by his peers, he led in tossing the iron rings, or, on his knees in the dust, in contesting the winning margin with wit and a straw; and when he died the membership of the club paid him the tribute of remaining one less than it had been while he lived.

A drama was enacted in Richmond through the summer of 1807 that focused the attention of the entire nation as had nothing else since the stirring fight for the Constitution. Thomas Jefferson, a Virginian, was president of the United States. John Marshall, a Virginian, was chief justice of the Supreme Court. They were uncompromising political opponents. Aaron Burr, late vice-president by virtue of a narrow-margined defeat for the presidency, when he contested for it with Jefferson and had received the support of Marshall's party, was suspected of an ambition to set himself up as emperor of Mexico and carry certain of the southwestern states with him out of the Union. For this he was accused of high treason, arrested and brought to Richmond where he was indicted and tried by a court over which Chief Justice Marshall presided.

The stage from the south, rolling into the Virginia capital on March twenty-fourth, brought former Vice-President Burr under strong guard. After preliminaries before a grand jury of which John Randolph, of Roanoke, was the foreman, during which Burr spent a part of his time in the jail and a part of it out on bail, the case came to trial on August third. During the whole period of his stay in Richmond, Burr was the recipient of social attentions and flattering hospitalities. His own distinguished bearing and magnetic address won many. Others appear to have patronized him from political motives. Though his was a trial for treason it nevertheless had a strong political savor. Jefferson hated Burr, which, it was believed, contributed not a little to Chief Justice Marshall's attitude as, for instance, when Burr's principal counsel gave a dinner party for him and the Chief Justice attended and was liberally criticized for the breach of his accustomed good judgment.

The trial was held in the Capitol of Jefferson's planning. A formidable gathering of legal talent was arrayed on each side. Among those who appeared for the defense were John Wickham, William Wirt, Edmund Randolph and Luther Martin. The press of the country sent an army of correspondents. Among them sat youthful Washington Irving who had not yet written the biographies of Columbus, Mahomet and Washington, or set the English-reading world laughing over his collaboration with Diedrich Knickerbocker. The court was packed throughout the trial. In spite of the hot summer the citizens remained in their town houses, crowded them with guests; and the taverns, the boarding-houses and every available place of temporary habitation were filled. Interest, as well as the thermometer, was everywhere at fever heat. Peoples' collars may have wilted but not their spirits. The country had never had a trial like Aaron Burr's, nor has it had such a one since, and expectation radiated toward Richmond from every direction.

The most sensational moment of the proceedings was reached when the defense asked that the president of the United States be summoned as a witness. President Jefferson took a week to refuse, with the reply that "To comply with such calls would leave the nation without an executive head, whose agency is understood to be constantly necessary."

The end of the trial was ambiguous. After continual battles between the opposing counsel, after the Chief Justice had with scrupulous care, passed down every one of his rulings in writing, on September first the jury found Burr "not proved to be guilty under the indictment by any evidence submitted to us." Nobody was quite satisfied with such a verdict. And so the thrilling drama ended; the country at large relaxed its tenseness; Richmond resumed her normal calm and ease; and Aaron Burr drove away into history: accused, acquitted, but not cleared.

It was nearly another forty years before Richmond again found itself the center of national curiosity. Then in 1845, the March number of Richmond's *Southern Literary Messenger* published a poem which convinced the citizenry not only of that city but of the entire country that a great poet had appeared among them. The author of it had been a contributor of short stories to the Richmond magazine and they had been well received, but national acclaim came to him only with this first appearance of *The Raven,* for its author, the author of stories and poems which had made him so long familiar on the streets and in the homes of Richmond, was Edgar Allan Poe.

Soon came the Civil War, and Richmond entered upon its great tragedy, and found itself with a new significance before the eyes of the whole world. During the bloody period from 1861 to 1865 the little capital of the commonwealth became the capital of all the seceding states. Here government on a large scale was set up, a war government surrounded by battle-fields, and here centered the aspirations and hopes of a cause that was to be lost.

Besieged during all these four years by operations of civil and military government; by the shifting armies of its own gray soldiers; by a pitiful procession of wounded and dying and dead; at last Destiny in blue came to its gates and it fell, and with it fell the hopes for which it had stood the citadel.

The wounds were deep, and they healed slowly. Gradually, through a long interval of peace, the old city has renewed itself and has become the commercial as well as the political capital of Virginia in the period of its greatest prosperity.

In the midst of its growth many of the sign-posts of its historic past have disappeared, but many others remain to remind one of other days. The James still rushes by over the rocks with the same roar that "deafened" Newport and Smith and Percy on the summer day in 1607 when these white men first looked on them. But gone are the Indian towns; the old forts called Charles and Lawares; Byrd's warehouse by the waterside and his Belvedere on the hill; and the old Academy where Madison and Mason and Henry battled, and where the fight for the Constitution was won.

St. John's still stands in the midst of the tombs of the fathers, altered by additions but claiming the identical pew in which Henry pledged his life to Liberty. One finds the columned old Capitol still commanding its green acre but no longer commanding its vista down the flatlands of Tidewater. It finds itself after so many years at the bottom of a well of sky-scrapers which obscure it from its ancient outlook and give their own high, many-windowed, squared-top lines to the sky-line of the city. It is still the seat of government and also the shrine of Houdon's matchless statue of Washington.

Memories of the nineteenth century survive in Chief Justice Marshall's former home; in a certain old Stone House that saw sights in its day and now, with its lovely garden, preserves the memory of the poet whose *Raven* took flight from Richmond; in the war residence of General Robert E. Lee, now the home of the Virginia Historical Society; in the war residence of Jefferson Davis, known as the White House of the Confederacy, and now sheltering the Confederate Museum; and in other old houses connected with the domestic history of the community.

Richmond has in other manifestations become the repository of the chief memorials of the Confederate cause, among which one finds the Confederate Memorial Institute, sometimes called the Battle Abbey; and monuments to Jefferson Davis, Robert E. Lee and J. E. B. Stuart. Other monuments in Hollywood Cemetery mark the graves of James Monroe, John Tyler, Jefferson Davis and Commodore Matthew F. Maury.

Richmond has long outgrown its three original hills. Large, modern and alive, it is stamped with most of the superficial

BROWNSVILLE-BY-THE-SEA, EASTERN SHORE

BOWMAN'S FOLLY, EASTERN SHORE

TIDE-MILL ON AN INLET OF MOBJACK BAY

MOORE HOUSE, YORKTOWN
In which the terms of Cornwallis' surrender to Washington were drawn

conventionalities of other American cities. In the midst of the roar of motor-cars and trolleys, behind a civil façade of tobacco factories, department stores, chain stores, sky-scrapers and apartment-houses, there still are other vestiges of another Richmond, which give the city an air and a flavor of its own. Detached, and a little apart perhaps from the obvious paths of traffic, venerable, dignified red and white houses stand in gentle reticent tolerance of the ostentatious new; here and there wistaria and roses mantle old walls and porticos and side galleries, joining their perfumes with the lilac and other homey garden familiars; side gates may be found giving on uneven foot-worn brick walks, laid in herring-bone pattern across patches of neglected lawn in whose cool shady corners lilies-of-the-valley lift their waxen cups, and where bees are busy among blossoming shrubs.

The people themselves, though they may have abandoned the homes of their fathers, for many-storied modernities, have carried with them an habituated courtesy; they bear themselves with a still recognizable manner; and the largeness of hospitality survives as a part of their lives.

Richmond treasures its traditions. It lives in the present, but it keeps a window open on the past, for its people seem to believe in the force of example and to value the thoroughbred strain in men as well as other animals, remembering the worth of worthies of other days.

CHAPTER IX

COLONIAL WILLIAMSBURG

The Mighty Mosquito—A Green and White City—Second Oldest College in America—A Table of Priorities—The Governor's Palace—The Capitol —"A Strong Sweet Prison"—Raleigh Tavern—Guests and Hosts—The Powder Horn—Old Bruton Church—The Social Season under the Royal Governor—America's First Theater—Moving Pictures in 1788—Restoring an Entire City—Old Homes of Great Characters.

 HE little city of Williamsburg has an inerasable past and now, emerging from nearly a century and a half of comparative neglect and decay, it seems on the verge of a future which in another and unique way will distinguish it from every other community in America.

Its more important past bridged the period between the colonists' defeat by the forces of Nature at Jamestown on the James and their own conclusive victory over the British at Yorktown on the York. Similarly its geographical position is on the way from Jamestown to Yorktown in the center of the peninsula between the James and the York.

It is seriously stated that the mosquito was one of the contributory internal causes of the downfall of the Roman Empire. With equal seriousness it is said that the mosquito, with the assistance of a devastating fire, drove the Virginia government from Jamestown and so was a contributory external cause of the foundation of Williamsburg. Jamestown never knew its real enemy. The discovery of the affinity between malarial and other fevers and the mosquito was waiting for the birth of young Walter Reed on the banks of the York near by.

The Burgesses, when their capital was burned to the ground, met in the home of Mrs. Sarah Lee, and voted to move to an inland site on high ground, called the Middle Plantation. Francis Nicholson was the royal governor and gave the project of the new city his enthusiastic support. He was a courtier and so an opportunist. He named the new city after his king. He had an imaginative pencil and he sketched its streets on paper in the ingenious monogram of the initials of William and Mary. His sheet of paper, however, showed no ravines. He found, nevertheless, that the site of the new city was a low ridge indented inconveniently on both sides by the head of depressions which led out to the inlets on its great flanking rivers. But Nicholson had made his courteous gesture, and for the new capital he forthwith adopted a new plan in the shape of an elongated checker-board. The broad central street he named for the Duke of Gloucester. The two streets paralleling it next on either side he modestly named Francis and Nicholson in honor of his not precisely shrinking self.

The College of William and Mary had already been seated at the then so-called Middle Plantation and now found itself at one end of the street named for this duke who was Queen Anne's eldest son. A mile away, at the other end of this street, rose the colony's new house of government, which accommodated the upper house, known as the Council, and the lower house, known as the House of Burgesses. This building was at once called the Capitol and so furnished the first instance on this side of the Atlantic Ocean of this use of the word. Between these two extremes gradually emerged the little city whose size has always been in inverse ratio to its importance. Williamsburg was the capital of Virginia when that colony was at its largest and extended westward indefinitely toward the Pacific Ocean, although the settlements and the arm of government reached little farther than the adjacent shores of Tidewater.

It became at once the focus of the interest and attention of the planters, for its heyday was the heyday too of life on the great plantations. The Governor built himself a "Palace" at the north end of a long esplanade, two hundred feet wide, at right angles to the main street. Public buildings rose at convenient points: a court-house, a church, a prison, some civic offices, and a round tower for the storage of powder. These at least were all of brick.

Williamsburg was, however, far from being a brick city. The leading planters were generally members of either the Council or the House of Burgesses, and they built town houses for the period of their residence in the capital for the sittings. Taverns or ordinaries offered transient conveniences. Nearly all such structures were built of wood, and seated back in their green yards, behind white paling fences and shadowed by great green trees. Their long, low, white fronts, with banks of dormer-windows winking out of steep roof-sides between massive outside chimneys, gave Williamsburg its character as a green and white city with an occasional flush of pink from the brick buildings sprinkled here and there. Like the lands of Tidewater about it, the little city was long and low and level. Nothing is or ever was high anywhere in Williamsburg except the spire of Bruton Church. Two stories was the accepted height of college, Palace and Capitol, and for the most part the second story of the dwellings shrank modestly behind a hipped and dormered roof in a way suggesting the then new fashion invented by the French architect, Mansart.

The beginning of Williamsburg was not quite the beginning of history on its site. History had already passed this way and left its mark. Nathaniel Bacon, Jr., held his convention here in August, 1676, with his fiery speeches arousing the people in rebelling against the British an even hundred years, lacking only one month, before another and more conclusive convention, with a similar purpose, was held farther north. Here in May, 1677, the Royal Governor came over from Jamestown and met the Indian Kings and Queens of all Tidewater, to make a lasting peace. Here the Indians finally signed obedience to the white man's rule. As a guarantee of good treatment the Governor presented to each of them a coronet or frontlet adorned with false jewels. One of these, the one presented to the Queen of the Pamunkeys, survives and is in the collection of the Virginia Historical Society. When the Capitol at Jamestown had been fired and destroyed by Bacon, the General Assembly met first at Governor Berkeley's mansion at Green Spring, but in October, 1677, it met at Major Otho Thorpe's house in Middle Plantation. In 1693, the crown granted a charter for the foundation of the College of William and Mary, and it was located at Middle Plantation.

Many distinctions attach to this venerable institution. In length of time of actual operation it antedates all other American colleges except Harvard. Its table of priorities recites that among American colleges it was the first that received its charter direct from the crown of England; the first to have a full faculty of professors (1729); the first to adopt the lecture system (1758); the first to establish the elective and honor systems, to broaden its scope into that of a university, to establish courses in municipal and constitutional law, modern languages and political economy (1779); and the first to establish a course in history (1803). Here in 1776 was organized the first Greek letter intercollegiate fraternity, the Phi Beta Kappa Society.

It claims proudly that its alumni exerted more influence on the making of the Union than did the alumni of any other similar institution. It points to a long list of historically distinguished graduates, among whom were Peyton Randolph, first president of the Continental Congress; Thomas Jefferson, author of the Declaration of Independence; Richard Bland; John Tyler, Sr.; Edmund Randolph; Chief Justice John Marshall; President James Monroe; and also President John Tyler.

Among the quaint traditions which attach to the college is that of the tribute of Latin verses paid to the Royal Governor as long as he was in residence in Williamsburg. The college was obliged by its charter to pay him these two copies of Latin verses on each November fifth, as quit rent for its lands. Well remembered among such verses were those of Arthur Blackamore who sang the praises of Governor Spotswood's expedition across the frontier and of his accompanying Knights of the Golden Horseshoe.

The brick Capitol was twice the victim of fire, even though warned by the first burning of the college and by the conflagration which destroyed Jamestown. Hugh Jones said in 1724 that the use of fire, candles and tobacco was prohibited in it. Obviously without candles there could have been no night sessions of the Council or Burgesses, and without fires the winter sittings must have been chilly enough. Jones provided a description of this first Capitol:

"The building is in the form of an H nearly; the secretary's office and the general court taking up one side below stairs; the middle being a handsome portico leading to the clerk of the Assembly, and the House of Burgesses on the other side; which last is not unlike the House of Commons. In each wing is a good stair case, one leading to the council chamber, where the governor and council sit in *very great state*, in imitation of the King and council, or the lord chancellor and House of Lords. Over the portico is a large room where conferences are held, and prayers are read by the chaplain to the general assembly; which office I have had the honor, for some years to perform. At one end of this is a lobby, and near it is the clerk of the council's office; and at the other end are several chambers for the committees of claims, privileges, and elections; and over all these are several good offices for the receiver general, for the auditor, and treasurer, &c., and upon the middle is raised a lofty cupola with a large clock.

"The whole surrounded with a neat area encompassed with a good wall, and near it is a strong sweet prison for criminals; and on the other side of the open court another for debtors, when any are removed from the other prisons in each county; but such prisoners are very rare; the creditors being there generally very merciful, and the laws so favorable for debtors that some esteem them too indulgent."

Only the foundations of the Capitol remain, but imperishable memories cluster about them. Here, as councilor or burgess, sat nearly every great Virginian of the eighteenth century. Here were conceived and utterance first given to many of the ideas which inspired and supported the Revolution, and others which found their way into the Declaration of Independence and the Constitution of the United States. Here Patrick Henry made his Cæsar-Brutus speech terminating with his famous challenge, "If that be treason make the most of it." In 1776 resolutions were passed here calling on the Congress to declare the colonies free and independent states. Here, the same year, were adopted George Mason's celebrated Bill of Rights and his Constitution for the new-born state of Virginia, the first of the constitutions of the new states.

One of the two prisons, to which Jones referred, still stands. After Blackbeard was defeated and slain and his head borne back into Tidewater on the prow of the ship returning with his captured henchmen, they were brought to this prison. They caught their last glimpses of this world through its little square, barred windows before they were led out and to near-by Gallows Road where they were hanged by the neck till dead. But this was no mere local jail. It was the prison of Virginia when the colony extended as far at least as the Mississippi River. When George Rogers Clark captured the British Governor Hamilton at Vincennes on the Wabash he sent him all the way east to Williamsburg to be locked up in this prison. The warden and his family resided in the dormered second story. As there is no surviving stairway to that upper story, or indication that there ever was such, it is now said that this was deliberate, and was intended to prevent the prisoners' access to their keeper in case of mutiny. Pressed for an explanation as to how the warden and his family established connection with the earth, such gossip offers "a removable ladder kept behind the upper doorway."

"A strong sweet prison," Hugh Jones called it, and a contemporary Williamsburger said: "Today it is stronger and sweeter than the prison erected here in 1901 and known as the 'honor jail,' because no one stays in it who doesn't want to."

On the north side of Duke of Gloucester Street stood the Raleigh Tavern, with a bust of the noble courtier, its namesake, over the front door. Its great moment came in February, 1769. Word crossed the Atlantic that the Parliament had advised the King to transport persons accused of treason in

America to Great Britain for trial. The Burgesses sitting in the Capitol at once passed warm resolutions denouncing the threat. Lord Botetourt, Royal Governor at the time, immediately dissolved the Assembly. Evicted from the Capitol they reassembled in the Apollo Room of the Raleigh Tavern and there astonished Botetourt, and advanced the independence of the colonies, by passing resolutions to import nothing further from England. Here also sat the famous Committee of Correspondence, "the immortal eleven," Peyton Randolph, Robert C. Nicholas, Richard Bland, Richard Henry Lee, Benjamin Harrison, Edmund Pendleton, Patrick Henry, Dudley Digges, Dabney Carr, Archibald Cary and Thomas Jefferson.

Mine host of this tavern at the moment was one Anthony Hay. He did not live to see his son, George Hay, prosecute Aaron Burr and marry the daughter of President James Monroe. Anthony Hay was not the only famous host of the Raleigh. Another, his predecessor by many years, was Henry Wetherburn, whose brews were so much admired that William Randolph sold two hundred acres of land to Thomas Jefferson's father in consideration of "Henry Wetherburn's biggest bowl of arrack punch."

Half-way along the broad street between the college and the remnants of the Capitol are three engaging brick survivals. The most modern is the court-house, an exquisite bit of architecture in line and proportion, inside and out. It dates only to 1770. Originally its pediment was unsupported by columns, and the whole composition was lighter for it and more in harmony with its diminutive size. The stones of the broad platform before the front door, and of the steps leading to it, were imported from England.

Across the street from the court-house is a quainter though

less beautiful structure called the Powder Horn. Governor Spotswood induced the Assembly to appropriate two hundred pounds for its erection in 1714 in order to have a proper receptacle for the arms and ammunition sent out by Queen Anne's government. It is an octagonal building whose walls, twenty-two inches thick, are laid in the colonially popular Flemish bond. Its roof tapers in the form of an octagonal cone.

The story of the Powder Horn was uneventful until the day after the Battle of Lexington. News of that event, however, had not reached Williamsburg. Lord Dunmore on that day caused the powder to be removed from the so-called Horn and placed on an armed schooner at anchor in the James River. This arbitrary act, a gesture of disarming the colonists, threw all Virginia into a turbulence and was the immediate cause of the assembly of armed forces throughout the colony in opposition to royal order. In its subsequent career this curious old pile has been a market-house, a meeting-house, a dancing school, a Confederate arsenal and a stable, until it was redeemed and has become a public monument and a museum.

Contemporary with this veteran is Bruton Church. In age, form, setting and history it is one of the most interesting old churches in English America. It rose 1714-15 on the site of an earlier church which was accounted too small "to accomodate the crowd of strangers brought together by the general assembly, the courts, the councils, and other public agencies." It is cruciform in shape and sits behind a great square tower which tapers off in a beautifully devised octagonal spire. In common with other churches of its day, its interior had whitewashed walls, stone-flagged aisles and rectangular, oil-painted, mahogany pews. What especially distinguished Bruton was the pew of the Royal Governor which was in effect a great chair suggesting a throne, overhung with a crimson canopy, and placed conspicuously near the chancel opposite the pulpit.

Bruton boasts the possession of three very old communion services. One of these came from the church at Jamestown and bears the date 1661. A second was presented by Lady Rebecca Gooch, and one of the pieces bears the date 1686 and the hall-mark of Peter Haraden. The pieces of a third set, presumed to have been presented by Governor Francis Fauquier, are dated 1764 and 1768, and they bear the arms of England used during the reign of King George III.

Old Bruton's walls and its churchyard are made picturesque by the tablets and tombs and monuments which adorn them. Among the names of conspicuous characters buried in and about this church are those of two royal governors, Edward Nott and Francis Fauquier; three members of the Council, John Blair, one of its presidents and an acting royal governor, John Page, of Rosewell, and David Bray; Secretaries of State Daniel Parke, who was grandfather of John Parke Custis, the first husband of Mrs. George Washington, Edmund Jennings, of Ripon Hall on the York, who acted as governor for four years, and William Cocke; a justice of the United States Supreme Court, John Blair, Jr.; a United States district judge, Cyrus Griffin and his wife, who was Lady Christine Stuart, daughter of the Earl of Traquair; a number of the presidents of the college, and others notable in their day.

Daniel Parke's epitaph refers to the "hopeful progeny" which he left behind him. They were two, Daniel, Jr., and Frances. Unfortunately for the credibility of the marble their reputations have survived them. George Fitzhugh called young

Daniel Parke "a violent man who for some offense fled to England and came to a violent death." The other "hopeful," Frances Parke, we shall meet presently on the Eastern Shore as the trying spouse of the eccentric John Custis, of Arlington, who chiseled her a nameless fame on his own unforgetable tombstone.

The pleasantest phase of colonial Williamsburg must have been its social life. The number of its permanent population at its most was only a little more than two thousand. But when the courts and Council and Burgesses were in session, the leading planters came from all over Tidewater and brought their families and set up for the "season." Its houses and ordinaries were full; its streets were inordinately active with coach, chariot, chaise and berlin; its church, theater, college and race-course were alive with citizens and visitors; and there was such social gaiety as for elegance and sprightliness was not excelled in any other colony.

The "season" took its cachet from the Royal Governor's entertainments at the Palace. Chief of these, in addition to dinners and courts and receptions for distinguished visitors, was the annual ball on the King's birthnight. On that night the double row of "noble catalpas," which flanked the great "Palace Green," were hung with colored lanterns. Lighted by them the coaches full of guests found their way to the great front door.

Inside the Palace the mirrors and polished floors multiplied the tapers twinkling in candlesticks, sconces and chandeliers. The eighteenth-century company was colorful in the pomp of brocade and the graceful sweep of full folded silk dresses. Men and women alike piled their heads with curled and powdered wigs. Jewels sparkled on those pinnacles as well as on shoe-buckles and knee-clasps, at the necks of the ladies and in the lace jabots of the men's courtly costume.

Social confusion and jealousy and heart-burn seem to have been known here, and complaint of it and prayer for relief carried to the court at St. James. For in 1774 was issued "Rules of Precedency for men and women in America, prepared by Joseph Edmonston, Mowbray herald." This order of precedence, which included "his wife" or "their wives," was: Governor of the Colony or Province, President of the Council, Counselors, Speaker of the Commons House of Assembly, Chief Justice, Treasurer, Associate Justices, Baronets, Attorney-General, Judge of the Admiralty, Secretary of the Colony, Gentlemen of the Assembly, Mayor, Aldermen and Members of the Corporation.

When "rank and precedence" had asserted its formal sway at the Palace, the artificial and mannerly poise of the period held itself as long as the fiddles and hautboys gave off the measures of the French and Italian minuets. But when the punch-bowls and wine-buckets contributed their quota, and so had done their part, the tempo quickened, there was a more democratic mêlée and the whole company ranged up for the friskier Sir Roger de Coverley.

The assemblies, or subscription parties, were held in the long Apollo Room of the Raleigh Tavern to which young Jefferson referred when he wrote himself as happy "as dancing with Belinda in the Apollo could make him." There were reflected similar scenes in a modified form in the other houses of the town, for simple and unostentatious as was the exterior of most of the houses of green and white Williamsburg, the interiors boasted spacious rooms and displayed abundance of paneling, polished mahogany, crystal, silver, portraits and other splendid appurtenances of cultured gentlemen's homes. The theater was early an active and appreciated feature of life at Williamsburg. Here midway the south side of the Palace Green was built the first playhouse in the colonies, about 1715. A second theater was built near the Capitol. From a modest, somewhat amateur or at least local, beginning the Williamsburg theaters eventually drew the leading companies which came out from England to act on this side of the Atlantic. Thus throughout the century the "planter in town" enjoyed the plays of Shakespeare, Beaumont and Fletcher, Jonson, Congreve, Wycherley, Farquhar and other English dramatists until the disturbing days of the Revolution.

But the acted play was not all the entertainment enjoyed. The *Virginia Gazette,* published in Williamsburg, and the earliest of all Tidewater journals, on August 29, 1788, announced an entertainment of moving pictures. This announcement read:

"EIDOPHUSIKON OR MOVING PICTURES—The Artist who has the above exhibition on hand has taken pains (as health has permitted) to render them particularly striking to those who shall become his auditors. At the same time he is obliged to inform those patronizers of his exhibition he cannot get it ready as soon as he proposed, and is sorry for a retrogradation of his last advertisement, but shall certainly inform his subscribers and the public in general, of the first Evening's performance, which will be early in the following week, as he has completed his paintings and machinery, and has only the space of time above mentioned to see their motions and movements completed in a manner that he flatters himself will not only delight the eye but his recitals and songs will charm the ear."

It was inevitable that the planters would have a race-course at their capital, and the Williamsburg racing season was as celebrated as any other in the colony. They bred and trained their own entries from the finest importable stock and, based on an ownership or acquaintance with every entry and its forebears, there was for the entire population an intimacy and an interest in the races which can not be approached by the vast impersonal race meets of to-day. The English traveler Smythe, passing this way, gave considerable attention to the horses and the races at Williamsburg:

"Very capital horses are started here, such as would make no despicable figure at Newmarket; nor is their speed, bottom or blood inferior to their appearance. Their stock is from old Cade, old Crab, old Partner, Regulus, Babraham, Bosphorus, Devonshire Childers, the Cullen Arabian, the Cumberland Arabian, &c., in England; and a horse from Arabia named the Bellsize, which was imported into America and is now in existence."

He called attention, too, to the quarter-racing between two horses hereabouts, and remarked of the breed of horses in general:

"They have a breed in Virginia that performs it with astonishing velocity, beating every other for that distance with great ease; but they have no bottom. However, I am confident that there is not a horse in England, nor perhaps the whole world, that can excel them in rapid speed; and these likewise make excellent saddle horses for the road. The Virginians, of all ranks and denominations, are excessively fond of horses, and especially those of the race breed. Nobody walks on foot the smallest distance, except when hunting; indeed, a man will frequently go five miles to catch a horse, to ride only one mile afterwards."

In 1779 the capital was removed to Richmond, and after more than a century and a quarter of comparative neglect, without political or commercial significance, visited only occasionally by pilgrims appreciative of its rich endowment of historic interests, Williamsburg is to-day on the threshold of its new phase. It has been made the object of a curious and interesting experiment. The private munificence of Mr. John D. Rockefeller, Jr., is making it possible to restore the area of the colonial capital to a semblance of its appearance as Washington, Jefferson, Henry, the Lees, the Blands, the Randolphs and the others of its more famous familiars knew it.

The Capitol and the Palace will both rise again, the one facing the college along the mile of Duke of Gloucester Street, the other looking down the length of its esplanade which has for over two hundred years retained its peculiar character as one of the town's several "greens." Old Raleigh Tavern will be reproduced and a new Apollo Room will help to visualize the memorable events which made the old one celebrated. Some modern excrescences will be removed to restore other buildings to their original settings. The main college will resume the lines which Hugh Jones said that it received from Sir Christopher Wren. No need to restore the statue of Governor Norborne Berkeley, Baron de Botetourt, to his post before it. Serene and unchanged he remains to suggest how well beloved he was of his subjects and to remind of at least one anecdote which sketches a facet of his character.

"You ought to be very unwilling to die," observed his friend, Robert Carter Nicholas, when visiting him one day during an illness.

"Why so?" inquired Lord Botetourt.

"Because you are so social in your nature," replied Nicholas, "and so much beloved, and you have so many good things about you that you must be loath to leave them."

When subsequently his Lordship was indeed on his death-

NELSON HOUSE AND GARDENS, YORKTOWN

bed he asked his friend Nicholas to come in and see him and reminded him of the earlier conversation, and said:

"I have sent for you merely to let you see that I resign these good things of which you formerly spoke with as much composure as I enjoyed them."

Best preserved of the private homes in Williamsburg is the splendid square brick residence known as Wythe House. Here lived Chancellor George Wythe, signer of the Declaration of Independence, and described by Randall as one of "the ablest and most profoundly erudite lawyers ever produced in a State which has been particularly famous for good lawyers." He was the particular teacher, friend and adviser of young Thomas Jefferson, and these two with Governor Francis Fauquier and Dr. William Small of the college made up the intimate and habitual supper parties at the Palace of which Jefferson wrote so appreciatively. Among many interesting events of which Wythe House was the scene was the meeting of Washington, Lafayette and other generals here to plan the Battle of Yorktown while it was the Commander-in-Chief's headquarters.

Other survivals, interesting alike for their age, for their suggestions of period architecture, and for the people who lived in them, are the Randolph house, the Peachy house, Bassett Hall, the Tucker house, the Paradise house, the Blair house, the Saunders house, the Page house, the Coleman house, Tazewell Hall, the Carter house, three Garrett houses and Jackson Hall.

Tazewell Hall was the colonial home of Edmund Randolph who was secretary of state and attorney-general in Washington's Cabinet and, before him, of his grandfather, Sir John Randolph, Speaker of the House. It stands on the Court Green, and near it is the Peachy house which was Rochambeau's head-quarters before the Battle of Yorktown. Colonel St. George Tucker, in a letter containing all the news at the capital, before the army moved on Yorktown, said: "Aunt Betty has the honor of the Count of Rochambeau to lodge at her house."

Others not far off were the so-called Coleman house, home of the Tuckers and of Judge Cyrus Griffin, member of the Continental Congress; and the Tucker house, home of the Tucker as well as of the Randolph families.

Washington was often entertained in Bassett Hall, for Mrs. Washington and Mrs. Bassett were sisters. We read: "Went to Williamsburg with Colo. Bassett, Colo. Lewis, and Mr. Dick. Dined with Mrs. Dawson—and went to the play." Vice-President John Tyler was living at Bassett Hall in 1841 when Fletcher Webster, the son of Secretary of State Daniel Webster, galloped down the long lane of trees leading to the front door to announce to him the death of President William Henry Harrison and his own succession to the office of chief executive.

The grounds about Bassett Hall are extensive. When the Irish poet, Thomas Moore, visited Williamsburg in 1804, he was so impressed by the lawns illuminated at night by the myriads of fireflies that he wrote his verses *To the Firefly:*

> "At morning, when the earth and sky
> Are glowing with the light of spring,
> We see thee not, thou humble fly!
> Nor think upon thy gleaming wing.

> "But when the skies have lost their hue,
> And sunny lights no longer play,
> Oh then we see and bless thee too,
> For sparkling o'er the dreary way.

"Then let me hope, when lost to me
 The lights that now my life illume,
Some milder joys may come, like thee,
 To cheer, if not to warm, the gloom!"

Near Bassett Hall is the home of Peyton Randolph, Attorney-General of Virginia, Speaker of the House of Burgesses and first President of the Continental Congress. Saunders house facing the Palace Green was the home of Robert Saunders, a president of William and Mary, who married one of the twenty children of John Page, of Rosewell on the York. During an interval when the Palace was undergoing repairs Governor Robert Dinwiddie was a resident here.

The Page house was the town residence of John Page, of Rosewell. It faces the Palace Green and stands just next the site of the first theater. Mary Johnston used both dwelling and theater conspicuously in her novel *Audrey,* and the Page house is now frequently pointed out as "Audrey house."

Modest little Blair house was the home of two John Blairs, one President of the Council and acting Governor, and the other, his son, a Justice of the Supreme Court of the United States. Similarly modest in its externals was the town house of Councilor Robert Carter, of the Potomac, who, like other gentlemen, belied such unpromising externals with the taste and finish with which they surrounded themselves behind their doors.

Not least interesting here is another charming little white house where the Cary girls lived and received their famous beaux. Young George Washington, in his surveying days, came courting Mary Cary. She did not encourage him, however, and she married Edward Ambler instead. Here, too, came George William Fairfax courting Sarah Cary, and with better success. He carried her off his bride to Lord Fairfax's Belvoir just next Mount Vernon on the Potomac. When Washington married the Widow Custis and came back to Williamsburg at first on his honeymoon and many times afterward to sit among the burgesses, he made his home in his wife's "six chimney house" which had been the Custis home for generations before her.

At the turn in its fortunes old Williamsburg is limited in area but expansive in effect. Its greens, and the broad lawns about so many of its houses, give it a suggestion of "magnificent distances," but only a suggestion. When approached, nearly every feature of it suggests projection in miniature. That is one of its charms. Another is its profligacy in chimneys that hug the white house-ends which they support and in their solid dimensions suggest the friendly fireside within. There is nothing ostentatious about the quaint and quiet and modest little colonial capital. It does not wear its splendid history on its sleeve. Even the most pretentious that it has to show is somehow obscured by the ingratiating repetition of its broad greens, its dormer-windows twinkling over clusters of shrubbery and the staunch security of its chimneys.

CHAPTER X

THE ANCIENT KINGDOM OF ACCOMACK

Eastern Shore—The Laughing King—The Salt Works of 1614—Curious Pages from the Oldest County Records in America—A Sheriff's Oath—No Representation, No Taxes—First Theatrical Performance in America—Superstitions—Ordeal by Touch—Twelve Women Jurors in 1679—The Headless Man—Quarrels of Mr. and Mrs. Custis—An Eccentric's Epitaph—Arlington and Mount Custis—Homes of the Wise Family—Other Colonial Homes and Churches—Chincoteague's Early Rodeos—The Aloofness of Tangier Island.

HE Eastern Shore is the name given, by the first English in Tidewater, to a long peninsula which divides the Atlantic Ocean from Chesapeake Bay. Its southern tip terminates in Cape Charles, opposite and about thirteen miles from Cape Henry. Thus the names of the two Prince-sons of King James were given to guard the sea-gate to Tidewater. The upper part of this peninsula is known as the Eastern Shore of Maryland; but the lower part, all that part below a line drawn eastward from the mouth of the Pocomoke River to the ocean, is the Eastern Shore of Virginia, terms which indicate the peninsula's relation to Chesapeake Bay. If it were not for this barrier there would be no Chesapeake Bay and the waters of the ocean would sweep directly up to what is now the "Western Shore," to the mouths of the tidal rivers there.

Although Virginia's Eastern Shore was explored in the second year of the English on and about the bay, and was settled immediately thereafter, it is one of the least visited and least generally known of any of Virginia's territory about Tidewater.

This peninsula seemed to the early settlers a place apart, remote from the rest of Virginia. So definitely was this idea established at first, both here and in England, that for many years, the kings of England addressed their decrees to the people of Virginia: "To our faithful subjects in ye Colonie of Virginia, and ye Kingdome of Accawmacke." Accomack was the name given to the Eastern Shore by the Indians, and in the Algonquin Indian tongue it meant "the other-side land." To-day the Eastern Shore of Virginia is divided into two counties: its lower half is called Northampton County, reflecting the English origin of the settlers; and the upper half is called Accomac County, perpetuating the memory of the native name.

Its entire length from Cape Charles up to the Pocomoke River is about seventy miles. Its mean breadth is only eight miles. It is almost as flat as the waters which surround it, for the land never rises far above the water level. It is composed principally of sand with a slight admixture of Clay but without rock, whose surface was originally covered with forests which have been extensively cleared off disclosing a most productive soil. Inlets make of its own eastern and western shores a constant succession of islands and smaller peninsulas. A single railway line trails down its spine to its land's end. Long white ribbons of oyster-shell roads pattern the view to the aviator, but to one on the ground the outlook is a monotonous succession of fields and pine forest except where the sunny water reaches in and dimples the landscape.

In June, 1608, Captain John Smith sailed away from Jamestown in a three-ton barge with "a physician, six gentlemen and seven soldiers" aboard, crossed the mouth of the bay and touched at the island called Smith's Island "after our Captaines name," and thence explored the whole length of its bayside coast. He found the Indians friendly as they ever proved on Eastern Shore. One of their kings, Debedeavon, was called "the laughing King," and his men "the laughing Indians." He dwelt half-way up the peninsula at the head of Craddock's Creek where now is the village of Nadua.

Salt being a staple much required by the colonists to keep their fish over winter, the briny ponds on Smith's Island were the site of a salt works about 1614, when entire dependence for its operation was placed on the heat of the sun. The first settlement was called Dale's Gift after the Governor, but it was afterward familiarly remembered as the Old Plantation, and the name has been carried down across three centuries in Old Plantation Creek, the inlet next south of the Cape Charles railway terminus. Administrative territorial divisions were established here at least as early as on the James River for, when the hundreds were set up there, St. George's Hundred was set up on Eastern Shore, the only hundred ever there.

The records of Northampton County are the oldest in America. They date back to 1632. The first entry has a familiar touch. In it "the Minister complains about having not having rec'd his tythes of Tobacco." The next year beaver skins were mentioned in payment of debts; and Agnes Williams was to pay Widow Hollens twelve hens for attending her in confinement, but the widow sued her for eighteen hens. Miscreants were "tyed by neck & heels" for punishment. Other early records of the seventeenth century disclose that one hundred pounds of tobacco was the fee for preaching a funeral sermon; Christopher Bryant was ordered to be whipped for milking good wife Powell's cow by stealth; a negro was here in 1636; Lady Dale's cattle were trespassing owing to the keeper being "off playing nine pins"; John Ford had to build a pair of stocks for having shaken his fist at a constable; and Thomas Powell said that in former times "Kings went to see wars, but this King is fitten for a Lady's lap."

In 1637 no one could leave Eastern Shore without a passport. One John for committing fornication had to build a ferry on Old Plantation. Richard Buckland, having published abroad a libelous poem on Ann Smyth, was ordered "at the next preaching" to stand at the church door with a paper on his hat and on it *Inimrius Libellos,* and to ask the forgiveness of God and in particular of Ann. Robert Wyart having slandered Alice Travvellor, to the extent of taking away the reputation of Mistress Alice, he was sentenced to appear in a white sheet, with a white wand in his hand, three several Sabbath-days, in church, and to ask Alice's forgiveness. Robert himself got into another scrape when he stole a pair of pantaloons and was sentenced to appear in church during the whole time of worship for three Sundays with a pair of pantaloons tied about his neck, and with the word *Thief* written upon his back. Walter Williams was licensed to keep "an ordinary and victualling house, & to sell strong water." For being tipsy Robert Warden was ordered to stand at the church door "with a great pot tied about his neck." Walter Williams is shown in another place to have found difficulty in collecting for the sale of his "strong water." When the Indians would kill the settlers' hogs their King was "obligated to pay 150 arm lengths of good and current Roanoke and 60 sufficient Indian mats made ready in 3 months." As early as 1667, in the case of a mother charged with infanticide at birth by "taking physic, bruising her body, etc.," a jury of "the most grave, creditable and judicious women" was impaneled, and gave the accused a verdict of "clear of murther, but took physic," and sentenced her to receive thirty lashes.

One can not ramble long over Eastern Shore, or pick below the surface of history and tradition here, without discovering that it has amusing claims to distinction of a kind unduplicated elsewhere in Tidewater. Here were not only the first salt works, but if the oath which William Stone, first sheriff of Accomack, took about 1640, be not the first sheriff's oath written out and subscribed to in America, it is at least the oldest one surviving. It shows human nature little different then from now, for those pioneers in the wilderness required their officials to take oath to uphold the state, to ignore class distinctions, and to refrain from taking bribes or graft. It is an altogether quaint old piece of paper:

"Ye shall sweare that well and truely ye shall serve the King's Magistie in the office of the Sheriff of the County of Acchawmacke, and doe the King's yffitt in all things that belongeth to you to doe by way of yor office as ffar as you can or say.

"You shall truely kepe the King's Right and all that belongeth to the Crowne.

"You shall truely and rightfully treate the people of the Sheriffwicke, and do right as well to the poore as to the Ritch in all that belonged to yor office.

"You shall doe no wrong to anie man for anie guift or other behest or promise of goods for favour nor hate.

"You shall disturb noe man's rights. You shall truely returne and truly serve all the King's Writts as ffarr forthe as shall be to you coming.

"You shall take noe Bayliffe into your service but such as you will answere for.

"You shall make such of yor Bayliffes to take such oath as you make yorseffe in that belongeth to yor occupation.

"You shall be dwelling in yor own yyn ysons [proper persons?] within your Bayliewicke for the tyme that you shall be in the same office, Except you are otherwise licensed by the

Governor and Counsell of this Colony. And you shall diligently and truely doe all of the things appertaining to yor sayd office of Sheriffwicke to the uttermost of yr power. Soe holpg yor God ye."

Perhaps there was an earlier statement of the fundamental principle of the tyranny of taxation without representation, on which the war of the Revolution was fought one hundred twenty-three years later, than the Northampton Protest, but this is at least the earliest one of which there is documented knowledge. It was framed and published in 1651. While the Eastern Shore was without representation in the Assembly at Jamestown, the Burgesses nevertheless imposed a tax of forty-six pounds of tobacco per poll on them; and, in lieu of it, received a statement from a duly selected committee of six, in the cause of which they said:

"Therefore that Llawe wch reguireth & inioyneth Taxacons from us to bee Arbitrarye & illegall; fforasmuch as wee had neither summons for Ellecon of Burgesses nor voyce in their Assemblye (during the time aforesd) . . . we conceive that we may Lawfullie ptest agt the pceedings in the Act."

Nor does all the combing of records from Boston to Charleston reveal so early an instance of a drama having been acted on this side the Atlantic as is found in the county records of Accomac. One evening at the end of August, in the year 1665, the first of all known American theatrical performances, was given here. The play was *Ye Bear and Ye Cub*. The actors in it were Cornelius Wilkinson, Philip Howard and William Darby. Nothing else is known of the circumstances of the occasion, whence the players came and whether they were even a part of a traveling troupe, or what afterward became of them.

They emerge from the dusty records "accused for acting a play" and, as the godly people of Accomack were not disposed to let the introduction of such an ungodly diversion take place without challenge, they were ordered to appear at the next session of the Court "In those habilemts that they then acted in, and give a draught of such verses, or other speeches and passages which were then acted by them." Darby was jailed "to answere for his maties suit." If they were itinerant then were they much inconvenienced, for they were detained in Accomack until the Court spoke, a few days before the Christmas following. But Accomack had justice as well as a court and at that sitting the players were found to be innocent of fault and the informer was required to pay all the costs.

While Bacon was leading his rebels against the royal government of Sir William Berkeley he succeeded in jockeying that unpopular character into such a situation that he saw security only in flight. Knowing the western shore of Tidewater to be inflamed against him, the Governor fled to Eastern Shore. Before a great while, however, a trick threw the little navy which Bacon sent after him into Berkeley's hands, and he was enabled to gather a force, terminate his exile and return to Jamestown.

Berkeley wished to reward his friends in Accomack who had been loyal to him, and dispatched a message to the Assembly directing that some mark of distinction be set upon his friends across the bay. He may have overlooked the fact that the Speaker was a partizan of Bacon's, and when that official read out the Governor's message, he remarked that he was unable to suggest such a "distinction" unless it be to give his friends over there "Earmarks or burnt marks," alluding to the prevalent method of branding criminals and hogs.

In a case similar to that of infanticide is revealed the practise of detecting murder by what was sometimes called the "ordeal of touch" and sometimes the "bier test." It was based on an old superstition prevalent in England and Scotland, that if the murderer were brought into the presence of his victim, the wounds would bleed anew. In this case again the jury was made up of twelve women, and their verdict is a quaint survival in a grim forthright superstitious fashion:

"Wee ye subscribers being sworne to view ye body of a dead bastard child confest by Mary ye daughter of Sarah Carter to be borne of her body, wch said child we caused to be taken out of the ground in the garden where it was very shallow put in, then we caused Sarah the wife of Paul Carter & mother of said Mary to touch, handle and stroake ye childe, in wch time we saw no alteration in the body of ye childe; afterwards we called for Paul Carter to touch ye s'd child and immediately whilst he was stroaking ye childe the black and sotted places about the body of the childe grew fresh and red so that blud was redy to come through ye skin of the child. We also observed the countenance of the said Paule Carter to alter into very much paleness; the childe also appearing to us to be very much neglected in severall respects as to ye preservacon of such an infant and we doe conclude if ye child had any violence it was by ye throat, wch was very black and continued so, though other places wch were black altered to red & fresh collered, to wch we subscribe our hands this first day of March, 1679."

This is believed to have been the last test of the "ordeal by touch" on the peninsula, but other superstitions have carried down to a recent day among the simpler element of the citizenry. The bogy of Craddock's Creek is such a one. Though never seen it was believed to leave peculiar foot-marks and to haunt the marsh with its weird cry of "Yahoo! Yahoo!" Armed parties have been organized to search for the "haunt," both by day and by night, extending over several weeks, and carrying torches by night to shine "in its eyes." But the bogy has always been too clever for the trackers.

About Taylor's Bridge they tell of the Headless Man who guarded its approach and exacted a toll of fourpence-half-penny of all who passed that way, and punished those who refused to pay. Usually such a one's horse went lame before he reached home. However little people professed to believe in this bogy the bridge was nevertheless a dreaded spot by night, and only the brave dared cross it.

Whoever heard elsewhere of Marriage Trees? They show them on Eastern Shore. They stand on the line between Maryland and Virginia. This division between the two colonies was made in 1663, and in running the line, Scarburgh and Calvert selected a number of sturdy old oak trees as boundary monuments. On the northern side of this line the Maryland justices and parsons made marriage easier for runaways from "farther down," and many young couples never journeyed into Maryland beyond the shade on the north side of the "marriage oak," where they found the joiner waiting for his fee.

At the head of any list of the great men of Eastern Shore must surely be placed that rollicking Indian king who made himself immortal merely with his laugh. It is a little surprising to be told locally that the gory pirate, Blackbeard, was born on this shore; and to have the very islands where he operated pointed out, including Rogue's Island whose very name is offered as convincing evidence of the fact; and to be left speechless, whether convinced or not, by the indisputable evidence that there are families of Teaches on Eastern Shore, as if that proved everything. Less picturesque but more credible was another great character here, Francis Makemie, the father of the Presbyterian Church in America, who lived the best part of his life at Onancock, married and died there.

Two other names are often heard on Eastern Shore. They are Custis and Wise. The Custis line linked itself to the name John, and in all there were five John Custises here. The first was the immigrant who arrived about 1640. His son John was a friend of Lord Arlington and named his estate, on Old Plantation Creek, Arlington after him. Governor Berkeley appointed him major-general of the King's forces in Virginia; a political stroke to engage on his side, and against Bacon, one of the richest men in the colony. Sir William made his home and headquarters at Custis' Arlington during his exile from Jamestown.

The fourth John Custis, whose son was the first husband of Martha Dandridge, later Mrs. George Washington, was the eccentric of the line. His quarrels with his strong-willed wife are attested alike by traditions and court records, but as will appear presently, he eventually had the last word, carved in the marble of his tomb where any one might read it there two hundred and more years until quite recently when time and triflers finally blotted out the famous epitaph.

In spite of their quarrels this Mr. and Mrs. Custis did not separate. But there were long periods of silence between them during which they are said to have communicated only by the butler. One day, according to one of the stories still told of them, Mr. Custis made an elaborate toilet, ordered his horse and chaise to the front door and, with rather much ceremony, asked Mrs. Custis to go for a drive with him. She was not the one to hesitate even where suspicion lurked.

"Certainly, Mr. Custis; certainly, sir," said his wife, "but when were you ever so courteous before?"

And off they drove.

The customary drive at Arlington was along the bay beach. Instead of taking the shore drive, however, "the gallant whip" drove straight out into the water.

"Where are you going, Mr. Custis?" asked his wife.

"To hell, Madam," he replied.

"Drive on," said Mrs. Custis, "any place is preferable to Arlington."

And on he drove into the gradually deepening water. Mrs. Custis next broke the silence when the water had risen to the floor of the chaise.

"Again I ask, where are you taking me?"

"To hell, Madam, as I have already told you."

Undaunted, however, she bade him "Drive on, Mr. Custis, the prospect is far brighter than a return home."

At last the horse was almost off his feet and preparing to swim when Custis drew rein and headed back to shore.

"If I were to drive to hell," he said with emphasis, "and the devil himself came out to meet us, I do not believe, Madam, that you would be frightened."

"Quite true, sir," she answered, "I know you so well that I would not be afraid to go where you would go."

They came to terms finally in a curious contract one may see recorded in the old record books of Northampton Court-House. There are nine paragraphs to it, settling business details, under a preamble which gave as its purpose that "all animositys and unkindness may cease and a perfect love and friendship may be renewed betwixt them," of which the second paragraph appears the pithiest:

"That Frances shall henceforth for bear to call him ye sd John any vile names or give him any ill language, neither shall he give her any but to live lovingly together and to behave themselves to each other as a good husband & good wife ought to doe. And that she shall not intermeddle with his affairs but that all business belonging to the husband's management shall be solely transacted by him, neither shall he intermeddle in her domestique affairs but that all business properly belonging to the management of the wife shall be solely transacted by her."

John survived Frances seven years, and these years he celebrated in his epitaph:

"Beneath this marble tomb lies ye body
of the Honorable John Custis, Esq.,
of the City of Williamsburg and Parish of Bruton
Formerly of Hungar's Parish on the Eastern Shore of
Virginia and the County of Northampton the place
of his nativity.
Aged 71 years and yet lived but seven years
Which was the space of time he kept
a Bachelor's House at Arlington
On the Eastern Shore of Virginia.
This information put on this tomb was by his
own positive order.
Wm. Colley, Mason, in Fenchurch Street, London, Fecit."

In modern times one of the most conspicuous sons of the Eastern Shore was Henry Alexander Wise. He was a member of Congress, minister to Brazil, governor of Virginia and a brigadier-general in the army of the Confederacy. He will be remembered longest no doubt for the last important act of his administration as governor, when he ordered the execution of John Brown.

There is an extraordinary survival of old English family names on the Eastern Shore. Of the names in the list of inhabitants who were there in 1624 there are twenty-two which are continued to to-day. Among them are some which are quite common at the present time. The members of the Savage family date their immigrant founder even farther back than 1624. He was the Thomas Savage who came over from England with Newport and Smith. At that time he was but thirteen years old. The next year he was traded to King Powhatan in exchange for an Indian. He was one of the first Englishmen in America to attain a command of the Indian language and so was of service to the colony as an interpreter. A contemporary said that he served the public "with much honestie and success . . . without any publique recompense, yet had an arrow shot through his body in their service." The Laughing King gave him, in 1619, a large tract of land, between two creeks, which has ever since been known as Savage's Neck.

The people of this section have found life easy. The climate is tempered not only by the sweep of the salty Atlantic, but the Gulf Stream passes near enough to give an added mildness to the air at all seasons of the year. The ground is low, none of it is far from and far above the water or its influence, so that this section of Tidewater has become one of the richer trucking areas on the Atlantic coast.

In spite of the solid solvency of nearly all the inhabitants, from the first years of settlement, it is curious how few pretentious houses have been built on the peninsula. Brick houses and large houses are especially scarce. Ship-carpenters were the first builders, and they followed a tradition of compactness, not to say of line, which has had an influence ever since. "There are today many old houses on Eastern Shore which resemble the pictures of Noah's Ark," says Jennings Wise, "and give plentiful evidence of the character of the builders."

Arlington, of the John Custises, long stood overlooking the waters of Old Plantation Creek which is the first important inlet on the bayside above Cape Charles, and south of the railway and the Cape Charles ferry terminals. It fell into decay and disappeared years ago. The impressive tomb dedicated to the fourth John's singular seven years of "life" stood up until very recently, but it too is now a memory confirmed, however, by many chronicles.

There have been numerous Wise places here, yet only one estate remains in the possession of a descendant of that family which has so long been associated with "the ancient Kingdom." Old Only missed the Governor, as Henry Alexander Wise was called, and was sold before the Civil War. Fort George and Clifton passed out of the family's control at the end of that war. The only place here now owned by a descendant of this family is Cape Charles Venture, recently rechristened Kiptopeake. It was not, however, originally a Wise place, but was purchased by a son of the Governor. This is now the home of Henry Alexander Wise, grandson of the Governor. Kiptopeake is situated at the extreme end of Eastern Shore just behind Cape Charles. It was so named after a brother of the Laughing King, who was a friend of the first generation of Wises out of England on the peninsula.

There are four other houses that stand out among the places in the lower county. One of them is Cessford at "the courthouse," Eastville. The name is derived from a seat of the Scottish border clan of Kerr whose descendants built and lived here. It is a solid brick house, standing high on its foundations and rising to a third story behind a line of dormers. Another is Duckington of the Corbins, about three miles east of the county-seat. A few miles up the peninsula on Church Creek is Hungar's Church. This is a simple brick building carefully restored, with some rather graceful architectural details, and it is said to have been built before the end of the seventeenth century. In Church Neck, not far from Old Hungar's, near the mouth of Hungar's Creek, is Vaucluse, home of the Upshur and Wilkins families. Across the peninsula, on its oceanside, is Brownsville, another Upshur house, this one built of brick, possibly of some of those brick which Eastern Shore used to import in the early years not from England but from "over on the main," the Western Shore of the bay. Brownsville came to the Upshurs from their ancestor, Thomas Brown, one of the Quakers who were numerous on this end of the peninsula at the close of the seventeenth century. It bore an earlier name of TB, which the first neighbors gave it because Thomas Brown, to mark the bounds of his lands, carved his initials on shingles and nailed them to trees on the boundary-line.

Crossing the line northward into Accomac County one finds that the modest church of St. George's, Pungoteague, asks attention as one of the very old churches of America. It was built about 1656. It was cruciform originally. For a long period it was a ruin. At the beginning of this century it was restored and rededicated to service, but, in rebuilding, the ruined transepts were cleared away and the old bricks therefrom were used to complete the main building.

Half-way up the county, east of the railway, is Accomac Court-House. Here is Roseland, a large house built something over a century ago and belonging to the Parramore family. East of the county-seat on Folly Creek, is Bowman's Folly, the most pretentious house in Virginia on this side of the bay. A house of this name was built on this spot about 1653, by Edward Bowman, Sheriff, Burgess and Major. A descendant, John Cropper, of the Revolutionary Army and later general of the Virginia Continental line, tore the old house down, set his slaves to hauling earth to make a mound on the site, and then built the surviving fine mansion on top of it.

Near by is Mount Custis, one of the two places conspicuously associated with the family of this name on Eastern Shore which have outlasted the vicissitudes of the centuries. It is a curious house, or really two houses, of three stories each united by a third of only one and one-half stories, forming the letter H. There are numerous domestic buildings adjacent, and it looks out on the waters of the Metompkin Bay, an inlet from the Atlantic. Its chief treasure is a portrait of Tabitha Custis, wife of John Custis the first and mother-in-law of the builder, which, Lancaster says, was painted by Sir Peter Lely.

The other place perpetuating the Custis name on this peninsula is Custis house, on Deep Creek, on the bay. It was built by a brother of John Custis, of Arlington, forty miles to the south. It is not large, but its antiquity shows in its condition. Its brick ends and the massive outside construction for fireplaces and chimney, with penthouse between, are interesting. It is one of those old houses which, as Wise pointed out, suggest the lines of Noah's Ark. Of a kindred sort is little West house on this same Deep Creek. These two are among the oldest houses on Eastern Shore.

On the oceanside at the northern end of Virginia's end of this peninsula is Chincoteague Bay, a name instantly suggestive of the oysters native to its waters. At the southern end of Chincoteague is little Wallop house, which looks as if it had come from the saw and hammer of the very first ship's carpenter here; and at its northern end is Welbourne as modern as 1780. Welbourne is a staunch, high, brick structure

given a touch of individuality by an arcade of four arches in-
set in one corner. Elsewhere in the county, of varying ages,
but all old and all quaint in simple ways, are Shepherd's Plain,
Mount Wharton opposite Assateague Island, Melvin house on
Chincoteague Bay, and Callahan house at Locust Mount.
Of all of them Shepherd's Plain appears most fittingly named,
for here, as in so many other places on this unvaryingly flat
tongue of sand, the shallow waters come over the land almost
to the door-step of the house and made the sward lusciously
green for the grazers. In such a land, however, the use of
the term Mount seems a pleasantly ingenuous bit of ostentation.

No one whose interest is limited to history and houses need
go any farther toward the ocean. But any one interested in
nature, life and people may find their interest accelerated by
an inquiring visit to the strange, sometimes weird eastern
half of Eastern Shore which is as much water as land, a land
of islands, and all of it so much a part of the Atlantic which
beats unceasingly against its bulwark of low sandy islands. On
these islands and in the protected inlets and bays behind them,
were the caches and repair bases of the pirates who in the
earlier colonial days preyed on the adjacent plantations as
well as on detached and defenseless ships coasting by.

Of these the ones of interest are Smith Island at the southern extremity, scene of those salt works which were the earliest
English effort at manufacturing in America, and later a part
of the extensive Custis domain; Assateague Island at the
northern extremity, a combination of tidal marsh and coastal
beach yet in its lee protecting smaller and more interesting
Chincoteague Island from the assault of the ocean breakers;
and finally Tangier Island off the northern end of the peninsu-

la's bay shore almost opposite the mouth of the Potomac River.

If one's first reaction to the mention of Chincoteague Island is oysters, one's second is surely wild horses, for this island, and its protecting Assateague Island seaward, both have a kind of celebrity for the little horses which for nearly three hundred years have been allowed to live in an unbridled state of nature in the pine woods and the marshy grazing stretches which yielded them an existence. Water has no terror for them. They are as much at home in it as in the salty marshes where they graze. Often they have been known to plunge into the waters and swim from one island to another.

For generations the great popular social event of Eastern Shore has been the "horse pennings" on these islands. Here long before the great West knew the cowboy and the round-up, these islanders rounded up their wild horses in an annual exhibition which was the occasion for thousands of mainlanders to sail across to join in the wild festivities. There is a pretentious but feeble imitation of this performance even to-day. But the glory of it is gone, even as the glory of the horse everywhere has declined before the advancing motor-cars.

The ponies have been the real lords of these islands. Man, remote and detached from civilizing influences, with little arable land, has made but a poor show of living. It was said, one hundred years ago, that the islanders were able to raise "only about one-third of their bread-corn" and that they took the remainder of their sustenance from the sea and from the wrecks which were cast on their eastern beaches. They were a fearless independent people who avoided contact with their neighbors "on the continent" but paid the price in the primitiveness of the mode of life here, which began to yield only in the early days of this century.

They used to live in rude one-story habitations of pine logs with the chinks plugged with mud. They had no windows. Their dirt floors they covered with washed sand or sometimes with dried sea-grass. Lamps were unknown. In their stead, the more prosperous burned candles made of the myrtle berries which grow wild in the marshes, but the less fortunate used either to forego artificial light or to make their lamp of lard or oil in a clam's shell with a scrap of cloth for a wick. Civilization has, however, crossed the waters of Chincoteague Bay, and the islanders are now in possession of their share of that "culture" which is represented by the radio, the filling station and the can opener.

Tangier Island, in the Chesapeake, and politically attached to Virginia's Eastern Shore, is in an even more detached position than the coastal islands. It is not less than ten miles from the peninsular county of which it is politically a part, yet the waters surrounding it are so shallow that no steamer can approach. The result is that all human contacts are made by small boats. This isolation has produced an individual and quaint population and mode of life.

The island is unique in that it has practically no place in history. Once, in 1814, the British passed this spot on their way to their repulse at Baltimore, but nothing else has happened here of significance to any one but the islanders themselves in the limited orbit of their own lives. No one apparently has ever come out of the island to make a figure on a larger stage. If a people without history are a happy people then are these Tangier Islanders to be envied. And they live as if they thought they were. Alone, aloof and independent, they present a social situation unlike anything about them.

Tangier is but three miles long by two miles wide, and it

is said, on what authority I can not add, that the island was bought of the Indians in 1666 in exchange for two overcoats. A high percentage of its limited area is devoted to marshes. There are no farms, no large houses. Some truck is raised on small patches, but the inhabitants are fisher-folk and they nearly all live in tiny cottages assembled in and about the little village of Tangier, whose population in 1920 was less than one thousand. It has its unique points.

On a spot to which the motor-car has not penetrated, to which even the horse has been a comparative stranger, and where the wheel-barrow and handcart have been the principal wheeled conveyances, it should not be surprising to find the principal street of the town is less than ten feet wide. It is lined on either side by low picket fences, and the little cottages sit back beyond a patch of yard. It is, however, a little surprising to find that these front yards are used by the islanders as their burying-grounds, so that when the families sit out before their doors to take the air and to enjoy the outlook, they observe life, that is the life of their village street, across the tombs of their ancestors.

CHAPTER XI

YORKTOWN AND THE YORK

Where the Revolution Ended—Nelson House—Moore House—Cornwallis
Surrenders to Washington—Rosewell and the Pages—Carter's Creek and the
Burwells—Young Thomas Jefferson's Unrequited Love—Home of Walter
Reed—Werowocomoco, Powhatan's Capital—Pamunkey Indians To-day—
George Washington's Courtship—A Rector's "Ungovern'd Rage"—Patrick
Henry's Haunts—Rib of King James—Along the Mattapony—How
Berkeley Hated—Mobjack Bay—Hesse of the Armisteads.

HE York, for a time at first called the Charles,
is the shortest of the four major rivers in Tidewater Virginia. The distance from its mouth
on the bay northwestward to West Point, where
the Pamunkey and Mattapony Rivers join to form it, is not
more than thirty-five miles. Over this distance its average
width is about two miles. Its depth, however, is such that
ocean-going vessels find secure harbor in its waters almost
anywhere. During the recent World War the United States
Navy had its principal base in the lower York which is capable
of accommodating at one time all the naval ships of any character.

Although the peninsula between the James and the York is
in one place not broader than twelve miles, the first white
settlements were not made here until 1630. It took twenty-
three years after the landing at Jamestown for civilization to
reach twelve miles toward the north. Accomac had already
had a considerable English population, habitations, a manu-
factory and representation in the House of Burgesses. One

of the reasons for Accomac's early settlement was the friendly attitude of the Indians there, and for the York's deferred settlement was the unfriendly attitude of King Powhatan whose capital was on the north bank of this river.

Once civilization reached it the development of plantations and the building of fine houses on its shores was rapid. It became the theater of some of the most picturesque and important events in our early colonial history and of the closing days of the Revolution; and many of its family names have been made nationally famous by the eminence of the bearers of them.

After entering the York the point to focus interest first is Yorktown on its western bank about ten miles from the bay. The great fame of Yorktown is in direct disproportion to its size. It has never been more than a village. A glance at the map shows its reason for being, for here the York is momentarily at its narrowest, not more than three-quarters of a mile, and continually, from the earliest settlement of Tidewater, a ferry here has provided the main means of land travel between the James on one side of it and the Rappahannock and Potomac on the other.

The genesis of Yorktown was similar to that of other Tidewater villages in similar circumstances: a plantation, a landing, a ferry, an ordinary, a church, a few stores and the necessary dwelling houses. Few like villages advanced beyond such modest expansions, for the heart of the Tidewater country is devoted to plantation life. And Yorktown is found where Tidewater is most unaffectedly its simple self. But before the Revolution Yorktown had a considerable shipping business and several inns, and a few of her residences were excellent specimens of the best building of their period.

Its great claim to fame came to it one mid-October day in 1781, when it was the scene of the closing act of the Revolutionary War. Lord Cornwallis, commanding the British Army, was in possession of the town which was besieged by the American forces under Generals Washington, Lincoln, Knox, the Marquis de Lafayette, Count Rochambeau and Baron Steuben. At the mouth of the river stood the recently arrived French fleet under De Grasse, ready to cut off the possibility of the flight of the British by water. Cornwallis, thus checkmated, surrendered to Washington on October nineteenth, and so, here at Yorktown, the Revolution was finally crowned with success and the colonies were made finally free to enter upon their independent national life. So, too, on the shores of this narrow peninsula between the James and the York began and ended British dominion within the area of the present United States, the scenes of the first act and the last act within twelve miles of each other.

Yorktown bought its immortality at a price that left it damaged and decadent beyond revival. It was all but destroyed by the gun-fire during the siege. The Abbé Robin, one of the chaplains with the French troops, a few days after the surrender wrote:

"I have been through the unfortunate little town of York since the siege, and saw many elegant houses shot through and through in a thousand places, and ready to crumble to pieces; rich household furniture crushed under their ruins, or broken by the brutal English soldier; carcases of men and horses half covered with dirt: books piled in heaps, and scattered among the ruins of the buildings, served to give me an idea of the tastes and morals of the inhabitants; these were either treatises of religion or controversial divinity; the *history* of the English nation, and their foreign settlements; collections of charters and acts of parliament; the works of the celebrated *Alexander Pope;* a translation of *Montaigne's Essays; Gil Blas de Santillane,* and the excellent *Essay Upon Women,* by *Mr. Thomas."*

The interesting survivals in and near Yorktown are the Nelson house and the old Custom-House in the village, and the Moore house on the Temple Farm about three-quarters of a mile eastward on the river bank.

Nelson house takes its name from the builder, William Nelson. But it takes its fame from the later greatness of his son who, as a baby, in 1740, was brought to the beginning of the house when he was only one year old and was assisted in laying a brick in the foundations of his future home. This child was Thomas Nelson, "Scotch Tom," as he came to be affectionately referred to by his contemporaries.

As a youth he was sent to England and was educated at Cambridge. When he returned he married Lucy Grymes, of Brandon, and at Nelson house they became leaders in the civil and social life of Tidewater. The spacious rooms of this massive mansion, with their deep window-seats and handsome wainscoting, provided the setting for splendid entertainments. The Nelson horses and the Nelson hounds were famous, and fox-hunts often started from Nelson house across the lowlands.

He was a leader, too, in all that led to the Revolution and its consummation. He was a member of the Continental Congresses of 1775, 1776 and 1777; a signer of the Declaration of Independence, a general in the Revolutionary Army and a governor of Virginia. Among the stories told by his biographers of his ardent and practical patriotism is one of the siege of Yorktown.

Observing that Nelson house, one of the most conspicuous

targets in the little town, was untouched by American fire he inquired for an explanation and was told that it was spared out of respect for him. Whereupon he called attention to the fact that Lord Cornwallis and the British staff were using it as headquarters and requested that it be not spared. Two cannon were accordingly pointed against it and the balls began tearing through it. The British officers were at the moment at table and two of them were killed by the first shot. The subsequent shots caused the staff to abandon the house.

This Nelson was a rich man at the beginning of the Revolution, but he spent his fortune freely in his country's service. Yet such was his integrity that when, as governor, he tried to raise money for the soldiery he was told: "We will not lend the governor a shilling, but we will lend you, Thomas Nelson, all we can possibly raise." Against these loans for Virginia's contribution to the continental cause he pledged his entire private fortune over his own signature, and in the end he was left to pay, and Lucy Grymes, of Brandon, died beyond her eightieth year, blind, infirm, poor and possibly disillusioned. On his tomb in the yard of the old Yorktown church, his story is told in five words: "Thomas Nelson, Governor of Virginia. He Gave All for Liberty."

The old Custom-House has been standing since 1715 and is accounted "the first Custom-House in the United States." The present church replaces the one which was built in 1697 and was burned in 1814. But in it is the old bell, the same one that rang for "Scotch Tom" Nelson and Lucy Grymes. It is inscribed: "County of York, Virginia, 1725." The final survival of interest here is the Moore house on Temple Farm on the river bluff less than a mile east of town. Though built of wood it is older than Nelson house, for one is told that it was erected in 1713. Sir Alexander Spotswood, Governor of Virginia and aide-de-camp to the Duke of Marlborough at the Battle of Blenheim, is cited as the builder. In it were drawn up the terms of Cornwallis' surrender to Washington. Hereabout a century earlier, stood the home of Captain Martieu, an ancestor of General Washington and Governor Nelson. This ancient was no less liberty-loving than his celebrated descendant, for when, in April, 1635, the Tidewater colonists thrust the unpopular Royal Governor, Sir John Harvey, out of office and sent him back to England, Nicholas Martieu joined in this first American rebellion against the British colonial methods.

Beyond Yorktown, to the northwest, are two houses which are often pointed out. The first is Ringfield on the peninsula where Felgate's Creek and King's Creek join the York. It is a large, solid, seventeenth-century, brick house of two and a half stories with a roomy wing of one story and a half. Beyond the adjacent Queen's Creek is Porto Bello. This is a smaller and less pretentious house than Ringfield, but it possesses a rather more distinctive interest for it was built by Lord Dunmore in 1773 as a retreat on the water to which he might escape from Williamsburg, only five miles away, during the summer heat. But this last British Governor in Virginia finally "escaped" two years later, in another direction, down the James, driven back to England by the rising tide of American freedom.

Above Yorktown the east bank of the York is decidedly the more interesting. Here, just opposite Ringfield, is an estate called Timberneck. Though the present, spacious, rambling white house was built after the Revolution, it stands on the site of another house put here and lived in here by the Mann

family in the middle of the seventeenth century. Here Mary
Mann was born and here she married Mathew Page, and they
named their son Mann Page. Though the surname Mann has
died out in this family, there has been a Mann Page in every
generation.

The Pages also owned an estate called Rosewell just across
Carter's Creek some two miles farther up this side of the
York. On it they lived in a simple wooden dwelling. But

Rosewell

the Page fortune increased until it became one of the greatest
in Tidewater, and the first Mann Page erected on Rosewell,
and gave that name to the house, one of the most splendid
mansions of colonial Virginia.

"It was constructed in the most massive style," said Lancaster in his description of it, "of brick and white marble
casements. There was a great square, thick-walled, high-chim-
neyed, central building, flanked by wings—since torn down—
which formed a court and which gave the house a frontage
of two hundred and thirty-two feet. The central building
stands three stories above a high basement and is capped by

a cupola. It contains three wide halls, nine passages, and twenty-three rooms and the wings had six rooms each. Externally Rosewell House is severely plain, but with its ample proportions and its splendid brickwork, the absence of ornament makes it the more impressive.

"In striking contrast to this outside simplicity, was the interior, where, upon crossing the threshold of the main entrance, the visitor found himself at once in a great hall paneled with polished mahogany into which swept down, with generous and graceful curve, the grand stairway which eight persons could comfortably ascend abreast, and whose mahogany balustrade was carved by hand to represent baskets of fruits and flowers."

In this house, and to the Page family, generation after generation, were united the most distinguished names in Tidewater. Mann Page I married two Judiths. The first was Judith, daughter of Ralph Wormeley, of Rosegill on the Rappahannock, and the second was Judith, daughter of Robert ("King") Carter, of Corotoman, also on the Rappahannock. The latter Judith was the mother of Mann Page II who also had two wives: the first was Alice Grymes, of Brandon, and the second was Anne Corbin Tayloe, of Mount Airy on the Rappahannock. Alice was the mother of John Page, the next heir to Rosewell, who became one of the most distinguished men in the state, but was the last of the Pages to make the seat on the York his principal residence.

He attained additional, posthumous celebrity as the John Page to whom Thomas Jefferson addressed nearly all the surviving letters of his youthful days, so full of girls and gossip. They met as students at William and Mary College and became devoted friends, and young Jefferson was a frequent guest at Rosewell. Some of these letters were written from Williamsburg, but Jefferson playfully dated them from

MOUNT AIRY ON THE RAPPAHANNOCK
The central building with only a suggestion of one of the walls connecting
the wings

MARY WASHINGTON'S HOUSE, FREDERICKSBURG

KENMORE, FREDERICKSBURG
Home of Betty Washington Lewis, sister of George Washington

"Devilsburg." Among John Page's distinguished descendants are his grandson, Thomas Nelson Page, writer and ambassador, and his great granddaughter, Amélie Rives, Princess Troubetzkoy, also an author of distinction.

The decline of Rosewell is one of the saddest stories of any great Tidewater house. Neither time, nor the elements, nor unforeseen accident was the cause of the departure of its glory. About one hundred years ago it came into the possession of a man named Booth whose sole idea was to profit by wrecking it. The avenue of cedars which made such a splendid approach from the river landing to the front door he sold off to be made into tubs. The mahogany paneling throughout the house, the lead in the roof that covered it, and the very bricks from the graveyard wall and tombs were torn away and converted into cash. Even dismantled of its splendid adornments, it remained a great house. To-day, however, it is a ruin, fire having wrecked it in 1916. In that fire, according to Stanard, there perished also, though no explanation is given of how such a treasure was overlooked by the departed Pages or the devastating Booth, the portrait of Warner Lewis, of Warner Hall, painted by Sir Joshua Reynolds.

About two miles above the ruins of Rosewell there are on Carter's Creek the mutilated remains of another of Tidewater's oldest and most famous houses. It was known first as Fairfield, but later was called Carter's Creek and as such it is generally remembered. The date of its erection and the key to its builders were given in the figures "1692" and the initials "L. A. B." which were upon one of its gables. The initials stood for Lewis and Abigail Burwell, and he was the first of this prominent Virginia family to come out of England.

The house itself was different from any other in Tidewater

in that it represented a type of sixteenth-century, English manor house. It was built in the form of a rectangle, open on one side, the main building having two wings attached but extending at right angles to it.

Nathaniel Burwell, the builder's son, married Elisabeth, daughter of "King" Carter, of Corotoman, and their son, Lewis Burwell, was president of the Council and acting-governor of the colony. His son, Lewis, next master of Carter's Creek, educated at Eton, though his father had gone to Cambridge, was the last of the Burwells to retain the estate.

His sister, Rebecca, was one of the belles of Tidewater, and Thomas Jefferson unconsciously gave her an enduring fame. While he and Jacqueline Ambler were fellow students at William and Mary College, they were both in love with the beautiful Rebecca. Jefferson's letters to John Page, of Rosewell, and to another friend, Will Fleming, give the key to his infatuation.

In the course of a long and amusing letter to young Page, Jefferson, then in his nineteenth year, in writing of having slept in a room under a leaky roof with disastrous results, the principal one of which was the damage done to his watch and its precious contents, said:

"Well, as I was saying my poor watch has lost her speech. I should not have cared much for this, but something worse attended it; the subtle particles of the water with which the case was filled, had, by their penetration, so overcome the cohesion of the particles of the paper, of which my dear picture and watch paper were composed, that, in attempting to take them out to dry them, Good God! . . . My cursed fingers gave them such a rent, as I fear I never shall get over."

This evidently was a silhouette of his adored Rebecca for, further on in the same letter to her neighbor, he wrote:

"I fain would ask the favour of Miss Rebecca Burwell to give me another watch-paper of her own cutting, which I should esteem much more, though it were a plain round one, than the nicest in the world cut by other hands—however, I am afraid she would think this presumption, after my suffering the other to get spoiled."

When Page wrote him of young Ambler's attentions to Miss Rebecca, or to Belinda as Jefferson referred to her after the eighteenth-century fashion of bestowing a fanciful name on an inamorata, he again exposed his soul to his friend, in the course of which he said:

"Since you have undertaken to act as my attorney, you advise me to go immediately and lay siege *in form* . . . If I am to succeed, the sooner I know it, the less uneasiness I shall have to go through. If I am to meet with disappointment, the sooner I know it, the more of life I shall have to wear it off: and if I do meet with one, I hope in God, and verily believe; it will be the last. . . . If Belinda will not accept of my service, it shall never be offered to another."

To Fleming he proposed:

"You marry S——y P——r, I marry R——a B——l join and get a pole chair and a pair of keen horses, practice the law in the same courts, and drive about to all the dances in the country together."

But the future author of the Declaration did not marry Rebecca, nor did he keep his threat never to offer himself to another woman. She married Jacqueline Ambler and became the mother of a group of daughters who were just such belles as their mother had been, and one of them became the wife of a young attorney who later became celebrated as Chief Justice John Marshall.

The Burwells were for generations buried at Carter's Creek. But when the place fell on evil days their remains and their monuments were removed a few miles east to the yard at Abington Church where these impressive tombs and monuments may now be seen in their restored state.

About four miles from the ruins of splendid Rosewell, opposite the crossroads post-office which is called Belroi, stands a modest white frame house where was born one who, estimated by that true measure of greatness, service to one's fellow man, was one of the great men of all America. His name was Walter Reed. It was his destiny to be acclaimed as the discoverer of the source of some of the greatest physical curses which have afflicted mankind and to make it possible to eradicate them.

Here, within twenty miles of his own neighborhood, the first English permanent settlement was almost frustrated by the "sicknesse" which they did not know how to name, much less how to combat. Three months after the first landing in 1607 it made its appearance.

"There were never Englishmen left in a forreign country in such miserie as wee were in this new discouvered Virginia," wrote George Percy. "If there were any conscience in men, it would make their harts to bleed to heare the pitifull murmurings and outcries of our sick men without reliefe, every night and day for the space of sixe weekes; in the morning their bodies being trailed out of their cabines like Dogges, to be buried." The malady was so destructive that when Captain Newport returned the next year he found but thirty-eight of the colonists alive. Decimation in this same tragic proportion went on for several years until the surviving colonists became in a measure "seasoned."

Not only had the tragically helpless colonists no idea of the origin of their affliction; no more had any one else up to that time, nor during the succeeding three hundred years, until Walter Reed proclaimed the epoch-making discovery that the fly and the mosquito were the bearers and distributors of the germs which produced malaria, typhoid fever and yellow fever. This brilliant scientific achievement has made it possible to eradicate scourges of yellow fever and to minimize almost to the vanishing-point the spread of malaria and typhoid; it has opened the tropics and the semi-tropics to colonization by immigrants from the temperate zones; and it has already saved thousands of lives, and it will save innumerable lives in the future.

This modest little house in which Dr. Walter Reed was born has been taken by the medical profession of America and has been restored as a public shrine in perpetual remembrance of their mission and of the attainment of one of them.

On this northeastern shore of the York above Yorktown the first English in Tidewater found Werowocomoco, the capital of Powhatan, ruler of all the Indians along the rivers on the western side of the Chesapeake. Its actual site has ever since, until quite recently, been assigned to various localities.

There is a heap of brick on the east side of Timberneck Creek where it angles on the York. Until a few years ago they stood up, one upon another, in the form of a stout old chimney. It was called Powhatan's Chimney, and loose tradition said that it stood on the site of Werowocomoco. Facing the ruins of Rosewell across the mouth of Carter's Creek is a house on land which belongs to the Page family and was once a part of Rosewell estate. It is called Shelly, a name which derives from extensive beds of oyster shells found there. From these same deposits of shells derives not only the plausible tradition that on this site stood an old Indian settlement but also the untenable tradition that it was Werowocomoco. There have been many careless statements even that Rosewell house was built on the site of great Powhatan's capital.

Scientific documentation has recently put an end to guess-work and tenably located the site of the historic spot a few miles farther up the York, on the same side, on the bay from time to time variously called Purton, Purtan, Portan and Poetan. These names all derive from the most ancient of them, Poetan. And Poetan derives from Powhatan.

Here on Purtan Bay lived the terror of the first English to settle on this continent, a great monarch who, surrounded by an imperial savage splendor, ruled over a wide realm. It was here that John Smith was brought after his capture on the Chickahominy, and it was here he was condemned to die and his life was saved by the Emperor's daughter, Pocahontas. All superficial traces of Werowocomoco, in common with those of all other Indian towns, have disappeared. Deposits of oyster shells, and a few imperishable stone implements occasionally indicate the site of the Indians' vanished settlements. But they built their shelter of perishable wood and skins which, even had man and accident spared them, the forces of Nature would long since have reduced to their elements.

Advancing up the York its termination is found to be marked by two water openings and a point of land between. The opening on the west is the mouth of the Pamunkey River, and that on the east is the mouth of the Mattapony River. On the point between the two stands the only considerable town on either of the three rivers. It is West Point. A rail-road from Richmond, twenty-one miles west, terminates here and the life of the little town is based on the fishing industry and on its value to Richmond as a secondary seaport. Its population, according to the last census, numbered 1635.

West Point was the seat of that other great Indian, Opechancanough, Chief of the Pamunkey tribe, brother of Powhatan, and the leader of the massacre of 1622, in what Howe called "the Sicilian Vespers of the colony," and which came so near to exterminating every Englishman in Tidewater Virginia. He was a dauntless warrior and fought to the end of a long life, until he was nearly blind and quite infirm, when he caused himself to be borne into battle on a litter in order that his presence at least might inspire his braves.

The army of Powhatan's confederacy, which the handful of English in the first years in Virginia had to face, consisted of twenty-four hundred warriors. The largest of the tribes making up the confederacy was the Pamunkey and their numbers were estimated as being one-eighth of those following Powhatan. Nearly all traces of this great Tidewater King's tribes have disappeared, save less than twoscore of the Mattapony living in a small reservation on the south bank of the Mattapony River, and about one hundred of the Pamunkey living on a reservation on the north bank of the Pamunkey River twelve miles, in an air line, above the head of the York.

The Pamunkey Indian Reservation is situated in the arms of two bends of the river that secure the inhabitants a peninsula which is very nearly an island. No member of this tribe is now of pure Indian blood. Copper-colored skin and long, straight, black hair show decidedly in some individuals, but there are others whose Indian origin would not be detected by any other than an expert. The race pride is strong and, though they would acknowledge the white man as their equal, they regard the negro as far beneath their social level. They are not particularly robust physically, and their longevity is below that of their neighbors, which may be attributed to their effort to keep their Indian blood free of further foreign admixture and the consequent frequent marriages between near relatives. Politically they retain their tribal formation and acknowledge the authority of a chief. This office is elective for a term of four years. The tribe's council of four men names two candidates to be voted for. Those favoring the election of candidate number one deposit a grain of corn in the ballot box and those favoring number two deposit therein a bean. The election of either candidate is determined by counting the corn and the beans.

This little remnant of the tribe of Pamunkey Indians each year makes a visible sign of their allegiance to the state. The Chief and eight other Indians, clad in their native hunting garb, carry a young deer, killed in Tidewater, to the Governor at Richmond. The custom dates from the seventeenth century, but owing to the disappearance of wild game it becomes increasingly difficult to carry out this manner of fulfillment.

Three miles farther up the Pamunkey is Piping Tree Ferry whose proper name, Pipe-in-tree, is thus explained by a tradition of the surviving Indians:

"On one occasion the Pamunkey braves met a committee of white settlers at this place and negotiated a treaty. When all the terms had been agreed to, the consummation of the treaty was solemnized in usual Indian fashion by handing around the same pipe to the representatives of both nations, each taking a puff as indicative of friendship and good faith. The pipe was then deposited in a hollow tree near by, and ever afterward, when the colonists disregarded their agreement, the Indians would remind them of pipe-in-tree."

Just across the Pamunkey, on its south bank, is a neighborhood whose story is always diverting to any one interested in the private life of George Washington. It lay in the path of the main route over which Washington customarily rode or drove between Mount Vernon and Williamsburg. The young Colonel had on one occasion left troops on the western frontier and was on his way to the colonial capital to seek aid for his regiment from the Governor and Council. He was traveling on horseback accompanied only by Bishop, a military servant. In crossing the Pamunkey in this neighborhood he fell in with a Mr. Chamberlayne who lived near by and who persuaded him, in spite of his hurry to reach the capital, to stop at his house for midday dinner.

Among the guests there was Martha Dandridge Custis, the rich and attractive young widow of Daniel Parke Custis, son of that last John Custis, of Arlington on Eastern Shore, who had "lived" only during the seven years of his freedom after the death of his wife. Washington had refused to stable his horses, urging his need of reaching Williamsburg before night, and Bishop awaited him before Mr. Chamberlayne's door while the Colonel dined. The orderly's vigil was unexpectedly protracted. When night came on the travelers were not even on their way. The first word Bishop had of his master was an order to take the horses to the stable as he was not going to move before morning.

Actually, it was on this occasion that Washington, hitherto so often and so vainly in love, met his fate. He did go forword on his errand next morning, but only to complete it with all possible expedition and then canter back again to see the Widow Custis at her own house, called White House, which stood on the south bank of the Pamunkey just opposite the Indian Reservation. When actually he left for the north it was after he and the lady had become engaged.

Where they were married has always remained a matter of

conjecture; whether at White House or at near-by St. Peter's Church. The old house did not survive the War between the States. The crumbling foundation bricks are all of it that remains. St. Peter's, however, survives. It is of brick and was built in 1703. Centering on its front door is a huge square tower over an arched open porch, similar to the first two brick churches which rose in Virginia, St. Luke's at Smithfield and the church at Jamestown.

Washington and his bride were married by the Reverend David Mossom who was rector of St. Peter's for forty years. During that time he survived four wives, but his more enduring fame is based on his temper, and on an amusing quarrel with his clerk which it provoked.

On one occasion the rector assailed the clerk from the pulpit. The latter received the attack in silence, but when he rose, and gave out the psalm, he chose the one in which were these lines:

> "With restless and ungovern'd rage
>   Why do the heathen storm?
> Why in such rash attempts engage
>   As they can ne'er perform?"

In the same county of New Kent are three other conspicuous Tidewater houses, off the river however. One of them, Providence Forge, is a good specimen of a conventional colonial house of moderate size. The second is Cedar Grove, rather irregular architecturally, but oldest of the three and the home of the Christian family, one of whom, Letitia Christian, became the wife of John Tyler, afterward president of the United States. The third is Hampstead, built in 1820 and a pretentious brick mansion with terraced gardens and superb view over the valley of the Pamunkey.

There is, however, one other ruin here recalling the impressive homes of the colonial planters. This was Eltham, a splendid central house of three stories and two-storied wings at each end connected by curtains with the central structure. It was the home of the Bassetts and was destroyed by fire in 1876. A descendant of this family built Clover Lea in adjacent Hanover County, a house spoken of as one of the handsomest old houses of Hanover, a county which boasts Hickory Hill, Oakland, Scotchtown, the girlhood home of Dolly Payne who later became Dolly Madison, New Market and Edgewood among the more prominent of its older architectural citizens.

But among Hanover's most interesting buildings are the quaint, little, brick court-house with its porch of many arches, the tavern near it, and the old Fork Church between the two streams which form the head of the Pamunkey River. Patrick Henry made his first great speech, in the "Parson's Cause," in this court-house; his father-in-law was the proprietor of the tavern, but in his absence young Henry often acted as host there; and in his youth he worshiped at the old Fork Church as also did Dolly Madison.

In the court-house is recorded the will of Robert Bruce Honeyman, proved in 1823, in which this clause occurs: "I give and bequeath to my son my Thermometer, my diploma of Doctor of Physic, also a human Rib, which will be found in a small trunk in my chest, with my earnest request that he will carefully Keep the said Rib, which is of James the Fifth King of Scotland and carefully transmit to his descendants." The subsequent history of King James' rib has yet to be disclosed.

All the country lying between the Pamunkey and the Mattapony Rivers is King William County. Its name dates its rise under King William and Queen Mary, as do Williamsburg, William and Mary College, and King and Queen County on the north side of the Mattapony. In King William the better-known of the old places are Chelsea and Elsing Green, though Horn Quarter is one of the handsomest.

Chelsea was built by the Moore family claiming descent from Sir Thomas Moore, for whose seat in England the Tide-water descendants named their first American home. Bernard Moore, of Chelsea, became a prominent figure in the colony and married Anne Katherine, daughter of the Royal Governor, Alexander Spotswood. "Though her husband was loyal to Virginia during the evolution," Lancaster reported, "it is said that this fair and spirited daughter of a royal governor disobeyed the official prohibition of tea-drinking and defiantly sipped the tabooed beverage. She was prudent enough, how-ever, to shut herself up in her room for the indulgence."

Elsing Green is a sturdy old brick survival of many fires since first it was built in the middle of the eighteenth century. Its wings survive and, though now detached from the big house, they may earlier have been connected by curtains or passages. It was the home of the Dandridges, and it is believed that William Dandridge, of Elsing Green, was the uncle of Martha Dandridge Custis Washington. Her father, John Dandridge, and William Dandridge made their earliest appear-ance in Virginia together at about the same time and both finally seated themselves on opposite sides of the Pamunkey. Moreover these two Dandridges used the same coat of arms. Otherwise the records are vague about the ancestry of either of them. Elsing Green, after one of its fires, passed about 1758 to Carter Braxton, signer of the Declaration of Inde-pendence for Virginia, who rebuilt it and lived there. The house has, during its several lives, contained many artistic treasures, among them Gobelin tapestries presented by William of Orange to the grandfather of one of its chatelaines. The fire backs in the great fireplaces were unique in that each represented an historic episode. All are gone except one which shows the death of General Wolfe.

The north shore of the Mattapony is dotted with the homes of Robinsons, Corbins, Braxtons and other old Tidewater families. At Pleasant Hill lived the Henry Robinson who was for so many years speaker of the House of Burgesses and who, when on one occasion young Colonel George Washington modestly and hesitatingly gave the House a required account of his military operations, relieved him with the celebrated remark: "Sit down, Colonel Washington; your modesty equals your courage, and that surpasses the power of any language I possess."

Laneville stood just below and was the home of a branch of the Corbin family who remained loyal to the crown. It is said that at the outbreak of the Revolution, Governor Dunmore sent many of the valuable chattels of the colony over to Laneville where they were buried in one of the cellars. One of these Corbins at least is remembered as an eccentric. Tradition has it that he occupied rooms in the wing at one extreme of his great house, and his wife lived in rooms at the other extreme, and that when he paid her a visit he ordered his coach and four and drove in state the length of the house to his wife's apartment.

Brave Bacon made his last stand a little farther south at the house of a Mr. Pate in Gloucester, and soon after "surrendered up that fort he was no longer able to keep, into the hands of that grim and all-conquering Captain, Death." Tradition tells that, to save the body from the vindictiveness of Berkeley, Bacon's friends weighted his coffin with stone and lowered it into an unknown grave in the waters of the York.

How venomously Governor Berkeley hated the rebel is shown in an old letter of February 2, 1676-7, written by him "From on board Sir John Berry's ship":

"Bacon entered the Town, burned five houses of mine and twenty of other gentleman's, and a very Commodous Church. They say he set too with his owne sacraligious hands. But within three weeks after, the justice and judgement of God overtooke him. His usual oath was here sworn (at least 1000 times a day was God damme my blood) and Gode soe infested his blood, that it bred lice in incredible numbers, so that for twenty days he never washt his shirts, but burned them. To this God added the bloody flux, and an honest minister wrote this epitaph upon him:

Bacon's dead. I am sorry at my heart
That lice and flux should act the hangman's part."

Adjacent to the York on the north is a region of Tidewater which has a separate entity. It is Mobjack Bay, and its rivers and branches and inlets eat so into the flat lands that scarcely a point on any of the extensive terrain here is more than a mile from salt water. Hence, here land travel to many neighboring points is so abnormally far that except by boat the house just across the water can be reached only by long circuitous roads around the heads of many inlets. Nearly the entire east shore of the York bounds Gloucester County which, with Mathews County, once a part of it, and now between it and the bay, make up the land into which the watery tentacles of Mobjack reach like the many arms of an octopus. Between the York and the bay the principal so-called rivers are the Severn, the Ware, the North and the East.

On the Severn one finds Warner Hall, a long well-balanced series of united buildings erected on the site of the original brick mansion here, unique among other things for its roof of tile, which was destroyed by fire nearly a century ago. This plantation was the home of the Warner, Lewis and Clark families. The land was patented early in the seventeenth century by Augustine Warner in whom united those two genealogical lines which led to George Washington and Robert E. Lee and by whom these two men were remotely kin. His son, and the second of his name, was like him a member of the Council, and was the speaker of the reforming Assembly during Bacon's Rebellion. When Bacon, after the burning of Jamestown, went into Gloucester he made Warner Hall his headquarters. This second Augustine Warner's daughter, Mildred, married Lawrence Washington of the Potomac, grandfather of George Washington, and it was from him and his daughter that the Washington family derived the names Augustine and Mildred which thereafter appeared in nearly every generation.

Other conspicuous houses in this neck between the Severn and the Ware, are Sherwood, home of the Seldens, Dimmocks and Williams; Lansdowne, Severnby, Eagle Point and White Mast. Eagle Point was built by John Randolph Bryan, brought up by John Randolph, of Roanoke, whose niece he married. The Eagle Point burying-ground is unique in all Tidewater for it occupies a pine-shaded islet in the river near the house. White Marsh early became famous for its terraced gardens on which grew rose-covered arbor trees trained to grow in the shape of summer-houses. Sherwood is on the Ware, and along the shores of this same river are these colonial survivals: Level Green, The Shelter, Airville, Lowland Cottage, Hockley,

White Hall, Glenroy and Goshen. Under the gambril roof and tall chimneys of The Shelter was born Molly Elliott Seawell, the writer, and here she passed her girlhood. Lowland Cottage and Hockley were homes of the extensive Taliaferro family. White Hall was the home of the Willis family before the Revolution, but for some generations it has been the home of descendants of the Byrds, of Westover, among whom are conspicuous in the present generation Governor Harry Byrd and Commander Richard Byrd, pioneer aviator and antarctic explorer.

On North River's Gloucester side near its mouth is old

Toddsbury

Midlothian; and next above it are Waverly, Newstead, Exchange, Elmington and Toddsbury, homes of the numerous Tabb and Todd families, their family burying-ground on Toddsbury containing more tombstones than any other private cemetery in Virginia. Philip Tabb, of Toddsbury, was a typical sporting colonial planter. He gambled, hunted and drank. The neighborhood cherishes a tradition of his wife who joined the Methodists and, as the story goes, "after providing a bountiful supper for her husband and his guests, she

JAMES MONROE'S LAW OFFICE, FREDERICKSBURG

BROMPTON, FREDERICKSBURG
Much of the bloodiest fighting of the Battle of Fredericksburg took place
before and about this house

JAMES MONROE
From the portrait by Alonzo
Chappel

JAMES MADISON

JOHN TYLER
From the portrait by Alonzo
Chappel

WILLIAM HENRY HARRISON
From the portrait by Alonzo
Chappel

would retire to her chamber and pray for their souls, while they cast the dice, swore brave oaths and drank merrily till late into the night."

Elmington, one of the finest seats on this river, was made the scene of *Don Miff* by Virginius Dabney; it at one time belonged to George Wythe Munford, author of *The Two Parsons,* and later it was for a short time the home of another writer, Thomas Dixon. Near by are Belleville and Dunham Massie, quaint little homes of Booths and Taliaferros.

On the opposite shore of North River are Auburn, Ditchley, Poplar Grove, Green Plains and Isleham. Auburn and Ditchley were built by members of the Tabb family so numerous on this river. Poplar Grove is a long and spacious white frame house sitting almost at the water level among the trees which give it its name. Part of the house dates to Revolutionary days. It was enlarged by Thomas Patterson in the last years of the eighteenth century when feeling between Whig and Tory ran high. He was an ardent Whig and as an act of political faith, and perhaps as a challenge to some Tory neighbor, he surrounded his house with poplars, which tree was the Whig symbol. There is at Poplar Grove a picturesque old specimen of a grist mill whose big wheel is turned by the tide, and also an example of the serpentine wall of single brick thickness such as Thomas Jefferson introduced at the University of Virginia and Barboursville, and which also adorns the gardens at Folly farther on in the Valley. One of John Patterson's daughters married Christopher Tompkins and their daughter, Sally, born here at Poplar Grove, was Captain Sally Tompkins, the celebrated nurse of the Confederate soldiers.

Another daughter of this house went to live at Isleham near by. In the middle of the eighteenth century it was the home of Sir John Peyton, who came from Essex in England and was one of the few baronets to settle in Virginia. He actively espoused the cause of American independence and became a captain in the Gloucester militia.

Green Plains and Isleham cast their reflections in the waters near the mouth of North River. The former house was built about one hundred twenty-five years ago by James H. Roy whose descendants have lived there ever since.

Ware Church, in Gloucester County, is one of the old churches of all Tidewater. The date of its erection is attributed to 1693. Abington Church, in the same county but nearer the York, has in the older part of its walls a brick dated 1660 but the arch of the door carries the figures 1765. The vestry book of Ware records that in 1684, "His Excellency the Governor having given to the church one large Bible, one book of Common Prayer, one book of Homilies, the Thirty Nine Articles, and books of Canons of the Church of England, it is ordered that the Clerk of the vestry enter the same in the register, to the end His Lordship's so pious a gift may be gratefully remembered." Long before that year Augustine Warner II, of Warner Hall, had made the church a gift of "one silver flagon." Both these churches have been well restored as indeed have been most of the colonial churches of Tidewater.

In a remote part of original Gloucester where that county was once bounded by one of the smaller tidal rivers, the Pianketank, there stands on its south shore and very near its union with the bay, a house called Hesse. It was built at the beginning of the eighteenth century, and though it has fallen upon shabby days it was once one of the great social centers of Tidewater. Hesse was the home of the Armisteads who intermarried with the Burwells, of Carter's Creek, and the Nelsons, of Yorktown on the York, the Carters, of Cleve on the Rappahannock, and with other great families of the colonial period. Only the high central portion of the once pretentious mansion now stands, but even in its decayed state and remote situation it is still suggestive of the distinctions and gaieties which once attached to it.

The very early maps of Tidewater show twelve plantations on the Pianketank. On the same side of the river as the Armistead estate and very near it, there appears on these early maps the name of a Washington.

CHAPTER XII

THE RAPPAHANNOCK RIVER

First Visits of the English—"King" Carter, of Corotoman—Splendor of His Progress—Five Ralph Wormeleys and Rosegill—Mother of Washington and Her Neighborhood—Sabine Hall—A Colonial Pharmacopœia—Mount Airy and the Tayloes—Echoes of Ancient Leedstown—Uncle Jimmie Micou and His Scheming Clerk—Sir Thomas Lunsford, "Child-Eater"—Where James Madison Was Born—Cleve of the Carters, and Other Historic Homes.

HE Rappahannock River has several characteristics in common with the James. They are of about the same length. Each is broad and deep at its mouth but soon loses these features and creeps within its low banks over a narrow winding way to the falls which check its tides. The Rappahannock, however, has never changed its Indian name which means the "alternating stream," the "ebb and flow stream," or, in colloquial English, a tidal river.

Captain John Smith visited the river three times. His first visit was involuntary, just after his capture by the Indians on the Chickahominy, when he was paraded all over Powhatan's realm as a prisoner of war. His second and third visits were made the next year, 1608, in the course of his "discovery" of the Chesapeake, on which occasions his party ascended the Rappahannock as far as "a little bay" which they named Featherstone after one of their party who died there.

Indeed, even to-day, in approaching the Rappahannock out

of the bay, one is reminded immediately of the doughty John Smith's adventures here and of how near it came to being his grave. A lighthouse off the south lip of the mouth takes its name from low Stingray Point behind it. Had there been a light in Smith's day the point might never have had its present name. Unwarned of the shoals off this point Smith's boat grounded here, by reason of the ebb-tide, and he spent the time spearing with his sword the fish so plentifully in sight in the shallow water. One fish so taken gave him trouble. He did not know its character but likened it to a thornback, though it had a long tail, "bearded like a saw on each side, whereon the middest is a most poysoned sting, of two or three inches long," which she struck into his wrist "nearly an inch and a half." The chronicler of the party, continuing, said: "No blood nor wound was seen, but a little blew spot, but the torment was instantly so extreame, that in foure houres had so swollen his hand, arme and shoulder, we all with much sorrow concluded his funerall, and prepared his graue in an Island by, as himselfe directed: yet it pleased God by a precious oyle Doctor Russell at the first plyed to it when he sounded it with a probe (ere night) his tormenting paine was so well asswaged that he eate of the fish for his supper, which gaue no less joy and content to us then ease to himselfe, for which he called the Island Stingray Isle after the name of the fish." He did not yet know that the "island" was really a part of the mainland.

The first reaches of the Rappahannock on its northern shore, as far as Corotoman River, was the ancestral land of the Carters, one of the most important families in colonial America. The estate was called Corotoman. Earlier than the coming of John Carter to his grant here, the progress of English settlement on this river is none too clear. Lancaster County was so officially recognized in 1652, but already the first clearings and primitive houses must have been numerous. This Carter was a leader in his community and first appeared in the records as a major when he held the office of justice of the peace. Soon he was elected a burgess, then a vestryman, commanded the troops attacking the Indians, was promoted to colonel-commandant and eventually, in 1657, he appeared in the Crown Council. It is believed that he was one of the numerous "distressed cavaliers" who came over about 1649. In addition to accumulating a large estate and attending to all his official functions, he found time to marry five wives.

It was in the next generation that the Corotoman family blossomed into its greater distinction, and this focused principally in the emigrant's son, Robert Carter, who was a man of such character and consequence that his contemporaries called him "King" Carter, and as such he has been known ever since. He filled all the important posts in the colony up to and including president of the Council. He was enormously rich in land and slaves, and lived in a kind of patriarchal splendor. He built a church out of his private means. He allied himself by his first marrriage with the Armisteads, of Hesse, and by his second with the Landons, of Hereford, England. At his death he left an estate of "300,000 Acres of Land, about 1,000 Negroes and 10000 *l.*" His tomb in Christ Church, which he built, bears a lengthy biographical eulogy borne out by history. Naturally so powerful a man had his enemies, and tradition preserves this gibe chalked on his tomb:

"Here lies Robin, but not Robin Hood,
Here lies Robin that never was good,
Here lies Robin that God has forsaken,
Here lies Robin the Devil has taken."

His children carried on the social and official traditions of the name. The list of their marriages alone brings forward an array of the most conspicuous names and estates in Tidewater. John became a barrister in the Middle Temple, London, and married Elisabeth Hill, of Shirley on the James. Elisabeth married Nathaniel Burwell, of Carter's Grove on the York. Judith became the wife of Mann Page and so mistress of Rosewell on the York. Anne married Benjamin Harrison, of Berkeley on the James. Robert Carter settled himself at an estate called Nomini, on the Potomac. Charles built Cleve farther up the Rappahannock and married Anne, daughter of William Byrd, of Westover. Landon built Sabine Hall on this same river and married first an Armistead, of Hesse, later a Byrd, of Westover, and thirdly a Wormeley, of Rosegill, across the Rappahannock from Corotoman. Mary married a Braxton and became the mother of Carter Braxton, signer of the Declaration of Independence. Lucy married into the great Fitzhugh family and became the mistress of Eagle's Nest on the Potomac.

Christ Church, though somewhat dilapidated, still stands in its two hundredth year at the head of Carter's Creek, three miles from the site of Corotoman House. The building is cruciform, the brick walls are three feet thick, and the ceiling which forms a groined arch over the intersection of the aisles is thirty-three feet from the floor. Christ Church pews are old-fashioned and high, and two of them measure fifteen feet square.

Across the three miles of land between his house and his church "King" Carter built a straight road, thrown high, ditched on either side, and along it he planted a compact parallel hedge of cedar trees, many of which survive. Down this long formal alley he and his family made a kind of royal

235

progress as he went to worship God on Sunday morning. His coach was splendid; his horses and harness and liveried servants were splendid; and he, too, was splendid in a great wig, a velvet coat and lace choker, satin shorts, and silver buckles at his knees and on his shoes. It is said that the congregation never entered the church before his arrival but waited at the door until he descended from his coach and stalked splendidly up the aisle to his chancel pew; and then they followed after him.

Recalling similar departed distinctions, Rosegill, just across the river between Rosegill Lake and Urbanna Creek, still stands. As one approaches the central building it seems more impressive for its size and dignity than for any particular architectural beauty. It is supported at regular intervals by smaller detached houses, and the ensemble stands in thirty acres of lawn with an approach which discloses it at its best. A French visitor here in the eighteenth century said: "Arriving thither I might have believed myself entering a good sized town." If the exterior is merely impressive, the interior is both impressive and beautiful. There is a large square hall of entrance and another hall with eight large windows, and there are winding stairs on each end. The numerous great reception-rooms and halls are paneled in mahogany and oak, except the drawing-room which is in white. In the eighteenth century this great house held "a chapel, a picture gallery, and a noble library."

This library was one of the largest in Tidewater, and probably in all the colonies at the beginning of the eighteenth century, for in 1701, it embraced five hundred titles. These included "fifty comedies and tragedies in folio," *Every Man in His Humor, Don Quixote, Hudibras,* Hooker's *Ecclesiastical*

Polity, Burnet's *History of the Reformation,* Herbert's *Poems,* Camden's *Brittania,* and the works of Jeremy Taylor, Gower, Baxter, Burton, Montaigne, Bacon, Davenant, Quarles, Fuller and Waller.

Such was the home of the Ralph Wormeleys, for there was a line of that name, masters of Rosegill, with but a single interruption, from 1649 to 1806. They were all conspicuous characters. Educated for the most part in the English universities; occupying positions of the first place in the colonial government; and in one instance at least rivaling the glory of their "regal" neighbor across the water at Corotoman.

The builder of Rosegill and the founder of its picture gallery and library was the second Ralph Wormeley who, having entered Oriel College, Oxford, in his fifteenth year, in 1665, completed his studies, returned to Rosegill and eventually became a member of the House of Burgesses, a member of the Council, secretary of state, a trustee of William and Mary College, naval officer of the Rappahannock, and eventually president of the Council. According to a contemporary he was "the most powerful man in Virginia."

It was the fifth Ralph Wormeley who, having completed his studies at Eton and Cambridge, returned home about 1761 and became one of the greatest book collectors in all Tidewater. Rosegill had, too, like Corotoman, its Christ Church, on the lowland by the water southeast of the mansion, and there, beneath fine monuments, the departed Wormeleys lie buried.

Crossing again to the north side of the Rappahannock one has a quickening interest in finding oneself in a neighborhood associated with the birth, in 1708, of Mary Ball, the mother of Washington. Among the place names here is Ball's Mill

Pond, and at her home near it still live descendants of her family. This Ball estate has thus been in the possession of the same family for nearly two hundred fifty years. It is called Epping Forest.

The house in which the mother of Washington was born has several times been the victim of fires. Yet parts of the original dwelling, strong hand-wrought timbers, have survived, and they are incorporated in the latest building to rise on the same spot. The family burying-ground not far away is believed to enclose the remains of Mary Ball Wash-

Bewdley

ington's mother and father. He was Joseph Ball. He was born in England in 1649 and died on the Rappahannock in 1711.

Not far away, as distances go in this far-flung district, rose another Ball house, first cited as the home of Major James Ball, a cousin of Mary, of Epping Forest, and bearing every evidence of great age. This was Bewdley. It was a rectangular frame dwelling supported by two superb tall chimneys at each end. And what made it unique among all Tidewater houses was the high pitch of its roof and the double tier of dormer-windows which pierced it. This vast, dark, double-dormered roof was nearly three times as high as the wall which supported it,—an unusual spectacle among colonial houses and not to be forgotten. Only recently it succumbed to fire.

A third house in this neighborhood associated with Mary Ball's family is Belle Isle where lived a niece of Mary Ball, and hence a first cousin of George Washington, Fanny the wife of Raleigh Downman. Her father was that uncle of young George, who, when he heard that his sister "had some thought of putting" her son George "to sea," wrote from London that he thought the boy "had better be put apprentice to a tinker, for a common sailor before the mast has by no means the common liberty of the subject; for they will press him, from a ship where he has fifty shillings a month and make him take twenty-three, and cut and slash, and use him like a negro, or rather like a dog."

Some of the rooms of Belle Isle are over sixteen feet high. Once they were all paneled to the ceiling. But the old house was dismantled a few years ago when, it is said, twelve tons of paneling were sold and carted away to embellish a new house outside of Tidewater.

The church of this extensive connection of Balls was St. Mary's White Chapel and stands near all these plantations. It was originally cruciform, but during its varying fortunes the wings were taken down and the bricks were incorporated into the repairs of the alternating dull and glazed brick walls of what is now described as an "oblong square." White Chapel seems to have been built in 1740, to ease the crowding congregation of the much older parish. In it Colonel Joseph Ball, of Epping Forest, and Major James Ball, of Bewdley, were allowed to build a private gallery for their families. The church has interesting possessions given the parish as early as 1669. The churchyard encloses many old tombs and most of them bear the names of Washington's relatives on his mother's side.

In a more secluded spot elsewhere, however, is a Ball grave and a Ball epitaph which takes its place forward among the quaint carvings found on Tidewater tombstones:

> "The body of Capt. Richard Ball
> Lies entombed within this wall
> Thrice seventeen years, two months his age,
> He dwelt on earth. But from this Stage
> He was removed by God's great grace
> We hope into a nobler place;
> October was the month wherein
> He was acquitted from his sin
> Even the twelfth day at ten at night
> Death did deprive him of our light
> One from the date of twenty-seven
> The Lord (we trust) took him to Heaven
> 1726."

A house in this same neighborhood which obviously was once of considerable distinction is Edge Hill. Below its garden terraces a steep slope drops to Lancaster Creek down which it commands a lovely view of the Rappahannock. It is of brick, and its rectangular building still stands as do its connecting wings at each end, but of the wings beyond these only the front walls remain,—a suggestive old ruin of opulent days before the Revolution. But Edge Hill is young compared to Towle Point, the veteran house which gives its name to or takes it from Towle's Point just opposite Rosegill. It is sometimes spoken of as one of the oldest houses of Tidewater. It is a small, simple, conventionally quaint house sitting low among its four high chimneys in a way to suggest an architectural four-poster. Its dormered roof has not in over two hundred years known any other master than one of the Towles.

The next great houses here do not show themselves, to the traveler coming up the river, for another fifteen miles above Lancaster Creek. But then there are two, distinguished among the houses of all Tidewater, both for their architecture and their occupants, sitting back with aristocratic reticence on the distant first natural terrace above the broad flats through which the river makes its sluggish tidal way back and forth, back and forth. They are Sabine Hall and Mount Airy.

Sabine Hall was built about 1730 by Landon Carter, son of "King" Carter, of Corotoman, and none but a descendant in the direct line from the builder has ever owned it. Landon Carter built substantially but conventionally. The house had a simple rectangular base for a long time with a low extension on the east only. A recent discovery authenticated the fact that there were identical wings at each end and these are now being added in conformity, it is believed, with the original state of the mansion. The approach from the river is across a mile of fields and up through a terraced formal garden. The land approach is through a lovely park, and on this side the house is made more impressive by its noble high portico. The four columns, holding the pediment at the level of the roof above the second story, are of solid cypress.

The interior of Sabine Hall is wainscoted and paneled, and is enriched by the collection of Carter portraits and silver. Among those looking down out of the great frames is Robert "King" Carter himself, his head made enormous by the falls of curled wig, the splendid dark coat and shorts relieved by the lace jabot and cuffs. Near by is his first wife, Judith Armistead, of Hesse. Landon Carter looks out at the portraits of three Mrs. Carters, who were Elisabeth Wormeley, of Rosegill, Maria Byrd, of Westover, and Elisabeth Beale.

Apart from many larger pieces of silver bearing the Carter arms there are some quite unique spoons which are perhaps more characteristic of the patriot. These spoons bear an inscription extending the whole length of each handle. On those on which it has not been effaced by handling it reads: "After the repeal of the American Stamp Act—1766." It is the family tradition that Colonel Landon Carter, when sending a particularly reserved order to his London factors in that year, included directions to send out some tablespoons which were to be of silver if the Stamp Act were repealed, but if the act were not repealed to send them of horn. The obnoxious act was repealed, and the factor sent the spoons of silver with the reason why engraved on each of them.

Sabine Hall and its contents is an accurate reflection of the character of the man who built it. It has that same distinction without ostentation which made Landon Carter a figure who, from his retirement in the days before the Revolution, exerted a profound effect upon the minds and political and official conduct of those who were more conspicuously active than he was. His character as a patriot is reflected even more definitely in his letters to Washington, the Lees and other notable contemporaries, but his character, as a planter, and indeed as an observer of life generally, is revealed in the diary which he kept carefully for many years, after the fashion of Washington, Jefferson and some other colonial planters, telling of the crops, the shiftless servants, the disappointing parsons, the color of the coach or the rooms, the illness of the children, the tragedy of a daughter who married against his judgment, the heartbreak of a rebellious and insulting son, the barrels of oysters, the shipments of wine, the dinners and dances, and interspersed in a background of such universally human commonplaces, sage comments on people and conduct, and a spotty development of the state of mind of the Revolutionary patriots and of the progress of the war.

One of the recurrent complaints in this diary is about the doctor's prescriptions, which were annoyingly enigmatic to Colonel Carter. A few miles up-river from Sabine Hall one finds Doctor's Creek and wonders if it were named for the Colonel's bête noir; and if he were the same medico who furnished this list of medicines and medical books as set out in the old county records; and if so one's sympathy rather goes to the Colonel:

"Aq fort 3V's, Sp't sal arm, ol Cary:, 01 Jun, 01 ment, 01 cham ol pul, Bals hel Ter, Syr Sp Ceoro, Spt Nit Dul, Spt Vit, Pul Cast Rus, Spt Sal, Spt Sal Dule 2 Glass, Lap Contrary, puk [or pub or pul] Lental Rubr. Sal am vel, Gull Gamba, Bals Peru 2 viols, Sal mer Glaub:, Sp Ceti, Ther Venet 2 Viols, Precip Aur, Arg Vivum, Gum Camp, ol Ther, mer Ruper Precip, pul Gasconi, Tinc Cath, Bals Copre [or Copsie or Capsie] 01 Suc [or Sac] 01 Guf:, Gum Scam, ant Drap, Oc Canororum, Torch Echel cane, Alb Rhasis, Fl Benz, Pul grid flors, Turp min'r, Caux Lan, Sal vit, Bals Lucat, Ung Newtritum, 01 anisi, Gum Gall Col sptt, Emple ple minio, Gum Guiaci Gum By'r, Rad Satery, Lap Calam, Cro: mart. asting. Pul Castory, Cro. Argl 3 p'tt, Sal mart, Books: Jo. Jonstoni Thaumatographia Naturales, Martin ven Dis:, Sharps Midwifery, Shaws Physick 2 vol, Septuagint, Bezas Bible, Burroughs Phys, Barbetts Chirurg."

Mount Airy is one of the most distinguished old buildings on any of the shores of Tidewater. It is unlike any other house here. It does not even suggest the American colonial note.

It looks like a great English baronial house in its own setting. Unlike the generality of Tidewater mansions built of wood or brick, it is built of brown stone with light stone trimming, and all the details are scrupulously artistic.

This mansion is really three houses artificially united. Advanced a considerable distance before the central structure and set out beyond its ends, are two square two-story stone buildings which are united to the big house by covered curved passages. This ensemble encloses a grassy forecourt, and stands on a broad terrace rising some feet above the adjacent lawns and extending beyond the mansion in all directions. The outlook from the south loggia again suggests the baronial scope of the setting. The Rappahannock announces itself where the sunlight glints its waters three miles away across its own river-bottom lands.

Mount Airy has been, from the days of the patent, two generations before the mansion was built in 1747, to the present time, uninterruptedly the home of the Tayloe family. There was a succession of owners who conducted their lives on the large scale of their estate and their home. They held a conspicuous place in public affairs. The earlier owners added to their fortunes until John Tayloe, the grandson of the emigrant, became one of the richest men in the colony and expressed his fortune and his own character in this house which he built and in the brilliant social life and the expansive hospitality he conducted there. He had famous stables of blooded race-horses which included Belair, Grey Diomeck, Jenny Cameron, Jolly Roger and Yorick, the most famous racer of his day. Furthermore, Colonel Tayloe had his own private race-track on his own land, and a portion of his estate was set off as a deer park. He maintained a band of musicians

CHATHAM ON THE RAPPAHANNOCK

WOODLAWN, NEAR MOUNT VERNON

STRATFORD HALL ON THE POTOMAC

made up of his own servants whom he had instructed in music to play for the diversion of his guests.

There is the evidence or the suggestion of all this in the splendid interior of the house, with its array of portraits, its collection of prints of the more famous of the Tayloe horses, the sporting prints which hung in the rooms of the second and third John Tayloes while they were students at an English university, and the silver trophies won by the racers of the masters of Mount Airy in the distant days of the colony.

Rich as was John Tayloe, the builder, yet there is a suggestion of a "pinch" in the letter quoted below. He had eight daughters, and it is possible that he found it not too simple a matter to set them up in life under a social system which expected parents to establish their children on a scale commensurate with that in which they had been brought up. These eight daughters married into the most distinguished families in Tidewater: the Washingtons, the Carters, the Lees, the Pages, the Lomaxes, the Berkeleys, the Corbins and the Wormeleys.

A sample of the colonial gentleman's attitude toward his daughters' future is revealed in this letter written by John Tayloe to Ralph Wormeley, when one of the Misses Tayloe was about to marry the son of the master of Rosegill:

"Dear Sir:
"Mrs. Lee left a packet of great consequence to me in the chamber where she slept at your house, which I am obliged to send for. Therefore have the more speedy opportunity of returning my sincere thanks for your friendly letter by your son, who is well, and mine. I thank God, much better than he has been, though much reduced and looks very badly; but hope, as his thrush is gone, when his teeth come out he may mend fast, and hope to hear your lady is perfectly recovered and all the rest of your family well.

"The Provision you propose for your son in your lifetime, with what will be his after, is satisfactory to me, provided it be not too heavily encumbered with legacies and debts, and it is necessary to guard against any want that may possibly happen; therefore approve of your proposal with respect to a settlement, in case you should survive your son, in either way you please. I only wish my daughter's change in life to be made comfortable to her and guarded against every contingency. I am satisfied she can live happily with you, yet my tenderness for her creates fears, I must own, and hope they may never be more. But the subject is too tender to speak more plainly upon. I proposed the only mode in my power to give my daughter a fortune, and if not accepted I will not engage to do what depends on the will of others and not my own; for it will not suit my convenience to pay her fortune in any other manner than from moneys due me, of which I have not been able to collect a sufficiency to pay my eldest daughter's fortune, who, though in affluence, is yet entitled to the preference and must have it from me unless otherwise proposed by her husband, or shall think I do not do justice. My second is otherwise provided for. Nannie stands next in turn but, having no offer yet, may be provided for in time, perhaps as soon as wanted. My desire is to make my children as happy as I can and as soon as possible.

"Our best respects attend your family.

"I am, dear sir, your obedient humble servant,

(sgd) "JOHN TAYLOE.

Mt. Airy, Aug. 4th, 1772."

Not far from Sabine Hall and Mount Airy other Tidewater homes, though off the river, are Belleville, Bladensfield and Menokin. The first of these has from colonial days been a home of the Brockenbroughs. Bladensfield was a Carter place and reserved its name from Anne Bladen, wife of "Councilor" Carter, of Nomini Hall. According to tradition, which is well accredited, Bladensfield was once the home of Nathaniel Rochester, a native of this neighborhood, for whom the city of Rochester, New York, was named. Menokin was built and lived in by one of the six celebrated sons of Thomas Lee, of Stratford Hall, on the other shore of the Neck and of which more in another place. His name was Francis Lightfoot Lee. He was four times a member of the Continental Congress and was one of the only two brothers who were signers of the Declaration of Independence. His wife was Rebecca Tayloe, of Mount Airy. He died without children and left Menokin to his nephew, Ludwell Lee, a son of his signer-brother, Richard Henry Lee.

Opposite Mount Airy is the spectacle, strange for Tidewater, of a great river bridge. This one, like the bridge across the James above Norfolk, is of the present decade, and with it furnishes the only instances of bridges which span the James, the York, the Rappahannock or the Potomac below the head of their tidal reaches. At its southern end stands the aged town of Tappahannock.

This name is believed by some to be a corruption of Rappahannock. There was an Indian town of this name here when the first white men came up the river. Then it became known as Hobb's Hole (or Hold?) and so appears in the letters and diaries of many distinguished colonials. Self-conscious citizens later preferred the Indian name and under it the little town enjoys life with a lean core but a large margin.

Above the bridge on the eastern side of the river is Naylor's Point behind which lived the Fauntleroys. The first of this family here, in 1651, made a contract with the Indians by which he gave "ten fathoms of peake" and "thirty arms' lengths of Roanoke" and received title to a vast domain which extended from the Rappahannock to the Potomac River and some distance along both of them.

The domestic survivals along this stretch of the Rappahannock are largely on the western hills. Here are Kinlock, Blandfield, Brooke's Bank and Elmwood. Kinlock is a superb four-story structure built by Robert Naylor in 1845 in the center of a vast domain still held together. Its main hall is sixty feet long and fourteen feet wide under a ceiling fourteen feet high. Brooke's Bank is named for the family which built it and lived here so many generations. It dates to 1731. Its old brick walls bear the scars of the shot from gunboats on the river during the Civil War.

Blandfield suggests both the Blands and the Beverleys, for it was built by a Beverley who named it for his wife who was a Bland from the James. The builder was the son of Robert Beverley, the first native historian of Virginia, and of Ursula, daughter of William Byrd II, of Westover. It is a noble brick structure with large, solid, central building and spacious connected wings. The sequence of Beverleys as masters of Blandfield remains unbroken from the builder to the present owner and occupant, who is named for his distinguished forebear, Robert Beverley.

Elmwood began its career brilliantly, before the Revolution, as the home of Muscoe Garnett; it survives untenanted and decaying but none the less romantically. It is said that this house has rarely been opened for fifty years. All its furniture, pictures, plate and books remain in their places. It is spared the wear and tear of occupancy. It reminds one of Satis House in *Great Expectations*. It might be the home of another Miss Havisham, deserted by her lover in the midst of her wedding preparation, with one shoe on and never to put on the other, never to change her bridal dress or veil, never to remove the bridal feast from the table, never to allow anything to be altered. But things left alone do alter; even unmoved, untouched, they change.

Where the river next is narrowest there is a landing against the north shore, laid parallel with it as if it might block the channel, if it reached at right angles into the stream. About it are a few houses. And this is Leedstown. Nothing for the eyesight. But history did not pass it by. It is perhaps a mere historical curiosity that Leedstown has been in five counties. At first it was in Lancaster, when Lancaster was nearly all the Northern Neck, extending "back to the China Sea." As territorial divisions broke up the Neck,—gerrymandered is probably the proper word,—the village of Leedstown found itself successively in Rappahannock, Richmond, King George and Westmoreland Counties. Leedstown came into corporate being the same year as Philadelphia, which was 1681, and its babyhood was not the less prosperous of the two.

It had several ordinaries, one at least of which was superior, for George Fisher traveling this way in 1751, wrote of his stay here:

"I put up at one Mrs. T——ts, esteemed the best ordinary in town, and indeed the house and furniture has an elegant appearance as any I have seen in the country, Mr. Finnays or Wetherburnes in Williamsburg not excepted. The chairs, tables &c of the room I was conducted into were all of mahogany, and so stuffed with fine large glaized copper plate prints that I almost fancied myself in Jeffriess' or other elegant print shops."

George Fitzhugh said, in 1859, "when we studied geography, which wasn't so long ago, Leeds was enumerated as one of the big towns of Virginia. Now, Marius might philosophize amid its ruins (if he could find them)."

Its memorable day was in February, 1766, when Richard Henry Lee and one hundred fifteen "gentlemen of Westmoreland" assembled here. In the recorded list of them appeared such names as Monroe, Brockenbrough, Fauntleroy, Turberville, Roane, Thornton, Carter, Mountjoy, Mason, Bland, five of Lee, two of Monroe, two of Ball, and four of Washington. In his pocket Richard Henry Lee brought a set of Resolves which was the first "gun" of the Revolution. In its terms appeared the germ of the Declaration of Independence. The one hundred fifteen ventured the penalties of treason, and boldly wrote their names to it. Two of them, Richard Henry Lee and Francis Lightfoot Lee, ten years later journeyed up to Philadelphia, and there they put their signatures to another document of similar import and thereby they became signers of the Declaration of Independence.

Above Leedstown the Rappahannock gives a brief imitation of the "Curles" of the James, and momentarily the place names are "Ports": Port Micou, Port Tobago, Port Royal and Port Conway.

Port Micou once stood, a domestic sentinel, above the water where now twin chimneys are the only remnant. But the name Micou carries on in the neighborhood. One who bore it was for years clerk of the county and a character, if all the tales they tell of him be true. As his nose followed his pen scratching across the pages of the records he habitually murmured: "Oh, Lord, I wish I was in Heaven!"—a pious wish belied by his acknowledged dread of getting there, at least by lightning, which was his besetting terror.

This Mr. Micou had a deputy named George Croxton who knew him well enough not only to call him Uncle Jimmie, but also to ride the old gentleman's fears of the elements for a holiday. When copying court records irked him and his passion for fishing called him to the river, George would slip out of their office to the jury room overhead where he kept a prodigious cannon-ball. This he would roll across the floor a few times and then descend to note the effect on Uncle Jimmie, whose ear was nervously alert for such sounds.

"George," he would say, "didn't you hear it thundering a while ago?"

The designing clerk admitted as much and hinted signs of a storm in the west. Then he would tiptoe up to the jury room again and give the cannon-ball another ride. He could depend that on his return to the records Uncle Jimmie would have his hand near his hat, and a release phrased something like this:

"George, I heard it thundering just now. Ellen is all alone at home. You better lock up for I am going home." And George would lock up, and then go and spend the rest of the "evening" baiting and fishing.

Not so simple was the dynamic emigrant who patented Port Tobago. He was Sir Thomas Lunsford, one of the Cavaliers who fled to Tidewater Virginia from Roundhead terrors, and lies buried in the shadow of Bruton Church, Williamsburg. He brought with him the record of a lawless youth, of years of campaigning about western Europe in any army that would pay his price, and bearing the epithet of the "child-eater."

Before he left England for the Rappahannock the political versifiers had sung:

> "From Lunsford eke deliver us,
> Who eateth up children."

Royalist Cleveland had ridiculed him thus:

> "The Post that came from Banbury,
> Riding on a red rocket,
> Did tidings tell how Lunsford fell,
> A child's hand in his pocket."

And the same Cleveland, in another place:

> "They fear the giblets of his train,
> Even his Dog, that four-legged cavalier;
> He that devours the scraps that Lunsford makes,
> Whose picture feeds upon a child in steaks."

Sir Thomas was a royalist first and last, fighting and commanding for the King against the Puritans, and was famous and feared the length and breadth of England. But his life became too insecure, and he and Lady Lunsford sailed over the ocean and set up on the Rappahannock. His reputation as a child-eater could not have been taken seriously here. He became one of the first gentlemen of the colony and married his daughter to Ralph Wormeley, of Rosegill. She inherited Port Tobago, and through her daughter and her connections it passed to John Lomax, "of Essex, Gentleman," father of the line who gave it its best years of prosperity and gaiety.

Ports Micou and Tobago were estates and houses. Ports Royal and Conway were towns, or at least attempts at them. Port Conway had its beginning as a tobacco warehouse or "rolling house." This was a name given the places for deposit and inspection of tobacco on the river in the days when the leaf was the currency. Such places were called rolling houses because there were then few wagons, and the great hogsheads of tobacco were rolled to the warehouse at the landing. For a similar reason some of the first clearings were called rolling roads. James Madison, later the fourth president of the United States, was born in Belle Grove, at Port Conway, which was named for one of his forebears. It is said locally, and naturally without citing book or page, that Port Conway lacked only one vote of being chosen by Congress to be the capital of the

United States. But the same naive story is told of Port Royal on the other side of the river.

Port Conway's last distinction came to it in April, 1865, when John Wilkes Booth, having assassinated Abraham Lincoln, reached Port Conway in his flight southward from Washington, and here crossed the Rappahannock to Port Royal, to meet death a few days later in "Garrett's barn" not far from the river.

Below Port Conway are Walsingham, Woodlawn and Oaken Brow. The last was originally built by one of the Tayloes, of Mount Airy, for his son. It was burned some years ago but has recently been restored. Near it is Naugatigo, old and quaint, with a fine drawing-room.

Port Royal has otherwise little to say for itself. Yet its graveyard is not without a kind of quaint eloquence. There are several eighteenth-century tombstones there; among them one to the unnamed son of William and Anne Fox, on which is chiseled this stanza:

> "Beneath this humble stone a Youth doth lie
> Most too Good to live too Young to dye
> Count his few Years how short the scanty Span
> But count—his Virtues, and he dye'd a Man."

At a distance of two miles from Port Royal is Gaymount, a house whose exterior is without pretension but not without charm. The interior, however, with its handsome woodwork, reflects distinction, and the broad hall is notable for its landscape paper. The central building was put here in 1725, but the additions did not rise until 1798. The scope of its view across the hills and valleys on both sides of the river is not surpassed, if indeed it is equaled, by that from any other house on this river.

The Baltimore steamer, which "runs" the Rappahannock once a week in each direction, ties up for the night under a shady bluff at Hop Yard Landing, before advancing in the morning on its triumphal progress fifteen miles farther to Fredericksburg. This landing takes its name from the Embrey estate adjacent. Once it was called Feneaux and belonged to the Fitzhughs, a family whose numbers were as numerous and significant at this end of the Northern Neck as were the Washingtons and Lees and Carters at the other end. Next it on the southern rise is stately old Powhatan, and a little farther back are Rokeby of the Williams, and Cleveland of the Masons. Powhatan is another of the mansions built by John Tayloe for one of his sons; this one for Benjamin Ogle Tayloe, who, for a town residence, lived in Octagon House, Washington, built for him by Dr. William Thornton, architect of the Capitol of the United States. For a long time the table on which the Treaty of Ghent was signed was among the treasures at Powhatan.

On this bank, too, is Cleve, sitting on the first low terrace near the water which gives it a kind of friendly intimacy with the old river. Cleve is another of the seats of the four sons of "King" Carter, of Corotoman. This mansion was built by Charles Carter about 1750. He was married first to a Miss Walke, then to one of the Misses Byrd, of Westover, and finally to a Miss Taliaferro. The house was ruined by fire in 1800. It was restored, but minus the supporting buildings which gave the colonial seat the aspect of a village. From the Carters it passed to the Lewises, descendants of Fielding Lewis, of Kenmore, and his wife, Betty Washington, sister of the General. Among the treasures at Cleve for many years were a portrait of Betty Washington Lewis and a bewigged and scarlet-coated painting of the builder; but in the earlier days the walls were rich in Carter portraits, the long central hall having been hung with double lines of them.

Life at Cleve had all the distinction and gaiety of life at Sabine Hall, Nomini Hall, Shirley, Westover and the other Tidewater homes with which it was connected. Charles Carter seems to have set great store by dancing as an accomplishment. In his will he directed that his daughters be "brought up frugally and taught to dance" and that his sons remain in

Cleve

England, where they were at school, "to learn the languages, mathematics, philosophy, dancing and fencing."

It is not known how education weighed on the little Misses Carter, of Cleve, but in 1756 a letter came to one of them, Maria, from her cousin, Maria Carter, of Sabine Hall, which was no doubt received with understanding and sympathy:

"My Dear Cousin:
"You have realy imposed a Task upon me which I can by no means perform viz: that of writing a Merry & Comical

Letter: how shou'd [I] my dear that am ever Confined either
at School or with my Grandmama know how the World goes
on? Now I will give you the History of one Day the Repetition of which without variations carries me through the Three
hundred and sixty five Days, which you know compleats the
year. Well then first begin, I am awakened out of a sound
Sleep with some croaking voice either Patty's, Milly's, or some
other of our Domestics with Miss Polly Miss Polly get up,
tis time to rise, Mr. Price is down Stairs, & tho' I hear them
I lie quite snugg till my Grandmama uses her Voice, then up
I get, huddle on my cloaths & down to Book, then to Break-
fast, then to School again, & may be I have an Hour to my
self before Dinner, then the Same Story over again till twi-
light, & then a small portion of time before I go to rest, and
so you must expect nothing from me but that I am
"Dear Cousin, Most Affectionately Yours."

The writer of this letter became the wife of Robert Beverley
and the mistress of Blandfield. The recipient of the letter
married William Armistead, of Hesse. And so the knot of
Virginia cousinship tightened.

Houses which are conspicuous on the south side of the
Rappahannock in its last tidal reaches before the falls, are
Moss Neck, Hayfield, Belvedere, St. Julien and Mannsfield.
Moss Neck was built by the Corbins. During the War between
the States it was for a time the headquarters of General Stone-
wall Jackson, and here General Lee and General Stuart sometimes came for conferences. St. Julien was long another of
the seats of the Virginia family of Brooke. Lawrence Bat-
taile built Hayfield and called it for the family name of his
bride, Miss Hay. Belvedere rose under the direction of William Dangerfield. His children he gave into the care of an
imported tutor, John Harrower, of the Shetland Islands, and
to the survival of his diary and his letters to his wife is due a
lively acquaintance with the life at Belvedere before the Revo-

lution. This, from one of his letters, gives a glimpse of domestic and political conditions on a Tidewater plantation in 1774:

"As to my living I eat at their own table, and our wituals are all Dressed in the English taste. we have for Breackfast either Coffie or Jaculate, and warm Loaf bread of the best floor, we have also at table warm loaf bread of Indian corn, which is extreamly good but we use the floor bread always at breackfast. for Dinner smoack'd bacon or what we cal pork ham is a standing dish either warm or cold. when warm we have greens with it, and when cold we have sparrow grass. we have also either warm roast pigg, Lamb, Ducks, or chickens, green pease or any thing else they fancy. As for Tea there is none drunk by any in this Government since 1st. June last, nor will they buy a 2ds worth of any kind of east India goods, which is owing to the difference at present betwixt the Parliment of great Britton and the North Americans about laying a tax on the tea; and I'm afraid if the Parliment do not give it over it will cause a total revolt as all the North Americans are determined to stand by one another, and resolute on it that they will not submit. I have the news paper sent me to school regularly every week by the Coll.—Our family consists of the Coll. his Lady and four Children a housekeeper an Overseer and myself all white. But how many blacks young and old the Lord only knows for I belive there is about thirty that works every day in the field besides the servants about the house; such as Gardner, livery men and pages, Cooks, washer and dresser, sewster and waiting girle. They wash here the whitest that ever I seed for they first Boyle all the Cloaths with soap, and then wash them, and I may put on clean linen every day if I please. My school is a neate litle House 20 foot long and 12 foot wide and it stands by itself at the end of an Avenue of planting about as far from the main house as Robt. Forbes's is from the burn, and there comes a bonny black bairn every morning to clean it out and make my bed, for I sleep in it by myself."

Mannsfield presents a fine spectacle above the river. It is, however, a newer house on the site of the one built here by Mann Page, a member of the Continental Congress and one of the family from Rosewell on the York. Mannsfield has given up the vicissitudes of individual ownership. Its broad acres once devoted to cotton and tobacco are now devoted to tees and caddies, for it is now consecrated to the service of a country club, nor is it too exclusive to accept the wayfaring tourist.

The Rappahannock has for many miles below this point been a narrow brown ribbon overhung with broad branched trees which sometimes sweep the superstructure of the steamer as it passes. But the tides flow and ebb even here, eighty-odd miles from the bay, and even for another four miles when they succumb to the rocky impasse where salt water and fresh water, and Fredericksburg and Falmouth, meet.

CHAPTER XIII

FREDERICKSBURG REMEMBERS

A Colonial Crossroads—Royal Street Names—Wooden Chimneys—George Washington's Boyhood Home—He Swims While the Girls Rob His Clothes—The Washingtons Come into Fredericksburg—Kenmore and Mary Washington's Home—Chatham and William Fitzhugh's Hospitality —John Paul Passes—James Monroe Practises Law—The Slave Block— The Pathfinder of the Seas—Where Blue Met Gray—Old Falmouth.

REDERICKSBURG sits quietly along its gentle slopes above the Rappahannock and remembers. It offers the passing world little of the present that is pretentious, but it points to this house and that one, and tells its story. It is a quiet story, its pleasant serenity interrupted only once by a stroke from the forked lightning of war. It is, indeed, scarcely at all a story of events. Almost uninterruptedly is it personal, the chronicle of people, but of people acting conspicuous rôles in the life and development of the nation.

About the past of Fredericksburg there is something processional. It has stood at the crossroad. At first the traffic was stronger from east to west, ships bringing English manufactured goods up the river to the warehouses here at the tide's end where they were transported in covered wagons farther west to outreaching bands of pioneers on the highlands near the first mountains, at a later period into the Valley, and finally over the last range to the great basin where the Mississippi and its tributaries flow. Another current through the little town flowed between the north and south, land travel over the great if crude highway skirting the tidal rivers' heads; gigs, chaises, phaetons and not least often splendid silver-mounted coaches, with driver and postilion guiding the four and sometimes six horses, bearing nonentities often, but not less often the near-great and the great.

For the most part the celebrities performed their great acts on other stages, but before and after, many of them tarried here, became a part of the life and history of the town, and gave a sentimental significance to the places of their abiding.

It is not surprising to find the white man leading the procession here. The first white man whose appearance is well-authenticated, was the persistently exploring Captain John Smith. He passed by the mouth of the Rappahannock in June, 1608, but his encounter with the sting-ray, when using his improvised method of fishing with a sword, proved so nearly fatal that he sailed on to the James and Jamestown. But at the end of July he was back again and the evidence of the narrative written by his companions seems conclusive that he came up to the tide's end. It was on this trip that Featherstone Bay was named. Smith marked it on his map and it conforms reasonably to the locality of the present city of Fredericksburg.

"Betwixt Secobeck and Massawteck is a small isle or two which cause the river to be broader than ordinary," says the narrative. There they buried Featherstone and "left his name."

"The next day," it continues, "we sailed so high as our boat would float; there setting up crosses and graving our names in the trees."

There is no island of any size between the mouth of the Rappahannock and the falls except that one opposite the present city. To have sailed beyond this island so far as his "boat would float" would have carried the explorers to the inter-

MOUNT VERNON ON THE POTOMAC

MOUNT VERNON ON THE POTOMAC

Taken from the air at a point above the Potomac

cepting rocks over which in freshet weather the waters toss in foamy rapids. Smith was a thorough explorer. He sailed to the falls of the other rivers of Tidewater, and there is little reason to doubt this evidence that he was equally thorough in his exploration of the Rappahannock.

For another sixty-odd years, in so far as history is audible, the Indian was left in peaceable possession of his hills and streams here. Then the land was taken up by settlers, and after them came a little army to defend them in their possession. Palisades rose about a fort, and in it two hundred soldiers barricaded themselves. That is all the seventeenth century has left of itself in the chronicles.

In the sixteenth year of the new century a more picturesque cavalcade passed by. It was the first great exploring party off to the mountains. The French had penetrated far west by the route of the Great Lakes, and the Virginians wanted definite information of their own western contacts. Outward bound they dined with Austin Moore, and returning they spent the night with Mr. Woodford, both resident where now the city is. The leader was Spotswood, the Royal Governor of Virginia, himself. Accompanying him were ten Tidewater gentlemen, and they were escorted by four Indian guides and two companies of rangers. They took an extensive equipment. In it were "several casks of Virginia wine, red and white, Irish Usqubaugh, brandy, stout, two kinds of rum, champagne, cherry punch, cider," and, records the weary diarist of the expedition, "et cetera."

But more characteristic of the expedition was the great quantity of horseshoes which they were obliged to provide. In the stoneless sand and loam and clay of Tidewater, the horses were seldom shod. But for this rougher trip the mounts all wore iron shoes. When the Governor returned to Williamsburg he presented each of his companions with a miniature golden horseshoe, and his company has ever since been known as the Knights of the Golden Horseshoe.

Eleven years later, in 1727, such a community as had assembled opposite the island was incorporated as a town. It was named for the then Prince of Wales, Frederick, son of King George II. This act of fealty to the English royal family was accented in nearly every name as laid out on the original plat. Sophia Street was named for the King's sister; Caroline for the Queen, his wife; Princess Anne, Princess Elisabeth, Amelia, Frederick and William for his children; George, for the King himself; Prince Edward for his grandson; and Charlotte for the wife of King George III.

It is delightful to find that William Byrd II, of Westover, visited the new town five years after its birth, for if he wrote about it, he would surely have something saucy to say. Sure enough, his observations went into his journal made during his "progress to the mines." He came down from Germanna way in an early October evening storm:

"I was a little benighted, and should not have seen my way, if the Lightening, which flash't continually in my Face, had not befriended me. I got about seven a'clock to Colonel Harry Willis's, a little moisten'd with the Rain; but a Glass of good Wine kept my Pores open, and prevented all Rheums and Defluxions for that time."

The next day he saw the town:

"I was oblig'd to rise Early here, that I might not starve my Landlord, whose constitution requires him to Swallow a BeefSteak before the sun blesses the World with its genial Rays. However, he was so complaisant as to bear the gnawing of his Stomach, till 8 a'Clock for my Sake. Colo. Waller,

after a Score of loud Hems to clear his Throat, broke his
fast along with us. When this necessary affair was despatched,
Col. Willis walk't me about his Town of Fredericksburgh.
It is pleasantly situated on the South Shore of Rappahannock
River, about a Mile below the Falls. Sloops may come up and
lye close to the Wharf, within 30 Yards of the Public Warehouses, which are built in the figure of a Cross. Just by the
Wharf is a Quarry of White Stone that is very soft in the
Ground, and hardens in the Air, appearing to be as fair and
fine grain'd as that of Portland. Besides that, there are several
other Quarrys in the River Bank, within the Limits of the
Town, sufficient to build a great City. The only Edifice of
Stone yet built is the Prison; the Walls of which are strong
enough to hold Jack Sheppard, if he had been transported
thither. Tho' this be a commodious and beautiful Situation
for a Town, with the Advantages of a Navigable River, and
wholesome Air, yet the Inhabitants are very few. Besides
Colo. Willis, who is the top man of the place, there are only
one Merchant, a Taylor, a Smith and an Ordinary keeper;
though I must not forget Mrs. Levistone, who Acts here in
the Double Capacity of a Doctress and Coffee Woman. And
were this a populous City, she is qualify'd to exercise 2 other
callings. Tis said the Court-house and the Church are going
to be built here, and then both Religion and Justice will help
to enlarge the Place."

The projected church, to which Byrd referred, rose soon
after. It was the first of the churches here to be called St.
George's. The names of its two earliest rectors arrest attention. The first, who remained only a brief time, was the Reverend Patrick Henry, for whom his nephew, the great orator
of the Revolution, was named. The second rector was a
Frenchman, Reverend James Marye, who served this parish
for thirty-four years. He exerted a profound influence on the
character of one of the greatest figures in American history,
as will appear presently.

For a similar reason the progress of Fredericksburg at this

time is of equal interest. The records are lean, but they are significant. By the year 1738 the town had achieved importance enough to have the House of Burgesses pass a law directing that "fairs should be held in Fredericksburg twice a year for the sale of cattle, provisions, goods, wares and all Kinds of merchandise whatever." And an immunity of a kind was granted all who attended the fairs, for the act provided that all persons were privileged from arrest and execution during the fairs and for two days before and after them. Exception was made, however, of capital offenses, breaches of the peace, or for any controversies, suits and quarrels that might arise during the time. One not unnaturally wonders what there was left to arrest for. It looked as if the exceptions had swallowed the law.

However, the fairs were probably among the influences which made the town grow. In 1739 a new survey of Fredericksburg showed that it had extended itself beyond the fifty acres originally allotted to it as a site and it encroached covetously on the land of Colonel Byrd's host, Colonel Harry Willis, and over the owner's protest the Burgesses declared the Willis land, and other contiguous land, a part of the town. The Willis place went for five pounds. Colonel Byrd would probably have been surprised at the growth of his friend's town seven years after his visit to it.

Wooden chimneys must have been used generally in the early days in Tidewater. The case, already noted, of those at Suffolk was not unique. They were so generally used in the first houses of Fredericksburg that, in 1742, the Burgesses had to outlaw them. As brick chimneys generally preceded brick houses, it is probable that such buildings as rose in the little town up to this time were all of wood.

There came into the neighborhood of Fredericksburg about 1740 a "gentleman" and his wife and their six children, bringing a name and a character of which the little city was ever after to make its proudest boast. This "gentleman," for so he is described in the deed, who, two years before, had purchased a farm of two hundred eighty acres nearly three miles inland and northeast of the then small town, was Augustine Washington. To it he brought his wife, Mary Ball Washington; their eldest boy George, then only eight years old; and his brothers and sisters, Elisabeth, Samuel, John Augustine, Charles and Mildred. The father died here in 1743 and willed the farm to his son George. But George had already spent a few years on a tract, later to be known as Mount Vernon and at the time an elder half-brother's home, and he seems to have been irresistibly drawn in that direction. As soon after his father's death as it seems to have been reasonably possible, he sold his farm and moved to Mount Vernon which he was possessed of soon after. But these eight years on this farm near Fredericksburg started a lasting association between George Washington and that community.

To this period of his boyhood is attributed the writing of his celebrated *Rules of Civility and Decent Behavior,* which it is reasonable to believe had an important influence in the formation of his character. To the contradiction of some of Washington's biographers, who believed that Washington compiled these *Rules* himself, it has been discovered that they were translated from the French. The question as to how young Washington got them from the French leads directly to Fredericksburg where, in addition to whatever time he spent under the eye of Master Hobby, he went to a school "taught by French people" as the town records show, and hence obviously by the Reverend James Marye, who was the only Frenchman in the town at that time. The tie is bound tighter by the two singular facts that the French book in question which contained the original of the *Rules* was published in Rouen and that James Marye himself had been educated in Rouen. One writer, without citing his source, says Marye used that book as a text-book when studying in Rouen. Even without this last touch, it appears now well established that Parson Marye was the intermediary of Washington's famous *Rules* and so, and probably in other respects, was one of the prime influences on the boy's character.

While living on the farm, but traveling back and forth across the Rappahannock to school, the imagination of young George was touched by ships he saw at anchor opposite the town. They were ships from lower Tidewater, ships from Bristol, Plymouth and London. It was then he seems to have decided that his future life lay on the sea. The idea found favor with his older brother, Lawrence, but his mother opposed it. A strong letter from her brother in England, already quoted, quashed the notion, and George turned to surveying land instead.

After leaving the neighborhood and establishing himself at Mount Vernon, Washington was often in Fredericksburg. He came at first to see his mother and then to see his sister, Betty, in her new home. He found the city to be directly on his way between Mount Vernon and his seat as burgess in the Assembly at Williamsburg. When he affiliated himself with the Masonic Order he was initiated into the Fredericksburg lodge. When he married Martha Custis he brought his bride home by way of the little city on the Rappahannock for her to meet his own people.

But there is another authentic occasion of his earlier presence there which pops out of the old court records of Spottsylvania County. In 1751 he was down from Mount Vernon, and took a swim in the Rappahannock, and the record under date of December third suggests what happened on that occasion:

"Ann Carroll and Mary McDaniel, of Friedericksburg, being committed to the gaol of this county by William Hunter, Gent, on suspicion of felony and charged with robbing the cloaths of Mr. George Washington when he was washing in the river some time last summer, the court having heard several evidences are of the opinion that the said Ann Carroll be discharged, and admitted on evidence for our Lord the King against the said Mary McDaniel, and upon considering the whole evidence and the prisoners defense, the court are of the opinion that the said Mary McDaniel is guilty of petty larceny, whereupon the said Mary desired immediate punishment for the said crime and relied on the mercy of the court, therefore it is ordered that the sheriff carry her to the whipping post and inflict fifteen lashes on her bare back, and then she be discharged."

There is some ambiguity as to whether naughty Miss McDaniel stole the clothes or only the valuables out of them. Compared to other penalties inflicted for stealing at that time her "fifteen lashes" were comparatively mild, and may have been made milder, as they often were by the sympathetic touch of the sheriff. Young Washington, however, had nothing to do with the prosecution. He had sailed, the September preceding, to Barbadoes, with his dying brother, Lawrence.

Other contemporary and local methods of punishment, besides the whipping-post, were the stocks which stood in the public square, and the ducking-stool at the foot of Wolfe Street on the river bank. Crowds assembled before the victims of both stocks and ducking-stools, and the humiliation of exposure to the gibes and ridicule of the onlookers seems to have been the real sting in the penalty of being condemned to them.

When George sold his farm and left for Mount Vernon his mother is presumed to have moved to a farm called "Little Falls," a place on the river and not far from the town, which she had inherited from her father, and with her she took her three other children. The boys, Samuel and Charles, soon took up their homes on other lands which they acquired, and soon Elisabeth, or Betty as she is commonly called, in 1749 married Fielding Lewis, a prospering young citizen of Fredericksburg.

He built her a handsome brick mansion, on the northwest side of town, later to be known as Kenmore and which has ever since been one of the valued possessions of Fredericksburg. One of its most admired features are the ornamental ceilings done in stucco. They were the work of two Hessian soldiers captured in the Battle of Trenton. One of them died while working on the ceilings, his dead body having been found on the scaffolding.

Mary Washington found life lonely on her farm with the children dispersed, and soon, persuaded by her son, George, and doubtless by Betty Lewis, too, she abandoned her now solitary life in the country and moved into a modest frame house in the town only two streets from her daughter. There she lived until her death in 1789. Fredericksburg anticipated every other community in America in putting up a public memorial to a woman when they erected the monument near her house to the memory of their fellow citizen, "Mary, the Mother of Washington."

Soon after the Washingtons came to Fredericksburg there was activity on the heights across the river from the little town. A superb mansion was rising, comparable to any other in all Tidewater. The builder, newly come to the Rappahannock, was one of the great Potomac family of Fitzhugh. He was William, son of Henry Fitzhugh, of Eagle's Nest, and of Lucy, one of the daughters of "King" Carter, of Corotoman. His family owned vast tracts all over the Northern Neck, but he alone of all his kin of his own generation seems to have had the gregarious sense sufficiently developed to wish to live contiguous to a promising community. He wanted company. He got it. The splendid halls and numerous rooms of this great house, which he called Chatham, were rarely without visitors. Washington was frequently there, according to Lancaster who quotes the General as writing Mr. Fitzhugh: "I have put my legs oftener under your mahogany at Chatham than any where else in the world, and have enjoyed your good dinners, good wine and good company more than any other."

Though William Fitzhugh had the colonial gentleman's sense of public service, and sat in the House of Burgesses, the Continental Congress and other public sittings, he is remembered equally for his devotion to the turf. He had a great stable of thoroughbred horses, and like Colonel Tayloe, of Mount Airy, he had a private race-course on the highlands beyond his mansion. Here the gentry gathered from all the great houses in Tidewater, to dine, to drink, to dance, to meet their cousins, to arrange marriages, and to watch the fleet-footed Regulus, Kitty Fisher, Brilliant and Volunteer.

But, as Fredericksburg stood at one of the most traveled crossroads in Tidewater, when the racing parties broke up there was not the social lull at Chatham that might have been anticipated. So well known was this Fitzhugh, so generally connected with all the families in Virginia who traveled in their own coaches, that the stream of them up to the great front door of Chatham seemed never to cease. Finally William had all the company he wished; all he could stand. Among his lands, sprinkled all over tidal Virginia, he remembered a tract up in Fairfax, inland off the traveled highways, full of the promise of undisturbed retirement. There he built another house and called it Ravensworth, and thither he moved and spent his last years in peace.

Among others who came to Fredericksburg in the formative days before the Revolution were two young men born in Scotland. But they did not come together. One was Hugh Mercer and the other William Paul. Mercer became a great figure. Paul remained obscure, but his story is scarcely the less interesting of the two.

Hugh Mercer graduated in medicine at the University of Aberdeen, served in the army of Prince Charles Edward and emigrated to Pennsylvania in 1747. He served in the French and Indian War, and volunteered in Braddock's campaign where he was severely wounded. In the Revolution he rose to the rank of general and was killed in the Battle of Princeton.

On Braddock's campaign he met a young officer who became his life-long friend. This officer came from Virginia and his name was Colonel George Washington. It is not improbable that Washington suggested to Mercer that he move to Fredericksburg and practise medicine there. At any rate that was his next move after he left the army. A house by the river at the southern end of the town is pointed out as his residence. It was, and still is, known as the Sentry Box, because of its command of the river approaches to the town and its use in three wars as a point of outlook for the approach of an enemy.

The other Scot, William Paul, came to Fredericksburg in 1760. He was a merchant or a tailor, and had his place of business in the building where Washington was initiated a Mason. This would scarcely be worth telling were it not for William Paul's brother, John. It is often said that John came here on a visit to his brother William. Perhaps. However, what is certain is that a year after William's death here in 1772, John did come to Fredericksburg to administer his brother's estate. He remained two years. And it was while in residence here that John Paul received his commission as a lieutenant in such a navy as the revolting colonies then had. It was here, too, that John Paul, in token of the friendly act of Colonel Willie Jones, of North Carolina, who became his bondsman when he administered his brother's estate, took the name of Jones; so that if Fredericksburg was not the birthplace of John Paul, it may in a sense claim the distinction of being the birthplace of John Paul Jones, who left it to become one of the greatest sea-heroes of our history.

Nor is it without interest to find that the surgeon aboard the *Bonhomme Richard,* throughout her celebrated cruise under John Paul Jones, was Doctor Brooke whose family lived on the Rappahannock, below the city, at St. Julien.

In the procession through Fredericksburg one next recognizes many others of the most famous figures of the Revolutionary period. Jefferson, Pendleton, Bland, Randolph, Braxton, Mason, Richard Henry Lee, Francis Lightfoot Lee, Patrick Henry and others passed this way, for the most part on the way to that decisive independence-declaring congress at Philadelphia.

The day after news of the Battle of Lexington and of Dunmore's removal of the powder from Williamsburg, over six hundred volunteers from Fredericksburg and vicinity armed themselves and offered their services to Washington. Among them doubtless were Citizens Hugh Mercer, George Weedon and Gustavus B. Wallace, who all later attained the rank of general of the Revolutionary forces in the ensuing Seven Years' War.

Fielding Lewis, of Kenmore, Charles Dick, William Fitzhugh and others were at the head of a commission which established a gunnery and ordnance plant here to supply the army with arms and ammunition. "A hundred stand of arms a month" was the estimated output, in addition to a great amount of repairing done to damaged arms. In connection with it they took over "a mill house on Hazel Run" which they converted to the use of grinding bayonets and ramrods. In 1781, Dick wrote Governor Thomas Jefferson: "I have just time to acquaint you that the gentlemen of this town and even the ladies have very spiritedly attended at the gunnery and assisted to make up already about 20,000 cartridges with bullets, from which the Spottsylvania Militia and the Militia of Caroline have been supplied."

Presently the cry went up, "Dunmore is coming!"—and so he was, headed toward Fredericksburg to seize the gunnery works. But Lafayette intervened and kept him near the Mattapony. In spite of the good work done at the ordnance plant and the army's crying need of ammunition, public funds were not forthcoming to support it. It was then that Fielding Lewis, mindful of his brother-in-law's difficulties as commander-in-chief, came to the rescue, and lent the state every dollar he could raise from his private fortune.

When the Continental Congress adjourned in 1786 one of its Virginia members journeyed, with his newly wed bride, along the well-worn road to Fredericksburg and settled himself there. His law offices were in a rambling, one-story, brick building next to the Masonic burying-ground. His name was James Monroe. His destiny did not allow him to remain here long. It is said he served in a greater number of important public offices than any other American. Among his many services, he represented Fredericksburg in the Virginia Assembly and became progressively United States senator, minister to France, governor of Virginia, secretary of state, secretary of war and twice president of the United States.

At the beginning of the century the little city saw new kinds of processions passing through its street, for now it was an important center and distributor of trade. The West was opening. Not merely the near West of the Valley of Virginia which Spotswood and his Knights of the Golden Horseshoe advertised to the world, but the larger West beyond the mountains which the pioneers in buckskin were preparing to be transmuted into a beautiful and productive empire. The Iron Horse had not yet appeared. The freight trains of that period consisted of single wagons, with great arched canvas covers, drawn by from four to six horses or mules. Fredericksburg as one of the seaboard distributing points was as familiar with these great carriers as it is to-day with the pneumatic-shod motor-car. It is said that its streets and wagon yards often held as many as three hundred of these high-slung covered wagons at one time. Ships from many ports, sailing up the Rappahannock, brought the merchandise which was transferred here to these wagon trains and so passed on westward to the new pioneers.

The other procession was black, black men, on their way to the block to be sold to new masters. On market days the planters sent up slaves with their produce, and the auction of them on the public corners and before the public offices was a feature that, in the manner of the times, attracted no undue attention.

Twice a great conflagration threatened to wipe out the city. Once in 1807 and again in 1822. The first was the more destructive. It started within one block of the Mary Washington house, and consumed half the houses then standing. But a kindly fate seems to have looked after the city's more historic buildings, for all of them were spared.

Up from a country place south of town came, about 1830, a youth perhaps already infected with a new kind of fever for the sea by the weak remnant of brine in the feeble tide which reached him this far inland. His name was Matthew Fontaine Maury, and soon every one knew that he rode into town to court a Fredericksburg girl. He won her, and later he made Fredericksburg one of his succession of homes. Among these homes one was the sea, for he became another glory of the navy.

Maury did not fight men, nor did he deal death. His genius was a kinship with the elements. The currents in the air and the currents in the sea told him their secrets. He charted both sea and air, and he gave to the world the first description of the Gulf Stream. Orders and honors came to him from every important nation in Europe. On his monuments he is called The Pathfinder of the Seas. A naval official, one of his biographers, said: "No single individual has done more for his fellow man in lessening the hazards of navigation than Matthew Fontaine Maury."

At the end of nearly a century of peace two other processions came this way, one from the South in gray and one from the North in blue. The War between the States was on, and in 1862, Fredericksburg and its vicinity became one of its bloodiest battle-grounds. Already, in the spring of that year, the Federal forces had made it an easy prey, but operations elsewhere made it expedient for them to evacuate the town in the August following. The two armies faced each other across the Rappahannock in December, however, and the demand and refusal of surrender of the city precipitated the attack of the Federals.

Lee defended the city from the heights behind it with over sixty thousand troops. Burnside had at his disposal about one hundred thousand, massed on the east bank of the river above and below Chatham. The Confederate defense cost in lives about a third of the toll taken by the attack. The Confederates held the city, though General Longstreet is quoted as having said that such bravery and gallantry as was displayed by the Federal soldiers deserved success. The total losses were such that the slaughter about Fredericksburg was perhaps unequaled elsewhere during the war.

It is one of the town legends that General Lee, standing on the heights behind Fredericksburg during the battle, looked across at Chatham which the Federal commander occupied as headquarters and was urged to turn his fire on it. But, the story continues, Lee remembered that he had courted his wife, old William Fitzhugh's granddaughter, there, and had not the heart to unloose his guns against it.

Who were then at Chatham? Abraham Lincoln, they say;

and, nursing the blue-coated wounded and dying, was a young man named Walt Whitman, not yet the "good grey poet."

All these that have so known Fredericksburg either in passing by or loitering among its people, have left their landmarks which singularly neither fire nor war nor the elements have destroyed. They give the now old town an atmosphere all its own and a place unique among the minor communities of America.

The clapboards of Mary Washington's corner house still gleam white. Kenmore and its garden have come upon appreciative days. The low brick walls of Monroe's office have been pointed up. These three are now preserved as public monuments. Chatham, only partly hidden among its high trees, has been restored to such beauty as its builder first gave it. The proud citizens point these out first and then the home of Maury the Pathfinder, Mercer's Sentry Box, the Masonic building of Washington's first lodge and Scotch William Paul's store, the stone slave block on the corner on which the blacks were bid to new masters, and the old Rising Sun Tavern near the river where so many of the worthies in Fredericksburg's long procession rested and refreshed themselves. Even the street names remain as arranged two centuries ago when Frederick was Prince of Wales; and one threads one's way from Princess Anne to Caroline and Sophia and Prince Edward and Charles until one has only to observe the corner markers to be reminded of George II's entire family.

To-day the population of old Fredericksburg is about eight thousand. They are the living. Its larger population is below ground as one is reminded by its numerous cemeteries. Mayre's Heights which, living, the Federals could not take, they have taken, dead. A part of it is now a national cemetery, and

ST. LUKE'S CHURCH, NEAR THE JAMES
The oldest Protestant church in America, built about 1632

POHICK CHURCH, NEAR THE POTOMAC

ARLINGTON ON THE POTOMAC

GUNSTON HALL ON THE POTOMAC

there are the graves of fifteen thousand, two hundred ninety-four Union soldiers, among which twelve thousand, seven hundred ninety-eight are "unknown soldiers." Nearer the center of the city are gathered the Confederate dead. In the heart of town under the windows of Mr. Monroe's law office is a walled acre where two centuries of local Masons sleep. In the churchyard under the shadow of St. George's other worthies rest, and among the stones here two in particular arrest attention.

One of them rises over the grave of William, the brother of John Paul Jones. Another recites:

"Here lies the body of Col. John Dandridge, of New Kent county, who departed this life on the 31st day of August, 1756, aged 56 years."

He was Martha Washington's father, from the River York. Neither his daughter nor he were ever resident in Fredericksburg, and chroniclers have been hard put to it to account for his presence here. Not so hard put, however, as to account for another stone near by with this incredible inscription:

"Charles M. Rothrock, departed this life Sept. 29, 1084, aged three years"!

Old Fredericksburg is the center of a circumference of other appealing places. Westward the way leads shortly to the scenes of three other great events of the Civil War: the Battle of Chancellorsville, the Battle of "the bloody angle" of Spottsylvania, and the campaign of the Wilderness. Eastward is Traveller's Rest, a house whose name and history are less militant. Here Catherine Willis Atcheson became a widow in her fourteenth year, but shortly after mended that estate by marrying Prince Achille Murat, son of the exiled king of Naples whom Napoleon had put upon that throne, but did not quite cement there. On the hem of the town on one estate are two houses of interest, the Falls and Fall Hill. The former is the older and quainter, the latter is the newer and more pretentious. They have both belonged only to the Thorntons. An aunt and a sister of General Washington married Thorntons, as did his brother Charles.

Across the Rappahannock, at a distance of about a mile from the center of Fredericksburg is the village of Falmouth, its elder sister, once its rival, now a subdued but picturesque relic of its own past, clinging to the steep hillsides above the rocky bed of the "freshes" of the river. Falmouth received its charter in 1720.

In the early days of its commercial importance one of its citizens, Basil Gordon, accumulated the first million dollars made in America by one man. Here were the James Hunter's Iron Works in Revolutionary days, and of them James Mercer said in a letter to Thomas Jefferson:

"I am sure I need not tell you that it is from Mr. Hunter's Works that every Camp Kettle has been supplyed for the continental and all other Troops employed in this State & to the Southward this year past—that all the anchors for this State & Maryland & some for continent have been procured from the same works; that without these works we have no other resourse for these articles, and that without the assistance of the Bar Iron made there, even the planters hereabouts & to the Southward of this place wou'd not be able to make Bread to eat."

The father of the British poet, Thomas Campbell, was for a time a resident of Falmouth. Here still is pointed out the house in which was born Mrs. Delia Forbes Smith, grandmother of Consuela Vanderbilt, former Duchess of Marlborough. Where the hills seem highest stands Belmont, gleaming white in the frame of its four chimneys, bordered with box and bowered among its great old trees. It was built in the eighteenth century by William Knox whose daughter married Basil Gordon. Refreshed in all its aspects it is given renewed interest to-day as the home of the distinguished artist, Gari Melchers. Elsewhere Falmouth leans and crumbles, but not without a gentle picturesqueness which allures and surprises.

CHAPTER XIV

THE POTOMAC, WASHINGTON'S RIVER

John Smith and the Early Traders—Rising Tide of Population—Custis'
Epitaph Answered—Athens of Virginia—Tales of the Turbervilles—
Irascible Dick Cole—Nomini Hall and the Musical Councilor Carter—
Stratford Hall and Other Lee Seats—Wakefield, Where Washington Was
Born—Dick Hooe and His Ferry—Land of the Fitzhughs—A Christmas
Party—Quantico—Bell Ayr—Mount Vernon—Pohick, Washington's Par-
ish Church—Woodlawn—Gunston Hall—Alexandria and Its Past—
Arlington.

HE Potomac River bounds Tidewater Virginia
on the north. It is the river of the Lees, the
Fitzhughs, the Masons and the Fairfaxes. But
it takes its greatest glory from the name of
Washington. Here came, and made his home, the immigrant
from whom sprang the line which produced George Washington. Here, at a point not far from the mouth of the river,
that celebrated man was born, and at another point near the
head of the tidal reaches he had his home and spent nearly all
his years and died and lies buried.

By reason of its great breadth for the first forty miles above
its mouth, where it is often seven miles from shore to shore;
of its more numerous picturesque inlets, here as elsewhere in
this water system called "rivers" and "creeks," and especially
of its lofty shores in the upper sweeps, the Potomac has scenic
beauties not excelled and indeed rarely equaled by any other
river in Tidewater Virginia.

It still bears the Indian name which John Smith found or
gave it when he sailed up its waters in search of the "western

passage." The question has never been conclusively settled, whether the river took its name from the Potomac Indians who lived along its Virginia shore or whether the Indians took their name from the river. Patow-em-eke means "to bring again," or, in a freer rendering, "traveling traders, or pedlers."

There are some who accept the seeming identity of the place-names Occoquan and Axacan as proof that the Spanish explorers, who entered the Chesapeake and whose chronicles mention Axacan, came up the Potomac and entered Occoquan Creek.

There is no cranny of doubt, however, that John Smith came here in the first twelve-month of the English on the James, and it was he who literally put the Potomac on the map, for until his map was published in England the Potomac had had no place in cartography. Smith hopefully sailed all the one hundred twenty-five miles of the river's tidal reach and only gave up his search for the outlet to the China Sea when he encountered the impassable falls.

More than a quarter of a century passed after the English first settled on the James before the pioneers began to appear on the Potomac shore of the Northern Neck. Curiously they did not come here as the result of any push of population up from lower Tidewater. They arrived from another direction and for another reason.

In 1634 Lord Baltimore's colonists founded St. Mary's City on the Maryland side of the Potomac, near its mouth. In the course of some disaffection among them a few abandoned their Catholic brethren, sailed across the river and established themselves on the Virginia shore along the lovely inlet which has since borne the name of Coan River. These first settlers lived in a kind of social Eden, without government control or taxes, until the middle of the century when their trouble came in double rations.

They went untaxed because Jamestown was unconscious of the newcomers under its jurisdiction. But when the Council heard of them, and that they were prospering, it began to bestow attention on them and extended to them the beneficence of taxation. However, it took a military expedition to the Potomac to make the first collection. The newly discovered citizens were quick to remind that obligations do not travel singly but hooked up with rights. Thus very early they gave a local instance that the American colonist never approved taxation without representation, by electing one of their number to sail down the bay and up the James, and to speak for them in the House of Burgesses. That trouble was scarcely ironed out when another beset them.

Word one day traveled up to the Potomac to these dwellers on the Northern Neck that they were holding their land without title and so were liable to ejectment. The explanation was that their King, Charles II, at the moment somewhat remote from his crown, his throne and his capital, being in exile over the French way, had scratched his royal signature on a document which presented all the land between the Rappahannock and the Potomac to certain "favorites." The residents there were supported in their fiery protests by all Virginia, but it was only after many years that another royal grant corrected the situation, though it did not even then correct it quite satisfactorily.

Colonization, however, did not wait on such details. Once it began here on the Potomac shore, it marched straight up the river as far as the tide would float the ships. Land was taken in large units. Settlers flowed in. The first cabins and rough frame houses were soon succeeded by brick structures and, almost as soon as elsewhere in Tidewater, great mansions sprang up which rivaled those on the Rappahannock, the York and the James.

Along the first twenty miles of river there is not now a house which is a survival of the colonial period. Mantua, smiling down on the wide waters, from its corner on the Coan, is made over, however, from the bricks of old Northumberland house which was the earliest of the brick mansions here. It was the seat of William Presley who was the first burgess sent by the citizenry to say their say about the hitherto undiscussed question of their taxation and representation.

At no great distance, because no distance here is great, later lived a gentleman named Izatis Anderson, whose tombstone reminds of the eccentric epitaph of John Custis, because so different. It will be remembered that Custis proclaimed that though he died at the age of seventy-one he had "lived" but seven years, the years he lived as a bachelor. Anderson had a happier plight, for his stone reads:

"He was a worthy and estimable man
A Kind neighbor, a faithful friend
and good Citizen.
In other relations of life he might have been
Equally praiseworthy, but he died a bachelor,
having never experienced the comfort of being
a husband or father. This situation he found
So comfortless that in his last will he
directed this stone to be placed over his
remains, with an inscription
Warning all young men from imitating an
Example of celibacy,
Which had yielded to himself
No other eventful fruits
but disappointment and remorse."

Looking down on the head of the Coan is Springfield, a house which attracts attention on account of at least one architectural detail which it seems to possess as something all its own. The central building is flanked by one-story wings whose façades, curiously, build up toward the cornice above the central second story, in steps.

About the Yeocomico River, next above the Coan, there are two interests, one ancient and local, the other modern and national. The local interest centers in the tapestried walls and the gracefully turned roof of Yeocomico Church, for it is one of Virginia's oldest houses of worship. Not far away, at Lodge Landing, live a family with whom for many years every single American has unconsciously had contact. They are a family of engravers and, father and son, they have cut all the canceling stamps which are used in every American post-office anywhere.

The Yeocomico divides Northumberland County from Westmoreland County, and in crossing it and entering Westmoreland one comes into a county which, in the eighteenth century, on account of its galaxy of colonial celebrities, was called the Athens of Virginia. Along its stretch of shore were the lands and homes of the Washingtons, the Lees, the Corbins, the Fauntleroys, the Ashtons, the Turbervilles, the Marshalls, the Carters, the Monroes, and of others as highly esteemed in Virginia if not quite so well known beyond the Old Dominion.

Astonishment is often expressed at finding so many great men springing up here in so restricted an area. Scotland appears to present an analogy, for a Scot, Norman Douglas, was writing of his own country and not of Tidewater Potomac, when he said: "If you reckon it out it will be seen that the most of the great men of that country have been born within a remarkably small radius of time and an equally restricted one of space." Other instances may be added, perhaps, but they do not dull our wonder at Westmoreland.

Between the Yeocomico and the Machodic Rivers are Sandy Point which was the colonial plantation of Colonel George Eskridge, guardian of Mary Ball, the mother of George Washington; Hominy Hall, an Aylett house, and the birthplace of the first Mrs. Richard Henry Lee, of Chantilly; Springfield, the seat of General Alexander Parker, an important ally of General Wayne in the Revolution; Wilton, a venerable and charming survival on Jackson's Creek; Pecatone of the Corbins and Turbervilles, dating from 1650; and Cole's Point, presumably the Salisbury Park of Richard Cole, resident on the Potomac in 1659.

Weird and terrible are the traditions about old Pecatone in the days of a certain Mrs. George Turberville. According to the compiler of *Lee of Virginia:*

"Many wild stories were told, in my youth, of how a lady owner (Mrs. George Turberville) played the part of a petty tyrant among her overseers and negroes, confining the former in her dungeons beneath the house, and the latter sometimes whipped to death! How she traveled at night in her coach and four, armed with pistols and guns. How, in the last days of her recklessness, she, her coach and coachmen were borne aloft in a terrible hurricane, and lost to sight. From that day the house remained unoccupied for years. Then, in popular opinion, it was haunted: lights were seen passing from room to room, and awful groans and shrieks at night would assail the ears of the luckless traveller who happened to be in the vicinity."

This seems to have been the sprightly tempered Mrs. George Turberville who, in addition to "pistols and guns," carried axes, when she went abroad in her coach, to "remove all obstructions."

Fithian wrote down in his diary what the neighbors saw of Mr. George Turberville's lack of consideration:

"Mr. Carter dined at Squire Lees some few weeks ago; at the same place, that day, dined also Mr. George Turberville and his wife—As Mr. Carter rode up he observed Mr. Turberville's Coach-man sitting on the Chariot Box, the Horses off—After he had made his compliments in the House, he had occasion soon after to go to the door, when he saw the Coachman still sitting, and on examination found that he was there fast chained! The fellow is inclined to run away, and this is the method which This Tyrant makes use of to keep him when abroad."

It is pleasanter to run back to the patentee of old Pecatone, Henry Corbin, and to his neighbors. They loved life and their fellow man, and left a monument to that fact in a registered agreement which provided here on the Potomac in 1670 for what was apparently the first country club in America. John Lee, Isaac Allerton, Thomas Gerrard, and their neighbor, Henry Corbin, agreed to build them "a banqueting hall" where their estates cornered near Wilton on Jackson's Creek.

It was agreed that each party to the contract should "yearly, according to his due course, make an honourable treatment fit to entertain the undertakers thereof, their men, masters and friends. . . . Every four years to have a procession to every man's land for re-marking and bounding by line-trees or other particular divident or seat. . . . This for the better preservation of that friendship which ought to be between neighbours, each man's line, whenever anyone of us is bounded, one upon another, may be remarked and plainly set forth by trees."

Dick Cole, of Salisbury Park, was an irascible braggart who

fought with every one up to the Governor of the colony, Sir William Berkeley, whom he threatened to "kick from his place." "He formerly had a better man [than Berkeley] for his pimpe," he said, "for a Knight of Malta was his pimpe." His neighbors "Hardwick and Hutt were rogues." His neighbor Washington was "an ass—negroe-driver." The Gentlemen of the Council he proclaimed "a companie of Caterpiller fellows."

When, somewhat worn out with his choler no doubt, he came to lay himself down to die, he wrote his own epitaph with an unsparing first line, but on the whole in a rather more chastened mood:

> "Here lies Dick Cole a grievous Sinner
> That died a Little before Dinner
> Yet hopes in Heaven to find a place
> To Satiate his soul with Grace."

It was about the shores and hills on both sides of Nomini Creek that clustered most of the great eighteenth-century houses of Westmoreland. Here within a short radius were Nomini Hall, Bushfield, Chantilly, Hickory Hill and Stratford Hall. Except the last, all are gone, leaving only the traditions of the planters who lived there.

Nomini Hall was the home of Councilor Robert Carter, a grandson of "King" Carter, just across the Neck at Corotoman. Of the domestic life at no other colonial house have we so vivid a picture as of that at Nomini. It was all set down in his journal, day after day, and so preserved for us, by the young tutor there from Princeton, Philip Vickers Fithian.

Councilor Carter's public career is revealed in many places, but his private character is here set out bit by bit, photographically. He emerges a man of culture and kindness, in addition to sagacity and ability. He adorned his great house with the best importations from London, and his collection of pictures and plate and books must have been notable. Withal he was a modest man and as already indicated, he seemed to find his most agreeable diversion in music.

Fithian reverted again and again to the councilor's musical activities. He had, according to the tutor's diary, "a good Ear for Music; a vastly delicate Taste; and keeps good Instruments, he has here at Home a Harpsichord, Forte-Piano, Harmonica, Guitar & German Flutes.

"Evening Mr. Carter spent in playing on the Harmonica; It is the first time I have heard the Instrument. The music is charming. He play'd Water parted from the Sea!—The notes are clear and inexpressably Soft, they swell, and are inexpressibly grand; and either it is because the sounds are new, and therefore please me, or it is the most captivating Instrument I have ever heard. The sounds very much resemble the human voice, and in my opinion they far exceed the swelling Organ. . . .

"While we supped Mr. Carter as he often does played on the Forte-Piano. He almost never sups. . . .

"In the Evening the Colonel is busy transposing Music. . . . His main studies are Law and Music, the latter of which appears to be his darling Amusement. . . .

"The Colonel at Dinner gave Ben and I a Piece of Music to prepare on our Flutes, in which he is to perform the thorough Bass. . . . Evening we played in our small Concert our old Sonata, & besides Felton's Gavott; supped at nine. . . .

"Evening at coffee the Colonel shew'd me a book of vocal Musick which he has just imported, it is a collection of psalm-Tunes, Hymns and Anthems set in four parts for the Voice; he seems to be much taken with it & says we must learn and perform some of them in their several parts with our voices & with instruments."

The Councilor's modesty often came out, but on no occasion more delightfully than the evening when the children had retired, and the talk turned "on serious matters," and they discussed epitaphs and tombs. He probably had had his fill of the grandiloquent tributes which it was then the fashion to chisel on the tomb of every one apparently who could afford it. So, the Councilor said, according to Fithian who, with Mrs. Carter, was the only other one present, that "he would have no splendid nor magnificent monument, not even stone to say *Hic Jacet*. He told us he proposes to make his own Coffin & use it for a chest til its proper use shall be required—That no Stone, nor Inscription be put over him—And that he would choose to be laid under a shady Tree where he might be undisturbed & sleep in peace & obscurity.—He told us, that with his own hands he planted, and is with great diligence raising a *Catalpa*-Tree at the head of his Father who lies in his Garden." Whereupon Mrs. Carter "beg'd that she might have a Stone, with this only for a monument, 'Here lies Ann Tasker Carter.' "

General Washington's brother, John Augustine, lived at Bushfield, and George often came here both before and after settling at Mount Vernon. The Bushfield house which he knew burned down, but another and probably not less handsome one stands on its foundations. On higher land overlooking the Potomac and looking across Nomini Creek at Bushfield and Nomini Hall, was Chantilly, the home of Richard Henry Lee, who was one of the greatest minds and tongues of the struggle for independence. He was a member of the Virginia House of Burgesses and of the first general Congress; president of the Congress; mover of a resolution for independence in Congress on June 7, 1776; originator of the Committee of Correspondence; signer of the Declaration of Independence; member of the Congress which adopted the Federal Constitution and under it one of the first two United States senators from Virginia.

Just above, and near the site of Chantilly, the Virginia shore of the Potomac rises suddenly and abruptly to a height many times greater than anywhere below it on the river or anywhere above it for another interval of many miles. It is here called Nomini Cliffs. On them stands the Lee mansion which was erected here on the site of a former house early in the eighteenth century by Thomas Lee and called Stratford Hall. It survives to testify to its solid original magnificence when it was surrounded by its supporting buildings and long connecting walls.

Stratford is built of brick in the form of a letter H, with four great chimneys to the right and four others to the left of the center. These chimneys cluster and the brick masonry arches them together ingeniously, so that the ensembles have the appearance of open belfries or towers. The great house stood in the center of a large square at each of the four corners of which stood a two-story brick building devoted to domestic purposes associated with the mansion and the plantation. A brick wall united the four corner buildings and gave the central house the baronial appearance of a fortified house. Not all of the corner buildings survive, but there are remnants of the wall. Councilor Robert Carter built Nomini Hall on this same plan. The splendid stretch of highland between the mansion and the edge of the cliffs has grown up in forest, intercepting the superb view, across the Potomac here where it is seven miles wide, which Stratford Hall once enjoyed.

Stratford was the cradle of the Lee family. Here were born and lived a constant succession of able men. The builder was himself the president of the colonial Council and was acting governor of the colony in the absence of the royal appointtee. He was the father of six sons, all born at Stratford, who were unmatched in public service and attainment by any other six brothers in American history: Philip Ludwell Lee was a member of the House of Burgesses and of the colonial Council of which he was the secretary; Thomas Ludwell Lee was a member of the House of Burgesses, of the Conventions of 1775 and of the Committee of Public Safety; Richard Henry Lee and Francis Lightfoot Lee crowned distinguished careers as signers of the Declaration of Independence; William and Arthur Lee, the youngest sons, were in the diplomatic service of their country in Europe during the Revolution.

They were a nucleus of the great family of Lee whose contribution to American public life is thus summarized by Lancaster:

"To Virginia one governor, four members of the Council of State, and twelve members of the House of Burgesses; to the Colony of Maryland two Councillors and three members of the Assembly; to the American Revolution four members of the Convention of 1776 . . . two Signers of the Declaration of Independence, and their three other eminent brothers, Thomas Ludwell, William, and Arthur Lee; and the foremost cavalry officer of the Revolutionary War, 'Light-Horse Harry' Lee. To the Civil service of the United States the family has furnished one attorney general and several members of Congress, and to the State of Virginia, two governors, to the State of Maryland, a governor, and to the Confederate States, the great commander of its armies, three major generals, and one brigadier general. Later, during the troubles which culminated in the war with Spain, General Fitzhugh Lee gained added distinction as consul general to Cuba and as a major general of the United States Army."

Recently Stratford Hall, with twelve hundred twenty-two acres surrounding it, has been bought in order to restore and preserve it as a monument to the great men associated with it.

The other Lee places along or near the Potomac, in addition to Richard Henry Lee's Chantilly, were numerous. Richard, son of the emigrant Lee, lived at Mount Pleasant, and was buried in its grounds, near the big river about four miles east of Nomini Creek. Adjoining this estate in colonial days, though somewhat farther inland, was Lee Hall. The first Lee to reach America built and lived in a house called Cobbs, situated forty miles southeast of Stratford Hall in Northumberland, overlooking Chesapeake Bay. Near here was another famous Lee mansion, Ditchley Hall, built by Hancock Lee in the seventeenth century. The original house disappeared soon after it was erected, and the Ditchley Hall which took its place and survives to-day was built in 1765 by a grandson of Hancock Lee. About half-way between Stratford and the falls at the head of the tidal Potomac, is an estate called Leesylvania where "Light Horse Harry" Lee was born.

Where Nomini Cliffs have dropped away, a few miles above Stratford Hall, the lowlands open at the riverside and admit the waters of Pope's Creek. On its shore is the estate given an especial interest to all Americans from the fact that here on February 22 (February 11, old-style), 1732, George Washington was born. It has long been known as Wakefield, but that name was given it, some time after the event which distinguishes it, by the General's brother. The infant George can scarcely have known much of the place, for he accompanied his parents to a temporary new home farther up the Potomac when he was only three years old. Later in life, he visited his brother Augustine here and afterward his nephew William Augustine. The house burned down in the year 1780, on

CHRIST CHURCH, ALEXANDRIA

CARLYLE HOUSE, ALEXANDRIA

Christmas Day, while William Augustine Washington was entertaining a party of friends.

The Wakefield National Memorial Association was organized a few years ago to care for Wakefield and to promote general acquaintance with and interest in Washington's birthplace. One of its important projects is the erection, on the site of the burned house, of another house, as nearly like that one in which Washington was born as scanty dependable information of it makes possible.

A notable result of the studies made as to the probable appearance of the original Wakefield, has been some scholarly research about the actual character of that house. Up to this time there has been much loose writing about the house in which Washington was born, based largely on an alleged picture of it which came into circulation about the year 1850 and came to be accepted, erroneously, as representing Washington's birthplace. It showed a story and a half cottage, with an outside chimney at each end, and a one-story lean-to at its rear. Actually this is not a drawing of any house which ever stood on Wakefield's acres, but represents a house which, until 1832, stood on the banks of the Rappahannock, below Fredericksburg, on a tract which is locally referred to as the Washington Farm, on which, however, it is not substantiated that Washington lived at any time. With that bit of false history cleared away the projectors of the new house at Wakefield set about to find evidence of what the house which they proposed to reproduce was actually like.

In the main the plans, which have been drawn and accepted, are based on the list of contents of Wakefield house as set out in the will of Augustine Washington, Jr., elder brother of the General and father of the last owner and occupant of the house when it burned down. The new conception is a house which, at least, in no way suggests the cottage which for so many years was erroneously supposed to picture Washington's birthplace.

It is a simple rectangular building with half basement, full first story and a second story lighted by dormer-windows let into the roof. Two large chimneys support each end. It is hoped to build it of brick made from clay taken from the same pit as that which furnished the bricks for the house now being replaced. The Association is, moreover, planning to rebuild the old kitchen building, which stood near the burned house, and whose site is identified by the vestiges of the old brick chimney.

In general effect the drawings for the new house suggest several others still standing in Tidewater. The model is not an uncommon one. It resembles the house called Towle Point a few miles away on lower Rappahannock, the Warren house on the James River opposite Jamestown, Gunston Hall farther up the Potomac on the same side, a dwelling called Providence Forge in New Kent County, and Mount Wharton on Eastern Shore Virginia, in about the same degree as each of these houses resembles the others.

As if so many distinctions were not enough for one county, this Westmoreland presents the birthplace of another president of the United States, James Monroe, on an inlet named after him a few miles farther up-river; the home of Thomas Marshall, father of the great Chief Justice of the Supreme Court; and three houses all of which once belonged to a colonial clergyman and educator, Archibald Campbell, uncle of the British poet, Thomas Campbell. These three places are Pomona, Kirnan, formerly called China Hall, and Campbellton.

The last named house stands back on the highlands near Wirtland, seat of the Wirt family, and in it was kept a school at the end of the eighteenth century which was attended, according to Bishop Meade's somewhat ready methods of historical deduction, by George Washington, John Marshall, James Madison and James Monroe. It is scarcely remotely possible that any one of these sat at the Campbellton desks except young Monroe who seems to have spent his youth in the neighborhood of his birth.

The splendid sweep of the river northward, before it makes the first of its two great bends, is more alluring than any detail along the same shore. Passing this way one may be saluted by a great gun at the navy's proving ground, named after Admiral Dahlgren, and surely if in his reading one has stumbled on old Dick Hooe he will salute the shore here where his famous ferry touched. Hooe's Ferry was the main connecting link, in colonial days, between Williamsburg and all the Tidewater plantations on the one hand and Annapolis, Philadelphia and New York on the other.

Washington often used this route journeying south to his brothers at Wakefield and Bushfield, to visit his friends on other plantations, and to attend the Assembly at Williamsburg. Fithian wrote with particularity of his crossings here. A sample of many such directions is that given in 1779 to Henry Laurens, then recently appointed minister to Holland, in a letter from Richard Henry Lee, of Chantilly:

"I shall continue to entertain the very agreeable hopes of being honored with your company on your way Southward. Your route is thro Baltimore, across the Potomac at Hoes, and from Mr. Hoe you will get exact direction to my house."

The crossing was not always without peril. Isaac Weld, in his travels in America, came this way, and among his unhappy experiences was that with Dick Hooe's ferry. "The river at the Ferry is about three miles wide and with particular winds the waves rise very high," he wrote; "in these cases they always tie the horses, for fear of accidents, before they set out; indeed, with the small open boats which they make use of, it is what ought always to be done for in this country gusts of wind rise suddenly, and frequently when they are not at all expected: having omitted to take this precaution, the boat was on the point of being overset two or three different times as I crossed over."

There are many indications that Hooe was an eccentric. An amusing glimpse of him is given by a Mr. J. F. D. Smythe, of England, who traveled in America in 1783 in search of information for a book on the lately revolted colonies, in which, when later it was published, he had this to say of his experience of Dick Hooe:

"Here we were not a little diverted at a reply made by the owner of this ferry to a person enquiring after the health of one his nearest relatives. . . . 'Sir, (said he) the intense frigidity of the circumambient atmosphere had so congealed the pellucidaqueous fluid of the enormous river Potomack, that with the most eminent and superlative reluctance, I was constrained to procrastinate my premeditated egression to the Palatinate Province of Maryland for the medical, chemical, and Galenical coadjuvancy and co-operation of a distinguished sanative son of Esculapius, until the peccant deleterious matter of the Athritis had pervaded the cranium, into which it had ascended and penetrated, from the inferior pedestrial major digit of my paternal relative in consanguinity, whereby his morbosity was magnified so exorbitantly as to exhibit an absolute extinguishment of vivification.' This singular and bombastic genius is a near relative of the American General Washington, and it would certainly afford high entertainment to hear this gentleman's account of his relation's feats and prowess, and the unexepected success of the Americans."

Around the point above Dahlgren, the fifteen-mile stretch of Virginia shore, in sight as far as the sharp bend opposite Potomac Creek, once bore the neighborhood name of Chotank. This region was the almost exclusive domain of the Fitzhugh family. As planter, merchant, shipper and father the emigrant Fitzhugh was as much a "King" in his way as was Carter, of Corotoman on the Rappahannock, or William Byrd, of Westover on the James. His house, Bedford, stood on the first highlands west of the point, and there is a Bedford house there to-day, occupied by a Fitzhugh. William, the immigrant, in his will bequeathed forty-five thousand thirty-six acres of land on the Potomac shore, a trifle of forty-one hundred sixty-seven acres off the river but near by in this same Northern Neck, besides "other lands in Virginia, Maryland and England."

This William had five sons and they built plantation mansions which rival the Carter buildings and had features which were among the finest in Tidewater. Among the great Fitzhugh seats, in addition to Bedford, were Eagle's Nest on the Potomac not far east of the mouth of Potomac Creek; Marmion, near by; Boscobel, just back of Potomac Creek on the highest land between the Potomac and Rappahannock; Belle Air "of Stafford"; Chatham on the Rappahannock where it is not far from the Potomac; and Ravensworth on the highland back from the upper tidal reaches of this river. Only Chatham, Marmion and Belle Air remain. Boscobel survived until 1915 and Ravensworth until 1925, when both were destroyed by fires.

The surviving houses are suggestive of the magnificent fea‑ tures of those which have disappeared. Chatham is as beauti‑ ful to-day as the day it was built. Belle Air, however, still misses the hand of the sympathetic restorer. A sample of the interior decoration of Marmion is preserved among the ex‑ hibits in the Metropolitan Museum, New York City, by the installation there of the entire set of carved and painted panels from its drawing-room.

A Huguenot Frenchman, exiled for his religion, was travel‑ ing in Tidewater in 1686 and has left a lively though anony‑ mous record of his visits at some of the plantations. Included among them is an account of a Christmas spent with Colonel Fitzhugh at Bedford. The Frenchman had enjoyed Ralph Wormeley's hospitality at Rosegill and those two, with one other gentleman, traveled north together.

"It was agreed," wrote the Frenchman, "that all should go to spend the night with Colonel Fitzhugh, whose house is on the shore of the great river Potomac. . . . Mr. Wormeley is so beloved and esteemed in these parts that all the gentlemen of consideration of the country side we traversed came to meet him, and, as they rode with us, it resulted that by the time we reached Col. Fitzhugh's we made up a troop of 20 horse. "The Colonel's accommodations were, however, so ample that this company gave him no trouble at all; we were all sup‑ plied with beds, though we had indeed to double up. Col. Fitzhugh showed us the largest hospitality. He had store of good wine and other things to drink, and a frolic ensued. "He called in three fiddlers, a clown, a tight-rope dancer and an acrobatic tumbler, and gave us all the divertisement one would wish. It was very cold but no one thought of going near the fire because they never put less than the trunk of a tree upon it and so the entire room was kept warm."

One nearly always found an important church adjacent to so important a seat as was Bedford, and the lordly planters perpetuated their names in the inscriptions which they left on the altar service or on the decorations which they gave. Near Bedford rose St. Paul's Church, one of the finest in Tidewater, as it survives to testify. Among its treasures are "one large silver can, a silver chalice and bread plate" and on each the inscription: "Given by Henry Fitzhugh of Stafford County, Gent., for the use of your church." St. Mary's White Chapel, attended by Mary Ball's family, once had among its possessions "a cover of green velvet with gold fringe and in the center the Ball coat of arms heavily embossed in gold." But nothing else in Tidewater is so ostentatiously self-dedicatory as is found just beyond Chotank neighborhood at Aquia Church near the Potomac, where, under the Communion Table, is a marble slab inscribed: "In memory of the Race of the House of Moncure."

After the first Fitzhugh families came to Chotank the bearers of other distinguished names followed and made their homes there. The Washingtons built Hilton and Waterloo; Richard Stuart built Cedar Grove; the Alexanders built Caledon on one of the earliest grants on this river; and nearer Eagle's Nest, Colonel Peter Ashton built Chatterton, though it passed later to a branch of the Tayloe family, of Mount Airy on the Rappahannock.

One can not pass Potomac Creek, in the elbow of the river's turn here, whether in crossing its mouth by boat or its head by train, without remembering that the Indians whom Captain John Smith found here bore the same name as the river and may have given their name to it; or that Pocahontas once visited on its shore and here was taken prisoner by rough Samuel Argall; or that young Harry Spelman came here as the Indian King's friend and guest when there were no white settlers on the river; or that in those remote and dangerous days here Captain Harry Fleet came and brought baubles for the savages and in exchange took their corn and tobacco down the river for transshipment to England.

As far up the river as Potomac Creek there are on the Virginia side no communities of any size. Above the opening of Potomac Creek a few miles, however, there is a new and curious town on the site of an old village of the same name. It is Quantico by the mouth of the creek of that name. It stretches well back over the hill yet it is a restricted community for it is the principal post and training station of the United States Marine Corps. At Quantico, and along the shore a few miles above and below it, the railway comes to the waterside. Travelers between the north Atlantic and the south Atlantic coasts all pass this way and from the car windows may look out on the Potomac where it still averages two miles in width.

In the highlands behind Quantico is a charming old brick colonial derelict called Belle Ayr, home of the Ewells. One of the daughters of this family was married to Dr. James Craik, General Washington's life-long friend and physician, and another daughter was married to the eccentric "Parson" Weems, who preached and peddled and wrote popular biographies. In his *Life of Washington* he immortalized himself as the author of the cherry-tree story. But for all his eccentricity, Mason Weems was a capable man and knew much more about his subjects than he has been credited with knowing.

Above Quantico the river is diverted into devious ways by the hills which here rise higher than anywhere below. The banks often come within a mile of each other. The scenery becomes more diversified and charming, and just where the artless arrangement of land and water seems loveliest the traveler's ear is arrested by the tolling of the ship's bell and his eye is directed to the spot which is of all spots, not only in Tidewater but in all America, most cherished by Americans. High up among the trees on the Virginia shore, behind its many pillared portico and surrounded by its white village of little domestic buildings stands Mount Vernon, George Washington's home.

The story of that house is the narrative of Washington's whole domestic life from the days when he first came here from Wakefield a lad of three years with his father and mother. Later he came here from the family farm, on the hills back from the Rappahannock, which was his patrimony, to visit his brother. Finally he returned to become its master and remain, with only the absences imposed by his public service, until he died, and even after death, in the sarcophagus there which is visited annually by over half a million pilgrims. It is a story too long for this chronicle and I have, moreover, already told it in full in a volume all its own.*

Clustered about Mount Vernon are the remaining historic houses and estates of this section of Tidewater Virginia. Living with Mr. and Mrs. Washington at Mount Vernon from the time of their marriage were Mrs. Washington's two children, Martha and John Custis. Miss Custis died in her youth, unmarried. John married Eleanor Calvert, of Mount Airy, across the Potomac in Maryland. This young couple settled in a house called Abingdon farther up the river, opposite the southern tip of the present city of Washington. There four children were born to them. The elder two married and as

---

Mount Vernon, Washington's Home and the Nation's Shrine, by Paul Wilstach.

Mrs. Peter and Mrs. Law, lived, respectively, in Georgetown and in the city of Washington. The younger two, when their father, John Custis, died, came as children to make their home with their grandmother at Mount Vernon. They were Eleanor (Nelly) Parke Custis and George Washington Parke Custis.

When Nelly Custis grew to young womanhood she married Lawrence Lewis, the son of Fielding Lewis and Betty Washington Lewis, of Kenmore, Fredericksburg. General Washington cut off twenty-five hundred acres from the west side of Mount Vernon estate and gave them to this nephew. On these slopes overlooking Dogue's Creek and the Potomac River, Mr. Lewis built his home after drawings by Dr. William Thornton. He called it Woodlawn, and it is to-day, as it was when first built, one of the finest specimens of Georgian architecture in Tidewater.

A few miles beyond Woodlawn on the same hills stands old Pohick Church where Washington was a vestryman and where he brought the family and visitors from Mount Vernon for worship as long as it was open. It fell on evil days during the Revolution, but recent restorations have made it again almost as precious as an example of the finer colonial church as it is for its historic associations.

On Mason's Neck just beyond Pohick, and where it comes very near the great river, stands Gunston Hall, a comparatively small house but the home of a big man. George Mason built Gunston and lived there all his days and is buried in the Mason burying-ground on the estate. He was another extraordinary example of the culture of the colonial planters of Tidewater. He had not the educational opportunities of those young colonials who were schooled at William and Mary, or oversea at the English universities; yet he seems not to have missed such advantages. He was the principal opponent of Madison and Marshall in the great debate on Virginia's adoption of the Constitution; and he was the author of the Fairfax Resolves, of the Virginia Bill of Rights, and of the first Constitution of the state of Virginia.

Additional distinction was given the memories of Gunston Hall at the beginning of this century when it belonged to and was the home of the Kester family. Here Paul Kester wrote many of his dramas and at least one of his novels, and here, too, his brother, Vaughan Kester, wrote *The Prodigal Judge* and others of his celebrated novels. During the Kester's residence a constant succession of distinguished people came to Gunston to see them.

Between Gunston Hall and Mount Vernon there are two inlets which form an intervening peninsula of some three thousand acres. This was called Belvoir and it was the home of Lord Thomas Fairfax and others of his family in America. Here young George Washington was a frequent visitor, and it was here, after his mother had been dissuaded from sending him to a life at sea, that Lord Fairfax successfully interested him in the profession of surveyor, which engaged him until he began his military career.

Lawrence Washington, one of George's elder brothers and the first master of Mount Vernon, married a daughter of the Fairfax family, of Belvoir. From that time as long as the house stood there was always the most intimate intercourse between the families there and at Mount Vernon. The Fairfaxes remained loyalists at the outbreak of the Revolution and returned to England, and Belvoir was destroyed by fire toward the close of that war. When peace returned General Washing-

INDEX

INDEX

Butler
  Hudibras, 152
Byrd, Anne, 137, 235
Byrd, Evelyn, 130, 135, 137-138
Byrd, Evelyn Taylor, 130, 131
Byrd, Governor Harry, 228
Byrd, Jane, 137
Byrd, Maria, 137, 242
Byrd, Commander Richard, 228
Byrd, Ursula, 248
Byrd, Wilhelmina, 137
Byrd, William I, 131, 135, 152
Byrd, William II, 89, 93, 135-136,
  138, 155, 235, 248, 297
  diary quoted, 85, 143, 153-154,
  202-203
Byrd, William III, 131, 137
Byrd's Warehouse, 153, 163

Cabot, John, 44, 45, 46
Caledon, 299
Callahan house, 201
Calvert, Eleanor, 301
Calvert, Lord, 193
Calvert's Neck, 77
Campbell, Archibald, 294
Campbell, Thomas, 278, 294
Campbellton, 294-295
Candy Island, 114
Cape Charles, 23, 52, 185, 186, 187,
  198
Cape Charles Venture, 198
Cape Henry, 23, 49, 52, 102, 108,
  165
Carcassonne, 101
Carlyle, Colonel John, 304
Carlyle house, 304, 305
Carolina, 47, 70
Caroline County, 66
Carr, Dabney, 173
Carter, Anne, 146, 235
Carter, Charles, 137, 146, 235, 254,
  255
Carter, Elisabeth, 137, 214, 235
Carter, John I, 233, 234
Carter, John II, 146, 235
Carter, Judith, 212
Carter, Landon, 93, 137, 235, 241,
  242-243
Carter, Lucy, 235, 269

Carter, Maria, of Cleve, 255
Carter, Maria, of Sabine Hall
  letter quoted, 255-256
Carter, Mary, 235
Carter, "Councilor" Robert, 85, 88,
  94, 183, 246, 287-289, 290
Carter, "King" Robert, 88, 89, 117,
  146, 212, 214, 234-236, 241, 254,
  269, 287, 297
Carter, Robert II, 235
Carter house, 181
Carter's Creek, 211, 213-214, 215,
  217, 231, 235
Carter's Grove, 75, 117, 235
Cary, Archibald, 149, 156, 173
Cary, Henry, 149
Cary, Mary, 183
Cary, Sarah, 183
"Cavaliers," 67
Cawson's, 193
Cedar Grove, 222, 299
Centre Hall, 143
Cessford, 198
Chamberlayne, Mr., 221
Chamberlayne, Thomas, 137
Chancellorsville, battle of, 277
Chantilly, 285, 287, 289, 290, 292,
  295
Chapman, 121
Charles II, 120, 122, 282
Charles, 103
Charles City County, 66, 76, 77, 132,
  139
Charles Edward, Prince, 270
Charleston, 190
Chatham, 75, 269, 270, 273-274, 275-
  276, 297, 298
Chatterton, 299
Chelsea, 224
Chesapeake Bay, 18, 19, 23, 44, 45,
  46, 50-51, 101, 185, 203, 217,
  232, 281, 292
Chesapeake Indians, 50
Chickahominy River, 52, 66, 123,
  126, 127, 218, 232
Chickakony, 77
Chincoteague Bay, 200, 201, 203
Chincoteague Island, 201, 202
Chotank, 297, 299
Christ Church (Alexandria), 304

311

INDEX

321

INDEX

INDEX

Wayne, General, 285
Welbourne, 200
Webster, Daniel, 182
Webster, Fletcher, 182
Weedon, George, 272
Weems, "Parson"
Life of Washington, 300
Weld, Isaac, 296
Werowocomoco, 217, 218
West, artist, 131
West, Captain Francis, 151
West Fort, 151
West house, 200
Westmoreland County, 65, 66, 82, 88, 196, 249, 285, 287, 294
Westover, 75, 89, 93, 130, 131, 135, 136, 138, 140, 144, 153, 157, 235, 242, 248, 254, 255, 262, 297
West Point, 205, 218, 219
Wetherburn, Henry, 173
Weyanoke, 132, 133
White Hall, 228
White House, 221, 222
White Mast, 227
Whitman, Walt, 276
Wickham, John, 161
Wilkins family, 199
Wilkinson, Cornelius, 190
William, King, 224
William and Mary College, 120, 140, 149, 167, 169-170, 183, 214, 224, 237, 302
Williams, Agnes, 187
Williams, family, of Rokeby, 254
Williams, Walter, 188
Williamsburg, 93, 212, 224, 295
as Middle Plantation, 77, 167
beginnings of, 119, 244
Bruton Church in, 174-175
buildings of, 172-174
Burgesses in, 98
capital moved from, 156-157
capital of Virginia, 77, 150, 168
early history of site of, 169
English players in, 26
first Capitol in, 167, 170-172
first theater in, 99, 178
Governor's Palace in, 149, 168
green and white city, 168
prison in, 172

Williamsburg—*cont.*
racing in, 178-179
remains in, 181-184
restoration of, 29
social life in, 176-177
to-day, 180
Washington in, 221, 266
William and Mary College in, 169-170
See Chapter IX
Willing, Mary, 137
Willis, Colonel Harry, 264
Wilstach, Paul
Mount Vernon, Washington's Home and the National Shrine, 301n.
Wilton, 130, 148-149, 285, 286
Windmill Point, 133
Wirt, William, 161
Wirtland, 295
Wise, Governor Henry Alexander, 196, 198
Wise, Henry Alexander (grandson of the governor), 198
Wise, Jennings, 197
Wise plantation, 77
Witch Duck Point, 106, 107
Wolfe, General, 225
Wolfsnare Creek, 106
Wooden chimneys, 110, 264
Woodford, Mr., 261
Woodlawn, 253, 302
World's End, 152
Wormeley, Elisabeth, 242
Wormeley, Judith, 212
Wormeley, Ralph V, 237, 245, 252, 298
Wormeley plantation, 77
Wren, Sir Christopher, 180
Wyart, Robert, 188
Wycherley, 178
Wythe, Chancellor, 20, 156, 157, 181
Wythe house, 181

Yeardley, Sir George, 121, 134, 135
Ye Bear and Ye Cub, 190
Ye Merchant's Hope, 134
Yeocomico Church, 284
Yeocomico River, 284, 285
Yorick, 244